P9-DGR-289

# Categorization and the Moral Order

The International Library of Phenomenology and Moral Sciences

Editor: John O'Neill, *York University, Toronto*

The Library will publish original and translated works guided by an analytical interest in the foundations of human culture and the moral sciences. It is intended to foster phenomenological, hermeneutical and ethnomethodological studies in the social sciences, art and literature.

# Categorization and the Moral Order

LENA JAYYUSI

ROUTLEDGE & KEGAN PAUL
Boston, London, Melbourne and Henley

*First published in 1984*
*by Routledge & Kegan Paul plc*

*9 Park Street, Boston, Mass 02108, USA*

*14 Leicester Square, London WC2H 7PH*

*464 St Kilda Road, Melbourne,*
*Victoria 3004, Australia and*

*Broadway House, Newtown Road,*
*Henley-on-Thames, Oxon RG9 1EN, England*

*Printed in Great Britain by*
*Billing & Sons Ltd, Worcester*

© *Lena Jayyusi 1984*

*No part of this book may be reproduced in*
*any form without permission from the publisher,*
*except for the quotation of brief passages*
*in criticism*

*Library of Congress Cataloging in Publication Data*

Jayyusi, Lena.

Categorization and the moral order.
(The International library of phenomenology and moral
sciences)
Includes bibliographical references and index.
1. Social ethics.  2. Social interaction.  3. Categorization
(Psychology)  4. Analysis (Philosophy)
I. Title.  II. Series.
HM216.J39 1984    302    84-3448

British Library CIP data also available

*ISBN 0-7100-9720-4*

To Mother, Father,
and Jeff

# CONTENTS

# ACKNOWLEDGMENTS

I wish to thank the Social Science Research Council for making available funds which enabled me to pursue portions of this work and Dr J.M. Atkinson, who headed the project ('Community Reactions to Deviance'), for giving me my first research opportunity, supporting my work and making data accessible.

I also wish to thank the Manchester and Salford Probation Service for providing materials from the course of their work for my research. I particularly wish to thank those members of the Salford and Manchester local offices who personally took the time to gather the materials for me.

Thanks are also due to Dr Paul Drew for having made the transcripts of the Scarman Tribunal available to me.

Two persons were particularly significant for my intellectual development and work in the years that I was studying at Manchester: Dr Wes Sharrock and Dr John Lee. Each of them was a source of inspiration, guidance and encouragement; each transmitted a great respect for analytic rigour and an appreciation for detail that remain with me to this day. At the same time, both were fine friends and colleagues. John worked hard to help me gain access to the Probation Service and gave me much support at times when I needed it. For both John and Wes, I feel more appreciation than I can possibly express in a brief acknowledgment.

For his warm collegiality and confidence in my work I owe special thanks to my friend Dr Rod Watson.

On this side of the Atlantic, I wish to thank Earl Taylor of Harvard University for reading and commenting helpfully on a section of this work.

My deep thanks to the many friends here and to my sister May, who, despite the hard times we collectively faced on other fronts, nevertheless gave me constant support, help and encouragement during this last year of writing. Without that I might never have finished.

To my dear parents I owe a lifetime of support and guidance; both have been deeply inspiring for their critical spirit, my

father for the intellectual curiosity he tried to instil in me, my
mother for her irrepressible creativity and determination.    To
my mother, too, go special thanks for always finding material
ways of helping me accomplish this work.

My husband Jeff Coulter could not have been more wonderful in the depth and measure of his support and in the
genuine intellectual inspiration he provided me.    He has been
a fine friend and colleague: a steadfast source of argument,
questioning and insightful comment and, in his own work, a
challenging example of rigour and dedication.    On a personal
level he sacrificed a lot of his time and overrode his own
inclination to work during months in which he shielded me
from every mundane concern.    With constant good humour
and love he helped me towards conclusion.    Without him, this
book would not have been finished.

                                                    Boston, USA

# INTRODUCTION

My underlying concern in this work is with the sociological analysis and description of members' practical activities and their practical interaction. Such a project systematically encounters a set of problematics:

A Analytically: What is the phenomenon? How does one conceptualize, locate and individuate practical activities and courses of practical interaction? What specific sort of activities can provide a focus for the understanding of other sorts of activities? What further issues, questions, findings about the social order does any particular analysis open up? That is to say, what horizon of significance can one uncover?

B Methodologically: How does one locate and individuate the phenomenon - how is access to it achieved? By what steps can analysis proceed? What counts as a warrantable analytic inference?

It is not that the methodological and analytic problematics are discrete as traditional sociological work sets them up, so that methodology is reduced purely to the problem of *methods* for data *collection* (interview schedules, participant observation, etc.). Methodology has to do with the logical status and methods of analytic *inference*. Clearly, then, this is already a *constituent* of the analytic problem and rests on some solution to the initial analytic questions appropriate to any domain. In other words, the latter problematic is a species of the former - they are intricately embedded one in the other. The strategy for (B) hinges on some understanding and development of (A).

Let me then specify here, concretely and substantively, how (A) and (B) are organized in this work.

Firstly, I took as my initial focus of analytic interest members' activities of describing, inferring and judging. As a result of prior work and of the perspective from within which that work had been developed (namely, ordinary-language philosophy and ethnomethodology) (1) it had become clear

a that the study of practical activities can be broadly located within the study of communicative interaction (2) and

1

b   that the activities of describing, inferring and judging
were pervasive in the conduct of everyday life.   Indeed,
they seem to be *constitutive* of diverse social practices and
domains of social life.

How is the focus of analytic investigation then to be further
delimited and thematized?   One significant interest might be
in the study of how *persons* are described.   This was a
sociological interest rigorously developed in the work of
Harvey Sacks. (3)   Indeed, the description of persons turns
out to be intimately embedded in the description and ascription of actions, in the work of practical judgment in everyday
life and in practical inferential activities.   Thus, the categorization of persons (membership categorizations) (4) is criterial
and foundational in the understanding of members' practical
activities.   Further, in examining the ways in which persons
are described and the ways in which such descriptions are
used to accomplish various practical tasks - e.g. to deliver
judgments, warrant further inferences, ascribe actions, project possible events, explain prior events, account for behaviour, etc. - it becomes clear that categorization work is embedded in *a moral order*, how that occurs and *how* that moral
order operates practically and pervasively within social life.
Indeed, one can explicate in detail how it is that the social
order is a moral one.   As Phillips and Mounce say, '... the
very notion of social existence has moral implications.   The
relation between moral rules and society is not a contingent
one.' (5)   Hence, one is in a position substantively to
address and raise questions about issues classically located
within the jurisdiction of various 'official' domains of investigation, i.e. sociology of deviance, moral philosophy, etc.
We will elaborate on this presently.

In that the study of practical activities can be conducted (to
a large extent) as the investigation of communicative interaction (an insight developed from within ordinary-language
philosophy and sociologically pursued in the work of ethnomethodologists and conversation analysts), it becomes possible
to collect as investigable data a corpus of naturally occurring
activities and courses of interaction - either recorded *as* they
happen and subsequently transcribed (conversations, court-
room proceedings, radio broadcasts) or naturally inscribed *in
the course* of their production, i.e. texts of various kinds
(including reports, records and documents as well as literary
texts, television broadcasts and films).   Any corpus of such
data can then be analysed for various aspects of its production, its organization and the cultural properties it reveals.
Crucially, the practical activities that constitute the body of
data are examined for their *informal logic*. (6)   This is an
analytically consequential point.   A core analytic issue systematically becomes that of the *intelligibility*, in situ, of

various activities and their outcomes and character for members; the structures of, and the practical production of,
intelligibility are the abiding analytical concern.  Such a
concern opens up areas for detailed study and sociological
description that go far beyond the mainstream ethnomethodological concern with conversational sequencing and conversational activities, although rigorously grounded in that.  It
results in the systematic uncovering of various cultural conventions that *enable* the production of sense, of practical
actions, and that inform the organization of social relations
and the various practices of social life.  In the investigation
of the cultural structures of intelligibility and the practical
methods by which they are produced, displayed, understood
and *engaged* by members, the distinction between topic and
resource remains analytically operable.  It is maintained
through the very topicalization of the cultural resources by
which a first-order understanding of the phenomena under
study is achieved;  an understanding accomplished, that is,
from *within* the irreducibly natural attitude  of everyday life.

The properties and workings of an unrelievedly moral order
are elucidated both in a broad sense - through the explication
of the formal properties of culture and the in situ production
of practical activities - and in the focused sense - through
the study of the practices of membership categorization (of
the descriptions and judgments of, as well as inferences about,
persons).  This is the 'cutting edge' of the present work, its
horizon of significance.  Let me here outline, briefly, the
ways in which this is of relevance to the study of various
domains of social life - indeed, how it operates within the very
practices that are taken to constitute such domains (including
those practices by which domain boundaries are theoretically
set up).

*Sociology of deviance*

What constitutes the phenomena for this sub-domain of sociology?  It is the descriptions of persons - specifically, the
morally displayed and premised descriptions of persons by
other persons (either 'lay' persons or 'officials').  Indeed,
the very sociological term 'deviant' is a normative description
of members produced by, and incorporated or presupposed
within, the corpus of sociological work.  'Labelling theory'
attempts to address the process of labelling someone 'deviant'.
However, the categorization 'deviant' obscures the very diverse
procedures, implications and consequences behind the production, use, display and practical intelligibility of various categorizations subsumed by that sociological rubric:  murderer,
marijuana user, prostitute, alcoholic, child molester, etc.  It
would be incoherent to propose that *one* and the same process

of categorization, one set of criteria or consequences, one 'career' could be formulated theoretically for these various practices and the descriptions contingent upon them. As a result, much actual empirical work in this area has tended to be restricted to ethnographic descriptions. Whilst these are both interesting and illuminating there remains a pressing analytic task: the detailed study of the production, use and practical implicativeness of different categorizations within the moral order, in this case, ones that specifically and explicitly are used to display moral standards and do moral work. Such categorization work is, clearly, descriptive and ascriptive and involves both judgmental and inferential practices. The logic-in-use of such categorizations as the ones indicated above may thus be explicated as an integral part of the study of the logic of culture.

## Sociology and philosophy of law

No one would seriously deny that the concepts and categories of law are embedded in a normative and moral framework. They are deeply tied to the practices of action and responsibility ascriptions. The procedures by which such ascriptions (and the consequent verdicts) are arrived at *within* the legal system (and which indeed, in part, *constitute* such a system) reveal and are embedded in the everyday moral and practical order: the properties and conventionalities of ascription, the distribution of rights and obligations (routinely categorially tied, as we shall see), the procedures for determining evidence, accounting for action, describing settings, adjudicating doubt and certainty, determining the grounds for action and allocating blame or responsibility, etc. The ties between descriptions of persons and descriptions of events are routinely available in the accounts produced within a course of 'legal' investigation and deliberation and routinely reveal such accounts to be morally and normatively organized.

## Political sociology

Work in this field is concerned, in part, with the description and categorization of events, activities, collectivities and social structures. Characteristically, the theoretical descriptions of conventional political theorists routinely stand in competition with, or in contradiction to, the accounts, political descriptions and judgments that other members routinely produce as a feature of their practical involvement within the conduct of social life.

A set of questions thus arises:

1 What possible claim to a higher truth-value, adequacy, intelligibility, etc. could such theoretical descriptions rationally have in contrast to the 'active' descriptions of members? Particularly as these theoretical descriptions and accounts turn out, routinely, to be used and usable in the service of the practical conduct of political life?

2 What possible claim to 'value-freedom' could they have? Some political sociologists and thinkers, particularly Marxists, do not claim value-freedom at all. Nevertheless we remain with the problem of how one is to assess their accounts as against others according to 'objective criteria', if any. What are these criteria? They turn out to be *practical* and in no way exempted from the self-same moral order from within which 'lay' members' political descriptions are generated.

One thing that seems important, then, for the study and understanding of political thought (both that which is generated 'on the ground', so to speak, and that which is 'theoretical') is the detailed investigation of the social practices of description, inference and judgment and the concomitant rigorous analysis of the logic of our practical moral order.

One interesting illustration of the normative logic of political description comes from Cheyney Ryan's excellent discussion, The Normative Concept of Coercion. (7) Having argued against the use of the notion of 'coercion' in a decontextualized manner by some philosophers of law, by whom it has been abstracted from its routine practical usage within a context of social and legal *rights*, Ryan proceeds to comment on the description by Western political theorists of Soviet institutions as 'coercive'. His point is that such a description is logically misplaced, since it is abstracted from the set of rights operative within the Soviet social and political system. In the Soviet Union, the right to private capital accumulation, free market competition, etc. does not exist. It is therefore pointless to describe Soviet economic institutions as inherently coercive, in consequence, since the use here of the notion of 'coercion' would presuppose the relevance of rights whose absence in the first place motivates that description. Ryan calls this illegitimate abstraction the State of Nature fallacy.

> The State of Nature Fallacy underlies any attempt to explicate the notion of coercion in abstraction from the rights and obligations of the parties involved. It underlies those arguments which would adjudicate fundamental disputes over rights by suspending assumptions about the latter and appealing directly to coercion or liberty. (8)

He is saying that the use of the concept of coercion rests on the existence of established legal (or moral) rights and that it

is thus a normative concept.   In this he criticizes the position of other writers (e.g. Dworkin) who hold that it is
purely a descriptive notion.   However, we can take Ryan's
point even further.   In describing Soviet economic institutions as coercive, Western political writers are not simply committing a logical fallacy - they are indeed presupposing that
the legal rights to private capital accumulation and free
market competition, for example, which are operative within
Western institutions and legal organization, are universalizable,
i.e. that they are rights (presumably moral ones) that everyone *naturally* has, and that, therefore, their institutional
absence is *coercive*.   The description here is a thoroughly
*normative* one.   It stands in contrast to the rights presupposed to be primary by Marxists - the right, for example, to
be free from capitalist exploitation and alienation.   It is such
rights, in their turn assumed to be universal, that inform
Marxist descriptions of certain regimes as 'oppressive' and
'coercive'.   Thus, the descriptions produced of collectivities,
social structures and institutions, movements and historical
events are unrelievedly *normative* in their organization.   This
does not mean that we can look around for a totally neutral
description from some Archimedean point, upon which such
evaluative descriptions can be predicated.   These are the
sorts of descriptions produced and they *are* embedded in the
contexts of rights, obligations, practical interests and moral
conventions that we can and do presuppose, or take for granted.   On the other hand, it does not mean that for members
there is no way of practically settling differences or assessing
the relative merits of different accounts and descriptions.
Indeed there are, for apart from the (normative) criteria of
consistency, logical coherence, truth-telling, factual relevance,
etc. there are other shared moral conventions and shared
understandings.   What these are and how they operate is the
very subject of our interest.   It does mean, however, that,
*ultimately*, there are no objective extrinsic criteria to deter-
mine right or wrong between the conflicting moral conceptions
that organize different descriptions of the world.   There are
only, and only ever will be, criteria from *within* a specific
morality.

## The study of history

It follows from the above that the writing of history is also a
practice that is normatively organized and embedded in our
accounting practices generally.   The production of an historical account is not something *dictated* by real objective events
and phenomena but one that is *variously* organizable so that
the same events, characters and phenomena can be constituted
in different, sometimes *competing*, ways.   Hayden White (9)
has shown how the same events (e.g. the events of the French

Revolution) can be constituted differently by various historiographers by the language they use to *describe* them. He
argues that historical narratives employ fictional modes of
representation and that part of the explanatory force of histories is to be located in their success in making 'stories' out
of chronicles by a process he terms 'emplotment'. (10) 'Emplotment' of a sequence of historical events can be accomplished in a number of alternative ways, so that the accounts
thus produced are, often, radically different in character and
are already prefigured by the very mode of language used,
e.g. metaphor, metonymy, synecdoche or irony. White
overemphasizes the literary origin of the story types and
practices which constitute historical narratives and the strategies of sense production made possible by fictional art. The
origin of both literary narratives and historical (or biographical) ones, their forms, organization and logic, lies in the
mundane practices of cultural members - accounting practices
that are not only methods of sense assembly, but also methods
of accomplishing various practical tasks, such as persuading,
blaming, exhorting to action, justifying, excusing, informing,
appealing for help, condemning, etc. Such practices, it is
clear, are moral practices through and through.

## Sociology of media

The study of the organization of media accounts also deeply
informs, and is informed by, the investigation of the normative
organization of descriptions and explanations, and of the
properties and methods of the moral order. The ways in
which accounts provide for their own 'evidence', 'veracity',
'consistency', 'objectivity', despite their normative character,
can be one pivot of study. The study also can provide for
an understanding of the ways accounts can produce, for members, their character of 'bias', 'incompleteness', 'one-sidedness', 'distortion', 'unfairness', etc. Such explications provide for us an understanding of the work of media accounts
(television, newsreels, radio broadcasts, newspaper texts,
etc.). In looking at media accounts it becomes clear, for
instance, that alternative categorizations of persons are critical for the character of the account and the work that the
account is meant to accomplish. Note, for example, the difference between two formulations such as

Terrorists exploded a bomb at a military installation today.

and

Freedom fighters exploded a bomb at a military installation
today.

BRIDWELL LIBRARY
SOUTHERN METHODIST UNIVERSITY
DALLAS, TEXAS 75275

In the first account there is an implied delegitimation of the actions of a group of persons; in the latter, implicatively, there is some form of justification (i.e. for the community of hearers who would avowedly take 'freedom' to be a right and 'terrorism' to be *absolutely* condemnable). In each case there is a different *account* being given of the same action/ event (the explosion of a bomb). But further, the character of the location under attack, by implication, is different. In the first, the 'military installation' may be taken to be 'legitimate'; in the second, it could be taken to be intrusive and illegitimate, e.g. an outpost of an occupying power. And in each case the hearer is invited to seek a different explanation and to project an alternative trajectory of events and actions, both prospectively and retrospectively.

One interesting point about media accounts and their analysis has to do with the sorts of collective attributions made on their basis, as in, for example, conspiracy theories. It is one thing, on the basis of some particular media account, or news broadcast, to locate a specific practical task that the account's production could, intelligibly, accomplish (through some analysis of the informal logic of the organization and selection of the account's particulars). It is another to attribute to some collectivity (e.g. the state) some particular purpose on the basis of one or more media accounts. However, in everyday life this happens routinely and must, therefore, have its own orderliness, its own intelligibility. It is an attribution which in everyday life is made, judged, disputed, agreed with, demonstrated, etc. Therefore, it is a phenomenon that bears analytic investigation in the same way as does the production of the media account itself. Its investigation consists in the explication of the methods of practical inferential work, the conventions of 'agreement' and the logic of the moves from specific to general, individual to collective, that organize much of our practical theorizing and our sense of social structure.

In terms of the analytic interests elucidated, the above substantive areas do not stand discretely. In practical life, judgment, inference and description do not come marked 'political', 'historical', 'legal', 'moral', etc. in accordance with academic boundary lines. The same sort of description or account could be part of political discourse or a feature of a legal investigation. Different tasks may be accomplished by it, and how that makes a difference, if any, to the organization of any particular account in situ is a matter for analytic explication. The investigation of the mundane practices of everyday life in their in situ production avoids treating these 'areas' as reified domains of practice and interest. It is *in* these practices and *through* them that boundaries, interfaces, specificities, commonalities, differences, etc. are drawn, produced, invoked and displayed.

*Moral philosophy*

Given that the study of the logic of the moral order is a significant feature of the present enterprise, I wish to devote a somewhat lengthier discussion to this disciplinary connection. One of the most pervasive debates within moral philosophy pertains to the issue of moral diversity and moral relativism. Another issue, intimately related to this, is the distinction between description and evaluation and the is/ought dichotomy. Yet another related matter that seems to be contentious is whether moral philosophy itself should be evaluative, i.e. should take sides on moral matters, or whether it must be purely 'analytic'. These points will be addressed through the body of analysis in the present work.

One of the significant things about an ethnomethodological approach to the study of social life is that members' commonsense understandings are neither ironicized and banished to the realm of irrelevance nor used uncritically as resources for mechanistic sociological description. They are, rather, transformed into phenomena. Our commonsense understandings are a resource in that they provide us with a first-order constitution of phenomena for investigation – a phenomenal map of the social world which is then to be analysed in detail for its organization, features, production and intelligibility. Let us then outline some basic premises here, drawing on our everyday commonsense knowledge of the social world and the moral order, and point out their initial implication for the present work:

1  Agreement on some moral matters seems to be operable.

2  Although there seems to be agreement on the moral significance of such matters as lying, murder, torture, etc., there is
a  disagreement on what constitutes a genuine instance of such, or on whether some particular action is an instance of the type;
b  disagreement as to what extent, if any, a particular such instance is excusable, justifiable, condemnable and/or otherwise qualifiable.
Both (a) and (b) have a strong bearing on the issue of substantive change *within* the moral order.

3  Despite the highly implicative social and moral character of such matters as torture, murder, theft, cheating and lying, etc., it becomes clear as a result of our ordinary substantive

knowledge of the social world and any empirical overview of
actual practices of individuals, governments and collectivities
that such activities are produced *in a massive way*.   This is
a mundane social fact.   And it is a fact of very special significance for our understanding and conceptualization of the
moral order.   It is simply no use relegating this fact to the
back rooms and basements of philosophical discussion or treating it as epiphenomenal.   That this is the case means that
those philosophers who take a position presupposing or se. ct-
ing *only* agreement are, essentially, constructing prescriptive
edifices or generating fallacies.

An example in point here may be Hare's argument, grounded
in his universalizability principle, (11) that a person's skin
color is irrelevant to our moral considerations.   But this is
not the case for everyone.   It is not so for the members of
the settler-colonial regimes in Africa.   Nor for the members
of the Ku Klux Klan in the USA.   Nor for the members of
the German Nazi Party.   It is not Hare's position, of course,
that such differences and stances do not exist.   He acknow-
ledges and indeed addresses them at length.   Nevertheless
his point is, finally, that they represent examples of *spurious
moral reasoning*, that they are a parody and a caricature of
moral thinking.   Here is where I would take issue.   To take
such a position involves the philosopher in taking sides, and
whilst this may be a legitimate avenue for some branches of
philosophy, it cannot stand for the logical explication of moral
reasoning.   It masks the very real, pervasive and 'moral'
character of much of the reasoning that we would not morally
*approve of*.   Hare writes that

> it is part of the meanings of the moral words that we are
> *logically prohibited* from making different moral judgments
> about two cases, when we cannot adduce any difference
> between the cases which is the ground for the difference in
> moral judgments.   This is one way of stating the require-
> ment of universalizability which ... is fundamental to all
> moral reasoning. (12)

Hare's formulation is much too strong.   Racism may be morally
unintelligible (for some people), but it is not conceptually or
logically so.   One must therefore understand the very ways
in which such massive differences are possible within moral
reasoning without dismissing them as logically spurious.   Universalizability is a requirement of consistency, which means
that it is *itself* a normative requirement of persons within a
social order.   Hare is engaged in stipulation here in which
all moral reasoning is defined by a specific set of moral principles, a particular morality, and in which all differences
(however massive and widespread they may be) are relegated
to the realm of the irrational.   In this way the detailed prac-

tices of the moral order are glossed over and left unanalysed.
Here Kai Nielsen's remarks are relevant:

> 'Moral' carries a contrast with both 'immoral' and 'non-moral'.
> The former contrast makes us reluctant to speak of some-
> one's views being moral views when we take them to be
> anathema or even views we strongly disapprove of.  But
> when we think about it in a cool moment and remember that
> 'moral' also contrasts with 'non-moral', we will acknowledge
> that an 'immoral morality' is not a conceptual anomaly. (13)

Similarly, that such activities and attitudes as we indicated
above exist on such a massive scale also faults that philosophical position (viz. Ms Foot's) which states that the evaluation of any action is *logically entailed* by the description of
it, for this would lead to the rather odd consequence of concluding that *all* who perform these actions (a not inconse-
quential number of persons) evaluate their own actions *and
themselves* in a morally negative manner;  i.e. that they condemn themselves.  I think that this is a serious *sociological*
problem for that school of thought.  Of course it is significant that persons who engage in these sorts of activities (as
individuals or in their capacity as members of certain collectivities) often attempt to *hide* that fact or *reconstitute* their
activities publicly in ways disjunctive with their perceived
character.  For example, members of US military teams engaged in the blowing up of villages and the killing of civilians
during the Vietnam war would describe their activities as
'search-and-destroy operations directed against Vietcong
guerillas'.  The Israeli invasion of South Lebanon in March
1978, in which 2,500 civilians were killed in saturation bomb-
ing of villages and 100,000 were made homeless, was described
by the Israelis (and US press reports) as a 'retaliation against
a terrorist attack'.  Members of the El Salvador junta deny
(among other ploys) the extent of murders committed against
the civilian population or else say they are fighting 'communist
agitators'.  In other words, in the very way that these descriptions are produced the morally implicative character of
certain sorts of activities is being oriented to.  *The description denies or masks the nature of the activities for which it
is generated*.  It deflects attention from the particulars of
the practices that occasion that description in the first place.
We will address related issues in more detail in Chapter 6.
Our moral notions are conventional – they have a conventionally powerful implicativeness, not a logically binding one.

So far, we have laid down some considerations that we, as
members of the culture, know commonsensically.  We thus
find ourselves in a position between two basic and omnirele-
vant premises:  that there are certain deeply conventional
forms and spaces of moral agreement;  and that there is also

a genuine and significant range of moral diversity.   We are,
then, arguing for moral diversity but against radical moral
relativism.   But how can we demonstrate the intelligibility of
this position in more detail?   And how are these two premises
displayed in the conduct of practical life?   How are they
possible?

Let me address this issue in more detail by taking David
Cooper's critique of moral relativism, (14) in which he draws
on an argument made by Donald Davidson against cognitive
relativism. (15)   Cooper wants to extend Davidson's argument
into the moral arena.   He quotes Davidson:

> We can take it as given that *most* beliefs are correct.   The
> reason for this is that a belief is identified by its location
> in a pattern of beliefs;   it is this pattern that determines
> the subject matter of the belief, what the belief is about.
> ... False beliefs tend to undermine the identification of the
> subject matter;   to undermine, therefore, the validity of a
> description of a belief as being about that subject. (16)

Davidson gives as an example the ancient belief that the
earth is flat.   He suggests, according to Cooper, that it is
not at all obvious that they believed *the earth* to be flat – for
if they believed none of the things we know about the earth
(e.g. that it is round, that it revolves around the sun, etc.)
it is not clear in what sense we can take their beliefs as being
about *the earth*.   Cooper restates Davidson's point thus:

> not many of our beliefs about $X$ can be false – for, if they
> could be, then it is conceivable that we should encounter
> someone most of whose beliefs *are* false.   But that is not
> conceivable, for we should shortly have to decide that his
> beliefs are not about $X$ at all. (17)

This is the incommensurability argument, and there seem to me
to be a number of problems with it:

1 Davidson's (and by extension Cooper's) point about the
*correctness* of beliefs is counter-intuitive.   It is not the
correctness of beliefs that is central here, or even relevant,
but rather intersubjective agreement as to their correctness:
intersubjective agreement about the world.   It is that which
characterizes our *network* of beliefs – so that it is indeed true
that 'a belief is identified by its location in a pattern of
beliefs' and, one wants to add, practices, conventions and
forms of life.   If the *correctness* of our beliefs is the deciding point, then one is at a loss to understand the history of
science.

2 In replacing 'correct' with 'intersubjectively agreed on' in

the above passage one is not begging the question.   For if a
person displays a massive enough difference in the pattern or
range of beliefs about some object, then that may still provide
grounds for doubting that she is talking about the same object
we are talking about, e.g. the earth.   But this is a matter
that is only decidable in situ.

Here another problem surfaces.   Davidson (and Cooper) are
of course talking about concepts and categories, not instances.
The example of 'the earth' is deceptive for that is a case
where there is only one instance of its kind.   For some concepts and categories it is often only a wide range of difference
that is the grounds for deciding incommensurability.   For
particular instances, however, it is another matter.   If A
and B are talking about a certain ball, for example, and B
discovers that A's beliefs about that ball are identical to his
in all but one tiny detail, e.g. that it has a red ink spot on
one side, he may be entitled to conclude that they are not
talking about the same ball at all.   That is also situatedly
decidable.   It is misleading, therefore, to talk in terms of
*objects* as Davidson and Cooper do.   Where a particular
instance is at issue, a difference in belief over one feature
could generate a problem of identity.   Where a category is at
issue, it would have to be much more than a difference in
belief that generates this problem.

3   It is not our beliefs *alone* that enter into our shared
understandings and considerations.   It is our practices and
our forms of life.   In Davidson's example it is still obvious
that the ancients believed *the earth* to be flat, for by '*the
earth*' they meant, as we do, that planetary body which they,
as we, *inhabited*.   And by *the sun* they meant, as we do,
that planetary body which illuminates *the earth*.   This is an
issue of a *de re* and a *de dicto* identification and is solved by
a resolution of scope and modality.   (For further discussion
of such see Chapter 6.)   Thus one may disagree in some (or
even many) beliefs about some object and still be understood
as talking about the same object we are, provided that other
sorts of beliefs *and* relevant practices are shared.   There is
a point, however, beyond which that ceases to be the case.
This is when too many other kinds of both belief *and* practice
are different.   There then ceases to be anything that *grounds*
our identification of beliefs, no criteria for ascertaining what
they are and what they are about.   But this is a matter for
detailed exploration, and no single formula will suffice for all
sorts of belief and for all specific cases - it is a thoroughly
situated and contingent matter.

The present argument, then, is meant to be aimed against
the claim for the radical and in-principle incommensurability of
different beliefs - both within a culture and across cultures -

whether it is used as a defence for a position of radical relativism or against it, as by Davidson and Cooper.

Let us now see how Cooper's transplant of Davidson's argument fares in the moral sphere.  Cooper suggests the following:

> we cannot suppose many of our moral beliefs to be false, or
> to have only relative truth.  If they could be, it is con-
> ceivable we should encounter people most of whose moral
> beliefs are incompatible with our own.  But this is not con-
> ceivable, for we should shortly decide their beliefs are not
> moral ones at all - or that we had misunderstood what they
> were moral beliefs about.  We can only identify another's
> beliefs as moral beliefs about $X$ if there is a massive degree
> of agreement between his and our beliefs.  Hence, there is
> no chance of radical moral diversity. (18)

1  Morality and moral agreement do not reside only in our
having *moral beliefs*.  We have moral concepts (such as, for
example, murder) and indeed it is in the context of such concepts and their conventional implications that one can talk
about moral beliefs.  We do not *believe* that murder is wrong
(although we may believe that it is a *sin*).  For us, if we
genuinely hold certain values, murder just *is* wrong.  Our
stance vis-à-vis murder is a value stance - our talk about it
reveals *values*, not, in the first instance, beliefs.  Although
one might in certain circumstances say, 'I believe that murder
is wrong', our saying that is, routinely speaking, not a belief
avowal per se, but a display of one's stand on a particular
case, a condemnation of another's stance, an accusation, a re-
minder, etc.  Such utterances cannot simply be taken as
statements, reports, descriptions or simple avowals, but have
to be seen as *interactional moves*.  However, in the context
of specific values, we may have propositional moral beliefs,
for example, that a specific murder was excusable;  that one
who kills even under great provocation is a weak person;
that taxpayers have the right to censor the kind of books
available on public library shelves;  that people have the
right to carry arms to defend themselves or to wage armed
struggle, etc.  The ties between values and beliefs are very
intimate and perhaps can be hinted at by the fact that many
moral beliefs can be formulated both propositionally (taking
the 'believe that:' form) and non-propositionally (taking the
'believe in:' form). (19)  One can say, for example, 'I
believe that taxpayers have the right to censor library books'
or 'I believe in the right of taxpayers to censor library
books' (also 'I believe that people have the right to wage
armed struggle' and 'I believe in people's right to wage armed
struggle').  But one cannot say, 'I believe in the earth's
being flat' or 'I believe in the French Revolution's taking

place in 1789.' The first has the character of a *religious belief* and the second is just plain odd. Thus, those beliefs that we can dub as moral ones display a complex and integral relationship to moral values, standards and criteria, a relationship which shows up in the very practices of social life. What in one setting can be displayed as a value in which certain beliefs are embedded can, in another setting and for different practical purposes, itself get produced as a belief grounded in some other value or set of values and standards. This, then, is an argument for detailed analysis of interactional contexts for their moral features – only in empirical investigation can we emerge with a genuine and adequate understanding of the moral order.

2 In what sense can one talk of the truth and falsity of moral beliefs? Truth and falsity apply, as predicates, only to propositional matters where routinely in assessment work some external consideration, authority, or evidence can be decisive. In moral matters, although some persons can be treated as having a kind of *moral authority* (one's mother, the Pope, one's commander, etc.), one may still intelligibly disagree morally with that person on some matter and be none the worse for it – indeed, one may thus revoke recognition of that authority (cf. Henry VIII and the Roman Catholic Church). Such an outcome over a purely empirical matter (as, for example, seeking a doctor's advice) would not be intelligible. Kai Nielsen's discussion of whether there could be an authoritative basis for moral claims is illuminating here. (20) He compares moral questions with other sorts. One way of locating a difference in *kind* between the two sorts of claim (moral and non-moral), such as between how to treat one's son and health claims, is in the following way: If someone seen to be swimming badly is told *how* to do the breast stroke properly and her answer is 'I don't care. I don't want to learn to swim any better', her expression of her wishes (provided she is in no danger of drowning) is directly and acknowledgedly relevant to the question of what she should do. This would similarly be the case if a doctor told someone, on the basis of her expertise, that jogging was good for his health, and that person nevertheless refused to jog, although he knew that failure to do so was detrimental. However, Nielsen says, if I was told that I was behaving unfairly to someone and I replied, 'I don't care. I don't want to be fair', then that reply is not only 'morally unhappy, it is conceptually unhappy as well. This "answer" is conceptually unhappy because it is plainly irrelevant. You can readily point out to me that it doesn't matter what I want.' (21)

I shall not take up everything raised by Nielsen in this claim. I shall only point out a difference that he has missed between the two sorts of case. It is true that in the latter

case my expression of wishes has a different *status* from that
in the former - it is more significantly implicative in a moral
sense.   Moreover, a rebuttal here carries with it a conventional moral authority that it would not in the former.   In
the former case one cannot insist, 'I wish to swim this way.
Your instructions are nonsensical.'   Such a stance would not
invalidate the techniques of proper swimming.   Nor would
saying 'I don't wish to jog.   Your advice is nonsensical'
effectively challenge a doctor's technical authority.   The
challenge here has no teeth, and indeed simply reflects back
on the challenger's assignable rationality.   But one can say,
'I want to do X.   Your calling it unfair is nonsensical' and
be making an intelligible and cutting challenge to the authority, not only of the person who is confronting, but of the
very moral stance espoused and defended by that person.   It
is true that such a position may in turn be seen as not moral
at all, or as immoral, depending on the case.   But that itself
is a display of a specific moral stance and reveals questions of
morality to be intimately tied to questions of 'membership'.
We shall have more to say on this in Chapter 8.   Such challenges are often only the first step towards the articulation of
alternative moral positions.   Think, for example, of the history and variety of moral stances on 'adultery', 'virginity',
'abortion', etc.

In other words, where a third party's moral position is consulted vis-à-vis some moral disagreement, that position itself
constitutes, *in the end*, no more and no less than a moral
agreement or disagreement with one (or both) of the two originally disputant positions, although up to that point *persuasion* is still possible.   However, one can talk of the truth
and falsity of certain moral facts - i.e. that a murder has
been committed;   that someone has betrayed his friend;   that
a certain act constituted cheating - as well as the truth and
falsity of certain *morally relevant* facts - that someone knew
that another had been very sick when he sent him on an
arduous mission, etc.   Our moral concepts have their logical
implications, their logic-in-use and their conventional known-
in-common criteria for application (albeit, and all importantly,
open-ended).   Many moral disputes are disputes over facts
of this kind (although in there being such a dispute one may
find, situatedly, grounds for reading moral differences).
While moral notions organize our descriptive practices and our
constitution of facticity, in the actual settings of practical
interaction they are also embedded in and supported by
factual agreements and considerations (whether moral or otherwise).   It is in the contexts of non-moral beliefs and facts,
as well as of moral facts, that moral beliefs and values are
displayed and that moral agreements and disagreements are
established.   And this takes place in specific practical contexts of interaction which situatedly provide the relevances,

tasks and parameters of common agreement within which disagreement surfaces.  It is in these contexts that the logic-in-
use of moral judgment can be explicated, so that Cooper's
extrapolation of Davidson's argument about beliefs into the
moral realm is extremely ill-advised (quite apart from the
other problems raised by that position).  Agreement and disagreement over moral beliefs can be grounded in our shared
conventions and practices, our empirical beliefs, our knowledge of the social and physical world (e.g. the material
irreversibility of death) and our standards of consistency,
formal logic, etc.  Ultimately, therefore, there can be massive and radical disagreement in moral values maintained intelligibly, i.e. within other shared reference points.  What more
radical disagreement can one get than that between a member
of the Ku Klux Klan and a humanist of the Bertrand Russell
Peace Foundation?  Otherwise, what is meant by radical disagreement?  Is it disagreement over a very wide set of moral
issues (from returning greetings to abstaining from torturing
others) or disagreement over basic and highly significant
moral matters (torture, murder, the right to be free from the
threat of starvation, etc.)?  I suggest that it is essentially
the latter which gives rise to judgments of radical moral disagreements in practical life.  We have a wide range of categorizations and descriptions for persons who are seen to differ
from us in various ways, ranging all the way from eccentric,
non-conformist, bizarre to brutish, inhuman, maniacal, etc.

Agreements and disagreements are produced, displayed,
pointed to in *occasioned* ways.  Disagreement is situatedly
grounded, by interactants, in conventional agreements that
provide the parameters of practical intelligibility on any particular occasion.  But the boundaries of agreement and disagreement are not clear-cut and rigid as between different
members - they are criss-crossing and may shift according to
different practical purposes.

The thrust of the preceding argument is to demonstrate the
importance of detailed analytic elucidation of the logic, properties and practices of our everyday moral order, an undertaking that is long overdue.  I am in agreement with Snare's
criticism of the traditional attitudes of many moral philosophers:

In its response to the investigations of anthropologists, his-
torians and sociologists, modern English-speaking moral
philosophy has shown itself to be, if not quite ethnocentric,
at least curiously sophistical.  Some have simply dismissed
the data of social science as irrelevant to moral philosophy.
'How can empirical data be relevant to a philosophical question?'  Others, who perhaps concede that the empirical
diversity of values would pose a problem, tend to dismiss
the data accumulated by some anthropologists by a number

of ploys verging on the sophistical.   It is not that they
know of further fieldwork or theory which would lead them
to reinterpret the original data.   Rather, they undertake
to show that, in spite of the data, there can be, or are,
certain uniformities in moral beliefs throughout all cultures. (22)

Philosophy has had its linguistic turn.   It is now time for its
sociological turn.   Winch's discussion of Sidgwick elegantly
demonstrates this need.   Discussing the universalizability
principle as put by Sidgwick, Winch writes:

In his premises Sidgwick asserts that if in certain circumstances I judge an action right for a third party, *A*, then I
am committed to judging the same action right for any other
third party, *B*, *given circumstances not relevantly different*. (23)

This is, of course, a much more sensitive and apt formulation
than Hare's.   And in this form one has to agree with it - it
is an elucidation of the *informal* logic of moral judgment.
But the very point is that if we wish to understand the
organization of the moral order it is precisely the questions of
*how*, in what way, and for what practical purposes are circumstances made out to be relevantly different or relevantly similar that are of analytic interest.   It is *that* which reveals the
nature of moral organization and interaction, and it is the
practices by which that is accomplished that inform us of the
logic and properties of the moral order of which we are members.   To turn the universalizability principle, then, into an
abstract condition that functions as a premise for moral philosophy, or as its finding, is *to obscure* the very nature and
force of practical moral judgment, inference and description.

An analytic project such as we are proposing immediately
begins to reveal for us the conventional foundations of both
moral agreement and moral disagreement.   Take an example
given by Phillips and Mounce of an instance of moral deadlock
- the captured warrior.   His captors want to send him to a
rehabilitation centre and he wishes to be allowed to commit
suicide.

Here we have a direct clash between what might be called
a heroic morality and a welfare conception of human life.
If one said to the warrior, 'We'll take you to a rehabilitation
centre', he might reply 'Don't treat me like a woman!'   In
the event of a discussion, the adherent to the welfare conception might make a final appeal to the 'truth' that all men
want to live, to which the warrior might reply, 'Not at the
cost of sacrificing dignity and valour.'   Here one has rival
conceptions of human dignity.   But when deadlock is

reached, that is that.   It is this admission which inspires philosophical protest. (24)

In each case the different notion of dignity is embedded in the category-identity made relevant by each party and the normative standards tied to that category.   One party is operating a specific category 'warrior (of culture X)', the other party the category 'man', or 'human being'.   The possibility of this kind of disjunction, then, is tied into our categorization practices - these seem to organize different moral conceptions and standards.   On the one hand we have categorizations such as 'persons', 'men and women', 'human beings', 'organisms', etc.   On the other hand we have ones such as 'warriors', 'Frenchmen', 'Palestinians', 'women', 'artists', etc.   We are both sorts of person at the same time. These are categorial  identities embedded in our forms of life and our cultural practices.   Thus, it is the very structure of our language and speech, as well as the logic of our activities, the *weave of our practices*, that generates the possibility of divergent moralities, of both agreement and disagreement. This weave is the foundation of the complexity and diversity, as well as the orderliness and conventionality, of social life. The analogy one thinks of here is that of the interwoven patterns of an oriental rug:   one might follow the different strands through many alternative paths, locating patterns which cancel, complement or criss-cross each other, but which are formed from the same strands and elements and constitute a *gestalt* whole.   Within the weave of cultural practices we have chosen to follow those of membership categorization. Let us then begin with the task.

Chapter 1

# Membership categorizations

## TYPE CATEGORIZATIONS

In introducing this first section I shall raise some matters
which will be dealt with in detail in later sections.   I will
begin to show some of the ways certain sorts of membership
categorizations work and through that to mark out some of the
differences between various kinds of categorizations.   For
this initial task, I have chosen to consider 'type' categorizations since this is also one way of showing that membership
categorizations do not fall into fixed sets but may be constructed in various contingent ways, some of these ways being the
situated construction of 'types'.   Further, this enables us to
make the distinction between membership *categories* and membership *categorizations*;   the latter term refers to the work
of members in categorizing other members or using 'characterizations' of them, whereas the former refers to the already
culturally available category-concepts that members may, and
routinely do, use in categorizational work and the accomplishment of various practical tasks.   The use of such category-
concepts, however, does not exhaust the use of categorizations and the conduct of members' categorizational work.

   Examples of category-concepts are:   doctor;   mother;   poet;
vandal;   saint;   murderer;   child.   Examples of other categorizations might be:   a nice man;   a nervous person;   a
pretty girl;   an intelligent woman;   a dangerous driver;   a
hippy type, etc.   Note that these are all Adjectives-plus-a-
Category.   Often the sense of the categorization depends criterially (as in 'dangerous driver') on both parts of the categorization.   The former are organized in such a way that
they can be seen (and treated) as relating to other concepts
as devices or as categories within a device (in Sacks's sense)
for various practical purposes.   The latter kind work, at
best, as *umbrella categorizations*, subsuming various sorts of
particulars and descriptions.   The distinction between the
two, important as it is, is not however meant to be taken as a
rigid one.   Let us now turn to our initial investigation.

   The data extracts I shall first use in this section (1) come
from a telephone conversation which turns on the discussion of
a specific problem - the use of a certain place (the Planet
playground) by a certain group of people (Hell's Angels and

dropouts) and their activities there. The conversation gets
initiated by *A*, who is seeking information on the problem from
*R* (a policeman). In the process of giving information and
the ensuing discussion of the 'problem', *R* provides some
detailed characterization of the persons concerned. This
characterization involves projected actions that these people
may perform, assessments of their characters, talk about their
habits, codes, etc., and throughout the talk *R* refers to 'they',
'these types', 'Hell's Angels', 'dropouts', etc., sometimes
apparently interchangeably. It is to this that we shall direct
our attention.

The first place at which *R* introduces some reference to the
people concerned is in utterance 4 (see Appendix 3):

3  A:  Ah, erm ... my name's Anderson and I'm chairman of
       the Trust and I'm really just trying to find out
       what's happening.

4  R:  Well, there's not much happening yet as far as I
       know.... The only thing we know is that the place
       is being used by er all these er dropouts and er
       Hell's Angels and they're prepared to have a battle
       royal complete with er weapons and goodness knows
       what with a load of skinheads.

There is a possibly noticeable source of equivocality here -
is the place being used by individual dropouts *and* persons
belonging to the group designated as Hell's Angels, both lots
joined in their intention to fight the skinheads? Or is 'dropout' being used as some alternative and elaborative characterization of the persons using that place, who are members of
the Hell's Angels? 'Dropout', we notice, is an *individual
designator*, and 'Hell's Angel' designates an individual *as* a
member of a self-organized group. There is a further difference that we can note here: 'dropout' delivers the *character*
or property (criterial feature) of the category *in* the category
name, 'Hell's Angel' does not. We may note further that the
character of the utterance part 'all these er dropouts and er
Hell's Angels' is that of a (short) list of categories. One
answer to the above questions may then be obtained by examining the nature and work of categorial lists and the tie
between individual designators and group designators in such
lists. We shall return to this presently.

The next point in the conversation at which the persons
concerned are mentioned specifically is in utterance 25 in
reply to a question from *A*.

25  A:  Of er of er of what ... who were the people who
        were arrested do you know I mean er ...

26  R:  Ooh, I couldn't say offhand, I think these were
         about seven in all...

27  A:  Yeah, were there some skinheads or ...

28  R:  No, no, not skinheads, these are Hell's Angels
         types.

One thing one may notice here is that although *R* could not
specify the particular individuals that were arrested, he
could specify a category incumbency for them.   That is to
say, while he cannot say *who* they were, he could say *what*
they were (although for some purposes specifying a *what* for
a person works in or as specifying a *who*).   But again it is
not clear whether the actual persons referred to are actual
members of the Hell's Angels group, (2) or whether they
*could* be members by virtue of their being the types of person
that make up Hell's Angels recruits, or yet again whether they
are simply *like* the Hell's Angels (perhaps copy or emulate
them).   *R*'s utterance does not provide that the uncertainty
of these persons' membership in the group is an issue that
needs resolution.   He then proceeds to elaborate on and
characterize the Hell's Angels *type*:

28  R:  No, no, not skinheads, these are Hell's Angels
         types.

29  A:  I see, er, do you get a lot of bother from skinheads
         as well?

30  R:  Not particularly.

31  A:  Yeah.

32  R:  Er the Hell's Angels types are the people who er
         *don't* stop at home ... they sleep out, they sleep
         rough, they're a dirty, scruffy idle shower, they
         live off social security er plus er thieving er things
         here and there.

Here we have the characterization of a *type* constructed or
formulated by reference to a *group*, the Hell's Angels.   But
the characterization itself is not of the particular group and
its members, but of a kind of person and a mode of existence
that *could*, in fact, fit a variety of persons or incumbents of
other membership categories - dropouts, tramps, vagrants -
irrespective of any group membership.

This set of habits and mode of existence are not the prerog-
ative of the Hell's Angels or any organized group.   However,
they are talked of by *R* as pertaining to the *Hell's Angels*

*type*, as though all such persons with the above habits and
way of life constituted a unitary type and moreover one that
could be recognizably seen as the type constitutive of the
Hell's Angels group.   The *description* of the type - for that
is what we get - proceeds through the production of a *list*
of traits and practices.   But it is interesting that in producing this description of the Hell's Angels type, *R* is also producing a description of what the skinheads are *not*.   This is
achieved by virtue of the contrastive work done in utterances
28 to 32.

Given that the description of the Hell's Angels type is produced in the form of a list, the question may arise:  Does the
category *'skinhead'* not take any of the list items (each and
every one of them is excluded) or not take some of them, i.e.
does it not take the list as a whole, as a *collection*? (3)    Is
it a finite or open-ended list?   In the construction of a list
(characterizing the Hell's Angels explicitly and the skinheads
implicitly) lies the possibility of generating a *disagreement*
(e.g. 'but the skinheads also live off social security'), thence
an *argument*, then the assignation or elaboration of *precedence*
to some list items over others.   We will deal more fully with
list constructions in Chapter 3.

In the last data extract *F* formulates a 'type' category with
reference to a specific self-organized group, the Hell's Angels.
Later on in the same conversation he formulates a 'type' category through the use of an individual rather than a group
designator.

86  R:  I mean to say that the object of it is a children's
        playground, isn't it, initially?

87  A:  Yeah.

88  R:  Well, all it's becoming is just a doss house for
        people who are a dropout variety.

I take it, commonsensically, that the idea of a 'dropout
variety' here works in the same way as 'dropout type', that
is, through designating a *class* of person by reference to the
descriptor 'dropout'.

To reiterate very briefly:  we have now located three
classes of membership categories:  *self-organized* groups (with
proper names), *individual descriptor designators* (like 'dropout'), and *type categorizations*.   Of the latter we have those
that are organized by reference to an organized group and
those that are organized by reference to a property or descriptor.   This listing of categories, of course, is not meant
to be exhaustive nor are the items to be seen as totally and

determinately distinct from each other and from other categorizations with respect to all their features, i.e. they do not
fall into rigid classes.   We shall see later that categorizations may be treatable as falling into different classes with
regard to different features, and that they are hugely complex phenomena which function differently in different language (and interactional) games.   But for now let us proceed
with these preliminary observations.

The use of a 'type' construction as a categorization is inter-
esting and has some interactionally noticeable consequences.
In a sequence following his characterization of the Hell's
Angels type, *R* uses it to make a guarded prediction:

50   R:   I don't think your windows would last very long.

51   A:   Oh ... you sound very pessimistic.

52   R:   Well (coughs) knowing these types and dealing with
          them er ... one can't look at it any other way.

*R* is presumably predicting that the windows talked of as about
to be put up at the Planet playground could be broken or
even taken out by some of these 'Hell's Angels types' sleeping
out there.   For *A* such a prediction is an expression of pessimism on *R*'s part, which is justified by *R* on the grounds of
*his knowledge of and dealings with those types*.   But notice
that in characterizing the Hell's Angels Type through a listing
of items that are 'typical' of the incumbents of such a category, *R* had not included violence or window breaking or vandalism in that list.   How then is it possible to predict that
probably the windows won't last on the basis of knowing these
'types'?   *A*'s charge of pessimism displays and achieves the
following:   that there are alternative possibilities expectable,
some of which are undesirable and others not necessarily so.
Because a predicted consequence of an action is at least a
possibility, but not a *certainty*, the projected action is thus
not *constitutive* of that 'type'.   In other words, the projected action is a possibility embedded in the features of that
categorization.   The projected action is provided for by the
guarded prediction of a *consequence* - this projection is then
tied to, and provided for, as having been generated by a
knowledge of, and familiarity with, a 'type' of person.   It is
not knowledge of *specific* persons that generates this projection, but knowledge of and dealings with 'these types', albeit
that this 'type' categorization may be generated in the first
place on the basis of particular persons' behaviour.   It is
not, however, what is specific to each but what is perceivedly
*common to all* that is the focus of such projections, typifica-
tions and inferences.   It is the features of a perceived *class*
of persons that is relevant and thus displayed as relevant,

not the features of various 'individuals'. In this way, the
prediction provided by R is accountably guarded - it is neither
of a specific temporally located action, nor, importantly, of a
specific person, but of a *consequence*, a projected outcome
that may be produced in one way or another, by one person
or another from a collection of persons with common character-
istics - a 'type'. That this 'type' is constructed with reference to a self-organized group ('the Hell's Angels type'),
however, makes its use also *implicative* for projections to,
inferences about and judgments of that group itself.

What R is doing here, then, is depriving the individual
biographies of each of the persons sleeping at the Planet
playground of any status or relevance for assessing and projecting their possible future actions. Instead, we have the
encapsulation of a particular set of activities and a particular
set of practices attributable to various different persons at
various and different times into a 'type'. And this 'type' is
then used to project future actions for any particular person
that is seen or made to fit the 'type'. The name, history,
problems, personal likes and dislikes, aptitudes, skills, etc.
of a John, Ken or Brian, for example, who happens to sleep
at the Planet playground are not brought into the conversation as being relevant; they are not consulted, investigated,
diagnosed or otherwise made operative for the issue at hand,
which is: 'What will happen next?' or 'What will happen to
the window when put up?' They are left completely out of
the picture. What is involved here is a transpersonal projection of attributes and expectable actions. A consequence
of this is that those activities performed, and habits engaged
in, by particular individuals categorized under the 'type'
rubric do not find their various explanations in their biography: they become de-historicized. Why Brian Smith, for
instance, sleeps out in the open and has no job is not made
an explainable and investigable matter - it is rather made out
as a given attribute of Brian Smith. That is to say, it is
not produced as being a fact contingent on prior biographical,
individually specific episodes, experiences, opportunities and
relationships of Brian Smith (even if a lot of other individuals
shared a similar set of experiences, e.g. as in the Depression)
but rather it is made out to be *constitutive* of Brian Smith
and so constitutive of him, if need be, *in spite* of his biography. Thus it can situatedly be turned into a non-treatable
and non-repairable matter.

Let us note a few issues at this point:

1 Actions and properties *tied* to a 'type' categorization are
not necessarily the same as those *constitutive* of it. Neither
can they be treated as necessarily the same as those which are
seeable as embedded in its features. Given a list of traits

for a 'type' (a collection of them), it is possible to generate further expectable type-embedded actions and properties.

2 For group-relative 'types', what is constitutive of the group category is not taken to be what is constitutive of the 'type' formed from it. Or, one can say that what is constitutive of the 'type' is not necessarily or exhaustively constitutive of the group relative to which that 'type' gets constructed. A self-organized group is set up on the basis of some set of beliefs, interests, attitudes, commitments, inclinations or whatever, but it is *further* constituted through a set of membership rules and procedures which admit persons to membership within the group, and thus to category incumbency. What is routinely taken to be constitutive of the 'type', then, are the features taken to be typical of the group's members.

A member's being formulated as a Hell's Angels type may then display an *indifference* to his/her actual membership within the group for some practical purposes (as it does in our data). But the individual's actions and traits are thence nevertheless projectable onto the group to which he/she is related or likened. Moreover, the group's history and character are usable to project, outline or discover those of the individual (it is thus that this indifference is achieved and displayed). On the other hand, being the intellectual or quiet type, for example, is already trait-marked. The type here is formulated with reference to a property, with a *descriptor concept*, as is 'dropout variety'. The constituent property or feature of the type is then given *in its naming*, unlike the type constructed by reference to a named group (where the constituent feature is hidden in the first instance and embedded in the discoverable character of the group). 'Intellectual', 'quiet', 'dropout' tell the hearer exactly what the characteristic of the type is. The *constituent* features and traits of that membership categorization are not expandable. Nevertheless, again, we will find that in the course of a conversational interaction, other properties and features may be situatedly generated as tied to, or expectable or possible of, 'type' incumbents. They are embedded within the features of the 'type'.

The availability of such categorization-embedded features as well as of further category-tied features brings us to a basic point about membership categorizational work that we will repeatedly encounter in the course of our investigation: (a) Categories orientably and conventionally carry with them a *cluster* (4) of expectable features - i.e. the constitutive trait in the last example carries with it a cluster of related possible actions, traits, preferences, haunts, appearances, places, times, etc. It is the nucleus of other categorization-tied or relevant features which all together provide procedures for situated inferences to a host of other issues regarding category incumbents in their settinged availability. Thus, the use of categorizations is not only descriptive of persons, but it is through and through *an ascriptive* matter.  (b) *This cluster* is itself embedded in the logico-grammatical relationships between concepts.

There is some difference between the categorization 'dropout variety' and one such as 'intellectual type' or 'quiet type'.  In the former, although the constitutive feature is available in the naming, it is a second-order availability. The *criteria* by which a person may be categorized as 'dropout' are not accessible;  in what way a person categorized as 'dropout' has 'dropped out' is not given;  from work, college, family, old friends, old pursuits?  The elaboration or presumption of further features of a particular incumbent of the type categorization therefore depends, in the first instance, on the particularization of what in this instance counts as 'dropping out', although then such features are producible as being type-embedded.

We will take up some aspects of this when we discuss the practical translation problem in Chapter 3.  Let us move on to another issue.

One sometimes hears the following kind of exchange:

A:  Why does he do those things?

B:  He's (just) that type of person.

Finding a reason for doing certain things is contrastable to being the *type* of person who does those things.  Many requests for explanation are answered (and answerable) by the provision, invocation or attribution of a category incumbency to the person for whose action or behaviour an explanation was being sought.  The category used need not be a 'type' categorization but could be any other;  what work the answer does depends in part on the sort of category provided in explanation, e.g., A:  'Why did they go on strike?'  B: 'They're militants.'  The explanation here, instead of providing a specific reason for the strike or grounds for the strikers' action (e.g. demands for higher wages, better working conditions, etc.), simply consists in a *description* that casts the strikers as 'militants', i.e. as a certain sort of person.  The second speaker is locating the answer to the first speaker's question in the character (in the widest sense of the term) of the persons involved, rather than in the situation preceding the action, other people's actions or character or a history of the issues involved, all of which could provide grounds or occasioned reasons for the action.  By depriving the queried action of an explanation-by-specific-reason (or grounds) the speaker may be involved in also depriving it of possible *excuses or justifications* should they be needed. And the actions are thus provided as offering a *clue* to the individuals' possible future actions.   Action projections are made possible.   Where an action is used to generate a character (or attribute) for persons involved in it, rather than an explanation by specific reason, that character or attribute is then usable to project *further* expectations of actions, stances or involvements of the categorized persons.   Categorizations, in other words, can work as umbrellas for the ascription of other features and actions. (5)

In political debates or polemics between different parties the negatively implicative actions of the opponent are often deprived of explanation-by-grounds and transformed instead into a feature of the opponent's character (in the wide sense of the term), whilst an exactly similar action by one's own party is provided with an occasioned *reason*.   (The categorization provided may be in terms of a 'type' or in terms of a descriptor categorization - if the former, the reading of the relevant features of the 'type' are routinely left to the hearer/reader to glean from the context of what actions are the focus of the talk/text.)

The contrastive use of attribute-specification rather than explanation-by-grounds or specific reason (good or bad, sufficient or insufficient) is a feature of talk about much 'deviant' activity as well as of political argument and counter-argument. The underlying asymmetry of perspectives involved is a logical feature of such formulations, and it points clearly and simply to the normatively and morally organized character of categorization work, accounts, descriptions, predictions and discourse-interactional work in general.   The categorization 'deviant' itself is one that is potentially (and regularly) used in essentially asymmetrical account constructions.   But we will deal with such issues at some length later on in this work.   Notice for now the character of the following account:

Like the rest of us on that street - who played the male role with other men - Pete was touchy about one subject - his masculinity.   In Bickford's one afternoon, a good looking masculine young man walked in, looking at us, walks out again hurriedly.   'That cat's queer', Pete says, glancing at him.   'I used to see him and I thought he was hustling, and one day he tried to put the make on me in the flix.   It bugged me, him thinking I'd make it with him for free.   I told him to f... off, go find another queer like him.'   He was moodily silent for a long while and then he said almost belligerently: 'No matter how many queers a guy goes with, if he goes for money, that don't make him

queer.   You're still straight.   It's when you start going
for free, with other young guys, that you start growing
wings.' (6)

The contrast here is between doing homosexual activity for a
specific reason, having a reason to engage in it (money)
*other than the activity itself* and engaging in homosexual
activity for itself.   'When you start going for free' indicates
then that the activity is not being engaged in for a reason
outside itself (although in principle it still could be);   that
activity would then constitute the character of the participant
as the sort of person who engaged in that activity for itself.
In the case of homosexual activity the individual may thus get
constituted as a homosexual, instead of, for example, a
hustler.

Thus, not only can a categorization be proposed as providing some reason for action in contrast to an explanation-by-
specific-reason, but where some action is seeable as being
engaged in for itself, rather than for a specific reason external to the action, this is productive of a corresponding categorization of the actor.   Note further here that this routinely
provides for the production of simultaneous double or multiple
categorizations.   In the preceding extract, we have both
'homosexual' and 'queer' as usable categorizations (where the
latter turns in the first instance on the former but may come
to stand for it in usage). (7)

Consider the following extract of data: (8)

Jay:      Wuhdidju think of, when Romney came out with
          his statement that he w'ss um, ... thet 'e w'z
          brain//wash//ed

George:   I *think* he *wa*:s
          (pause ca. 5.0 sec.)

Jay:      IN - in uhm, what *sense*
          (pause ca. 2.0)

George:   I don'kno:w, b't if he says he w'z *brain*-washed,
          (pause ca. 7.0)

Sy:       He's one a' these 'Rom//ney c'do no wro:ng.'-
          types.   hh

George:   *He*'s en honest *ma:n*

George:   This much I *do* know.

In that George could not provide a *reason* for his belief that

Romney was brainwashed *independent* of Romney's avowal, Sy can formulate George as being a 'type' who believes unquestioningly in Romney. He could also, of course, have further formulated him as the 'gullible' type, as 'naive', or alternatively as 'someone trying to cover up for a political "friend"', but he did not choose to do that. George provides (but somewhat belatedly) grounds for his belief in Romney, and they take the form of a character formulation 'en honest man' (which is a way of categorizing him). This works as a cutoff and can provide a shift in the conversation back to a discussion of Romney himself and an assessment of his character. It can be seen, then, that the 'type' categorization is producible as an ad hoc practical contexted construction on the part of participants in a conversation. There can be, therefore, theoretically any number or variety of 'types'.

Compare now the construction of a 'type' in the preceding section of data with that in the following: (9)

1 Q: You have described your actions on a number of occasions where it is apparent that you have been going to considerable trouble - and do not for one moment think I am being critical - trying to quieten down young people, mostly young men, young boys, from the Bogside who were causing trouble in Londonderry?

2 A: From the Bogside or outside it, people I did not recognize necessarily.

3 Q: You did not recognize them. Let me say people from your community, meaning by that the Roman Catholic community - and I do not by that suggest there are two separate communities. That has been an occupation that has taken much of your time?

4 A: Yes.

5 Q: Does that mean that there is a hooligan element in that community?

6 A: I am not prepared to use the word 'hooligan', I think it is a rather artistic term.

7 Q: What term would you prefer?

8 A: There are youths who can get so hot-headed that they are careless of what trouble they cause.

9 Q: Can you think of no other description for them than that?

10  A:  I would say irresponsible.

11  Q:  These are irresponsible youths.   You would not
        put it higher than that?   Are they vandals?

12  A:  I would not use the word 'vandals' either.   I think
        if we enquire they are quite law-abiding.

13  The Chairman:  Would you use the word reckless of
        other people's safety?

14  A:  Yes.

15  Q:  Would you use the word reckless of other people's
        property?

16  A:  Yes, I would.

17  Mr Chambers:  These are people whom you have had
        occasion to attempt to restrain in one way or
        another?

18  A:  Yes.

19  Q:  And with varying success?

20  A:  Yes.

21  Q:  Sometimes you have been unable to achieve what
        you set out to achieve?

22  A:  That is true, yes.

23  Q:  Would you accept that such people can readily be
        stirred up to violence against other members of the
        community and against the property of other mem-
        bers of the community?

24  A:  I would agree with that, yes.

25  Q:  Having heard the evidence that has so far been
        given, do you accept that it was those people rather
        than any strangers or people from outside who
        started the trouble in Londonderry on the 12th
        August?

26  A:  I would accept it was probably that kind of person.

27  Q:  That is, people in this irresponsible element of the
        Roman Catholic community?

28  A:  I do not know if it was the Roman Catholic....

29  The Chairman:  I do not know that the words 'Roman Catholic' apply, Mr Chambers.

Where we have a 'type' construction used in this data – 'such people' in utterance 23 and 'that kind of person' in utterance 26 – the specification of that type (its contexted construction) has been produced over a number of turns that include the application and rejection of discursive descriptions (utterance 8), as well as individual designator categories, e.g. 'hooligan element' (utterance 5).  The type is not constructed in one utterance where the use (invocation, application, attribution, etc.) of the typological categorization and its descriptive designation appear together, as in the previous data extract ('He's one a' these "Romney c'do no wrong" types'), but rather the descriptive work designating the type and the typological categorization use (which marks the completion of the 'type' category construction) appear in different turns at talk, in sequence.

Note now the tension between the work $Q$ (Mr Chambers) may be attempting to do through his questioning and the sort of work that the use of a 'type' categorization does.  $Q$ seems to be attempting to pin down responsibility for the disturbances of August 12 under discussion onto a section of the Roman Catholic community (some young boys) from the Bogside of Londonderry.  To do that he first attempts to secure a specific sort of categorization for that section of that community (which would thus be constituted as a separate section by virtue of that categorization:  the reflexivity of descriptive work is evidenced here) – a 'hooligan element', 'vandals', etc. But $A$ does not participate in this categorization (thus undercutting its *ascriptive* implications).  Rather he selects adjectival descriptions (rather than noun/category descriptors) and extended descriptions:  'youths who can get so hot-headed that they are careless of what trouble they cause', 'irresponsible', etc.  By this $A$ tones down the accusatory and implicative force which might emerge from the categorizational descriptions offered by $Q$. (10)  What follows is the provision of further such description agreed to by $A$:  'reckless of other people's safety', 'reckless of other people's property'.  Note that the latter two items may be seen as elaborative of the description 'irresponsible'.

We said earlier that 'type' categorizations are usable for doing certain kinds of predictive and inferential work.  In utterance 23, $Q$ uses the expression 'such people', thus completing and accomplishing the ad hoc construction of a typological categorization and uses it to project and elaborate further expectable behaviour from the persons who are thus categorized: 'such people can readily be stirred up to violence against other members'.   What is employed as a resource and displayed here is the *cluster* of category-tied and category-embedded attributes and actions carried by the type categorization as situatedly constructed.   Not everyone may assent to every item taken to be applicable and included within such a cluster by others.   There is a latitude for disagreement – the cluster structure is, in other words, openended, just as the logic of a concept can be open-ended. But *A does* assent here.   However, what is being produced at this point is talk about, and with respect to, a certain type categorization – and a type categorization constructed from features not produced in the conversation as being specific to a particular community (the Roman Catholic community).   We have seen that a 'type' construction may be used to do one or both of the following:

1  transform a specific grounded action or set of actions, beliefs, etc. into an attribute;

2  construct a *class* of persons with respect to that attribute.

Thus, a type categorization, besides being usable in some predictive work, and in spite of that, may nevertheless systematically allow for imprecision, equivocality and guardedness both as to *specific* persons' actions and as to the applicability of general predictions to a specific individual or group where the type categorization was not clearly constructed in the first place by reference to that group (e.g. Hell's Angels, Roman Catholics, etc.).   To achieve the latter, further work would need to be done on the part of categorizers.   In the data, when *Q* follows his type categorization use with a turn at talk in which he specifies 'those people rather than any strangers or people from outside' (utterance 25), *A* responds with the typological construction 'that kind of person' instead of a specifying term.   When in the next turn *Q* attempts to specify further 'people in this irresponsible element of the Roman Catholic community' (utterance 27), he runs into disagreement over *this* specification.   After all, a class of persons constructed by reference to individually designating terms (descriptor concepts) may be found amidst many and various specific communities.   In this sense, of course, the 'Roman Catholic community' turns out to be (or functions as ) a different *sort* of group term from that of Hell's Angels, Irish Republican Army, etc.   In other words, 'type' categorizations are usable to *deflect specification of individual or group identification*.   Note that the categorization eventually arrived at over the course of several turns at talk excludes the habitual practice of violence, as in 'vandals' or 'hooligans' (two categorizations rejected by *A*) – violence is rather projected as a possible form of occasioned behaviour ('stirred up

into violence') on the part of persons categorized as 'hot-
headed' and 'irresponsible' types.   What might be interesting
to follow up here is the consequence of categorial deletion
(denial of category application or refusal to make a specific
categorial attribution) for further work on the part of interactants in the course of a conversation.

One interesting consequence of the use of type categorizations is the following.   Suppose one said, 'He's a criminal
type', what would the use of such a categorization do in contrast with 'He's a criminal'?   Clearly, if one were told in
protest, 'But he's not committed any crime', one would be
more constrained to back down from the description 'He's a
criminal' than from the description 'He's a criminal type'. (11)
Although some grounds for the latter categorization must be
available, these need not include 'proven guilty of criminal
action'.   Take another example:   'He's a homosexual' and
'He's a homosexual type'.   The former is a more definitive
categorization - that it is simpler to produce a backdown by
the speaker on that description is grounded in the fact that
it is simpler to provide the warrant for the *latter* description
('He's a homosexual type').   Indeed, what would count as
warrant for this is more diverse and open-ended.   A member
may provide warrant for it simply by pointing to the *way*
another member walks, talks and gestures (thus observably
trading on category-bound knowledge), and not necessarily by
providing any knowledge of, or evidence for, an actual homosexual relationship.   One way of minimizing speaker risk
(and claim risk), then, is to opt for the latter kind of categorization ('He's a criminal type', 'He's a homosexual type')
rather than the former (although it is still possible for members to find such characterizations morally implicative of the
speaker, but this is another issue).

In summary, then, one way of minimizing such risk is to opt
for the use of [Category + Type] categorization where this
can work as a *lesser claim* than the use of the category on
its own.   Other examples here might be:   Hell's Angels type,
schizophrenic type, etc.   The claim provided (or warrant
presumed) by such a categorization may be treated as a downgrading on the claim available from (or warrant required for)
the use of the category by itself:   Hell's Angel, schizophrenic,
criminal, homosexual, etc.

One upshot of this is that where a *positively* implicative
category is used (the above are all negatively implicative) to
provide a 'type' categorization, that categorization may be
hearable as *downgrading* or ironicizing the categorized member:
'saint type', 'a hero type', 'a Good Samaritan type', etc.
Compare this to the use of an [Adjective + Type] categorization, e.g. 'a heroic type'.   This latter is not hearable as a

downgrading since an adjective by itself ('heroic') does not provide a categorization, it remains to be completed by some other term in order to work as one – a heroic woman, heroic leader, heroic person, heroic soldier, etc.

In concluding this section it may be said that the 'type' categorization is a *collective attribute categorization* which accounts for its guarded usability in prediction work, where the prediction is made in reference to *specific* individuals and actions. That also accounts for the fact that when used as an explanation (A: Why does he do X?; B: Because he's that type of person), it does not function as an explanation by virtue of a specific reason or grounds but simply by reference back to the 'type's' attributes, i.e. class features.

## CATEGORY-BOUND AND CATEGORY-CONSTITUTIVE FEATURES

We have already referred to the notions of 'category-bound' ('category-tied') and 'category-constitutive' features in the preceding text. It is important at this stage to clarify what we mean specifically by these notions and to analyse some conventional consequences of their use. The notion of category-bound activities, first introduced by Harvey Sacks, (12) has been extended by other analysts with the use of the notion of category-bound obligations and rights (e.g. D.R. Watson (13)) and category-bound knowledge (e.g. Wes Sharrock (14) in his discussion of the ownership of knowledge by named collectivities). In this text we have referred to the ties between categories and conventionally expected properties, habits, beliefs, etc. We have noted that, rooted in the implicative logic of concepts, there are a host of features that, as *clusters*, can be oriented to and conventionally expected to go together with some categories. It seems appropriate then to talk of category-bound *features* as providing a more abstract analytic framework which comprises all the above variants. What is situatedly provided for or invoked as being category-bound is, of course, an occasioned matter and a methodic achievement on the part of members.

Let us look at the following extract of data (S.T. Data C6):

Q: First of all if I understand correctly the questions which have been put to you here there is a rather oblique suggestion that there was something sinister about the setting up of this post [a first-aid post] in Sultan Street. Have you anything to say about that?

A: There was absolutely nothing sinister about it. It was one of those automatic things that a first aider does.

It is his duty to help wherever possible in whatever way
he possibly can.

Firstly, the prior discussion between $Q$ and $A$ (see Appendix
2) had involved the characterization of an ad hoc treatment
centre by $A$ as a 'first aid post initially' rather than a 'casualty clearance station', which had been $Q$'s formulation.  And
the question-and-answer sequence had involved a discussion
and assessment of the nature of the preparations that had
been made for setting up this post, as well as the activities
conducted under its auspices (S.T. Data A11):

Q: May we take it then, Doctor, you accepted the assurances of certain people living in the vicinity of I suppose
the lower Falls, as a general term, that there was a
necessity for this clearing station on the 13th?

A: It was not - well, any post that was set up - it was not
a clearing station then, it was purely a first aid post on
the 13th.

What $A$ has done in the data under consideration is to set
up the categorization 'first-aider', a category whose relevance
and nature can be seen to have been locally generated by the
specifics of the situation under discussion - namely, by the
object-category (first-aid post) and the bunch of activities
that were correspondingly engaged in, whose outcome was the
first-aid post (as an organization bounded by locality, resources and practices).  A place or institution (object-category)
can thus generate a relevant membership categorization, not
only in the way that one might generate the relevance of the
categorization 'doctor' from the place-category 'hospital', but
also as an ad hoc practical accomplishment in context, just as
a 'type' categorization can be generated from various contexted particulars.  For instance, we could have 'dog kennel',
for which one might situatedly generate the membership categorization 'kennel owner'.  Such ad hoc categorizations can
also be generated for activities: 'dog shearing'/'dog shearer'.
But their generation in context is an occasioned accomplishment. (15)  In our data, rather than talk to the reason, for
example, or the circumstances surrounding the setting up of
that first-aid post, $A$ has transformed the nature of the practical problematic by making this action out to be one that is
*generated by*, and directly following on, the work of a *first-
aider*.  (In generating the categorization 'first-aider' from
the specifics of the talk - the first-aid post - he can then go
on to provide that the post was an outcome *generated by* the
relevance of the category-incumbency in context.)  A first-
aider naturally prepares to give first aid.  It follows both
logically and morally.  But this work relies on the prior
establishment of the post as (its formulation as) a *first-aid*

*post.* In setting up the category 'first-aider', *A* has collected
and formulated a bunch of activities that were engaged in
there as 'first aid', and has formulated them as being category-tied or, more specifically in this case, as *category-gener-*
*ated activities.* (16) Of these, setting up the post is one
category-generated activity: 'It was one of those automatic
things that a first-aider does.' With this there comes the
formulation of a category-tied obligation: 'It is his duty to
help wherever possible in whatever way he possibly can.'
Now one may take a distinction between category-tied features
and category-generated features in the following manner.
Where features are formulated, explicitly or implicitly, as conventionally accompanying some category, we may talk of them
as category-bound (or -tied). Where they are provided for
(or providable) in discourse as having been situatedly *pro-*
*duced through* their tie to some category, we may talk of them
as being (or being treated as) category-generated – the latter
is a refinement on the former that is sensitive to the situated
use of category-concepts and display of members' category
knowledge.

Thus, in the above data, the provision of the membership
categorization 'first-aider', fashioned out of resources provided in the prior conversation, makes available an *account* of
the actions in dispute, but an account that is essentially
*simple and self-sufficient.* The tie between account and
actions is here located *in* the category, whereas in a discursive account *work* has to be done to provide for it. Here
the work has already been partly accomplished in the previous
talk by providing a characterization of the post as a 'first-aid
post' which can then provide the relevance of the categorization used by *A*: 'first-aider'. It is a very neat and economi-
cal way of accomplishing the task of accounting. Of course,
such accounting work may situatedly be seen or treated as
being deficient – it may be faulted. Simply providing a
membership categorization as an account for some activity may
work – as we indicated earlier – by being counterposed to an
explanation-by-reason, where indeed it is a specific reason or
grounds that are being sought. We mentioned earlier, however, that categorizations such as doctor (first-aider, mother,
etc.) can be seen as strongly providing for reasons for doing
certain things, in certain contexts, but not the particular
grounds for acting, nor indeed a *specific* reason for it that
can be formulated as a purpose or motive.

That one is supposed to do something (category-bound obligations, category-bound tasks), or one is entitled to do it,
can stand as sufficient explanation for why one is doing that
and is self-evidently available as a general reason for acting
in certain ways, in given contexts. To ask further for
grounds there can be curious and may be hearable as formu-

lating some problematic character to one's activity or action, as, for example, when a mother feeds a hungry child, and some person persists in asking for an explanation. In such contexts one may, and routinely does, get as a first and preferred account a specific reason for the *local and situated production of category-bound activities* (although even that may be self-evidently available from the tie between some activity, a membership category and some member standing in a conventional relationship to that category incumbent); for example, a doctor bandaging someone in a field, where the answer to a query may be 'Because he cut his leg badly on the fence'. A doctor hearing a request for explanation of the same sort of activity in a hospital context (bandaging a leg) may, on the other hand, hear some 'problem' being oriented to by the questioner. Another example might be someone's asking a policeman why he was arresting another person. The answer may be 'Because he's causing a breach of the peace'. A persistence for a request here may come off as a search for a *motive*.

*One way, then, to undercut a search for motive or for specific reason is to provide an appropriate membership categorization that can formulate the activity or action in question as category-bound or as category-generated through the operation of category-bound obligations and rights.*

If you can further furnish that categorization out of resources and features collaboratively produced (or agreed on) by co-conversationalists, then you can further *undercut the possible objections to its relevance and may provide for the self-evidence of your account.* This is what happens in our data - the categorization 'first-aider' has been fashioned out of, and generated by, the relevances and formulations already produced in the conversation in such a way that the activities under discussion are formulated in and through that work *as* category-generated. This is a strong device.

Such a device as the above may be used also to provide *excuses* - 'It was one of those automatic things that a mother does - she tries to protect her child' (even when it leads to another's injury?).

Let us now take up a further set of issues. Consider the following (S.T. Data A29):

Q: Perhaps it is a matter of emphasis; some people might think that bringing in 12 or 14 beds and ringing up for doctors and nurses and so on is making fairly substantial preparation for casualties?

A: I do not think I should be a director if I did not antici-

pate problems.   There is not much point looking for
beds at one or two o'clock in the morning if the trouble
escalated, as I felt it might, from the night before's
reaction.

It is not clear whether *A* is here making a statement of
*eligibility*, of how it was that he came to be a 'director'
(i.c. that he would not have *become* a director had he not
been able to anticipate problems), or about the character of a
director's work and duties.   Either way, it reveals something
of how that category gets constituted and used.   Together
with other categories such as 'doctor', 'nurse', 'painter', etc.,
'director' carries with its understanding a corpus of expectable
*skills and abilities* – such skills and abilities often function
as the category incumbent's *credentials of incumbency*.   They
are required and expected.   Now it is not altogether clear
which *specific* skills and abilities may be said to be constitutive for any such categories.   After all, they can take sub-
categories with differentiated abilities and requirements, e.g.
neural surgeon, ear, nose and throat specialist, orthopaedic
nurse, abstract painter, etc.   Furthermore, for each category, incumbency may be claimed and claimable by virtue of a
*domain of practice* (e.g. the person who paints most of his
time and does so for a living), formal membership or bestowed
right of practice (in the case of 'doctor', say, degree and
residency provide this right), etc.   Such things may be said
to be constitutive of category incumbency, but they are in
systematic and occasioned ways not necessarily, or always,
sufficient or adequate for category invocation, ascription or
use.   In his 'Philosophical Investigations' Wittgenstein makes
a point deeply relevant to our present concern:

164.   In case (162) the meaning of the word 'to derive'
stood out clearly.   But we told ourselves that this was only
a quite special case of deriving:   deriving in a quite special
garb, which had to be stripped from it if we wanted to see
the essence of deriving.   So we stripped those particular
coverings off;   but then deriving itself disappeared. – In
order to find the real artichoke, we divested it of its
leaves.   For certainty (162) was a special case of deriving;
what is essential to deriving, however, was not hidden
beneath the surface of this case, but this 'surface' was one
case out of the *family of cases* of deriving.

And in the same way we also use the word 'to read' for a
family of cases.   And in *different circumstances we apply
different criteria* for a person's reading. (17) [My italics]

I wish now to address myself to this issue:   categories like
other concepts (and categorizations like other descriptions) are
open-textured.   That there are multiple criteria (both formal

and substantive) (18) available to members of the culture in
the situated application, invocation, production and use of
membership categories provides for the multiplicity of language
games that can be played with them.   In the course of looking at these issues, we will also try to recover analytically
the unrelievedly judgmental character of descriptions and of
categorization work.

In our discussion of the use of the membership category
'director' in the data above, one relevant problem may be
located in the way that the concepts of 'skill' or 'ability' work.
'Being able to do X' is something that is displayed and ultimately ratified through the achievement of X.   An 'ability' is
taken to be *demonstrable* and so demonstrable through its em-
bodiment in appropriate activity - its practical application in
performance.   It is a species of 'knowing how' in Ryle's
terms. (19)   'Knowing how' often presupposes some elements
of 'knowing that'.   To 'know how' to ride a bicylce, of
course, one has to *'know that'* one has to put one's feet on
the pedals and move them in a certain direction.   But this
knowledge is not sufficient for being able to ride the bicycle.
Thus, we can still say of someone who knows what to do in
order to make a car move and who actually does make it move
through traffic, that 'he does not know how to drive a car'.
And, indeed, one may justifiably expect that such a person,
if given a prolonged driving test, would not be *certified as a
driver*.   So it seems that a certain ability or set of skills is
constitutive for the categorization 'driver'.   But the matter
does not end here.   Let us go over some of the parameters
involved:

1   For certain sorts of skills, some specific inadequate performances may result in a judgment that the person does not
have adequate possession of that skill.   In other words, a
cook, for example, may be said not to know *how to cook well*,
i.e. his cooking skills may be *gradable*, and not simply ratifi-
able, through the evaluation of the cooking performance.   A
person who may be said to be *a cook*, because he holds that
job at a restaurant, may then be said to be a *bad cook*, or
someone who does not know how to cook *properly*.   But if
the assessment of this cook's performance is negative enough
he may be said not to be really a cook at all, or not to know
how to cook.   This presupposes and displays a *standard* by
which cooking ability is judged and is demonstrable, and such
a standard is not a priori available in some rule book,
although there may indeed be more or less agreement on it.

2   Some skills and abilities, on the other hand, are not gradable but rather *verifiable*, by performance, e.g. knowing how
to count, being able to open a safe, etc.   The status of the
notion of 'mistake' is interesting in this context.   If a person

in trying to open a safe makes a wrong move and realizes it,
i.e. can see or tell that he has made a wrong move, this
move may be describable (and self-describable) as *making a
mistake*, and judgment on the person's ability to open the safe
may be held in abeyance.   But if the person does not realize
or seem to know (cannot avow) that he made a wrong move
(or cannot tell which was the wrong move), his ability to
open the safe is called into question on the basis of the perceived mistake.   Here first-person mistake avowal may be
criterial.   The same holds, say, for operating a machine or
for an electrician who makes the wrong move in repairing
some simple electrical wiring and cannot tell what misstep he
took.   One might here be inclined to say that he was not an
electrician at all, or that he did not know anything worth
knowing about electricity, rather than that he was not a very
good electrician.   In cooking, however, adding an ingredient
at the 'wrong' point even if not avowed or conceded by the
cook calls into question not necessarily the cook's ability to
cook, but perhaps his ability to cook this particular dish or
it calls into question his being a *good* cook or a *gourmet*
cook.   Alternatively, instead of the cook's being seen to
have made a mistake in the recipe, it is possible to say that
he has a *different* recipe, another version, and final judgment
is held in abeyance.   A similar set of issues can be mapped
out for, say, a music conductor.

3   A further basis for the open-endedness of these category-
concepts (20) is to be found in the fact that abilities and
skills are acquired or learned *gradually* and may be learned
*partially*; this is probably tied up with the fact that many of
them are *composite*.   As Ryle says, in comparing 'knowing
how' with 'knowing that':

> Learning *how* or improving in ability is not like learning *that*
> or acquiring information.   Truths can be imparted, proce-
> dures can only be inculcated, and while inculcation is a
> gradual process, imparting is relatively sudden.   It makes
> sense to ask at what moment someone became apprised of a
> truth, but not to ask at what moment someone acquired a
> skill.   'Part-trained' is a significant phrase, 'part-informed'
> is not.   Training is the art of setting tasks which the stu-
> dents have not yet accomplished but are not any longer
> quite incapable of accomplishing. (21)

So also do we have such a phrase as 'training on the job'.
A teacher, director, co-ordinator, etc., may become an incumbent of the category concerned by filling that social slot, so
to speak, but before she has acquired the abilities and skills
required for the performance of the work constitutive of that
category.   Such categorizations then are ones that work as
*domain-of-practice* (*activity domain*) concepts and display the

social slot the incumbent occupies, in addition to being usable
as *competence concepts*.

4  Now, for a categorization that involves a complex cluster of
skills and abilities such as 'doctor', 'director', etc., some skill
may be treated as being more 'basic' than others.   We can
take chess as an analogy here.   To say that a person can
play chess, she must at least demonstrate an ability to make
chess-correct and game-appropriate moves, i.e. demonstrate
that she knows how to move the chess pieces correctly (this
involves knowing that certain moves are permissible and
others not).   But if she does not make appropriate moves for
the specific game in progress, she will be said not to know
how to play chess *well*;   the same holds if she loses every
time she plays.   But perhaps she is unable to make *any*
appropriate moves at all (although all the moves she makes
are strictly correct in terms of the formal constitutive rules);
suppose she loses so quickly, can never foresee a threat from
an opponent's piece, never notice a good opportunity for
seizing an opponent's piece, etc., then it may well be that
this can provide rational and accountable grounds for saying
that 'she does not know how to play chess at all'.   In other
words, *for any activity, a certain standard of performance is
already embedded and implicit and is situatedly, practically
and accountably displayed in the perception of successful or
correct performance, indeed in the very notion of what counts
as a genuine performance.*

   Categorizations such as 'director', 'doctor', etc. are constituted both through the formal domain of practice and the
attendant abilities and required corpus of knowledge displayable through *performances*.   These features may be said to
provide the parameters of open texture for such category-
concepts.   The latter's application (ascription, invocation,
avowal, defeasance, denial, etc.) is decidable according to
alternatively available criteria whose relevance is situatedly
occasioned and achieved.   What and whether specific abilities,
properties, features (concerns and practices, etc.) are treated
and produced as being 'constitutive' for the categorization
(basic, in everyday parlance) or as preferential (see the distinction between constitutive and preferential rules in Searle
and Shwayder) (22) is only available in and through the
course of a conversation or interaction – this is not to say
that *any* such skill can intelligibly be made out to be constitutive or preferential at will, but rather that there is some latitude for this.   For example, in our data *A* could have said,
'I would not be a good director if I did not anticipate problems' instead of 'I do not think I should be a director if I did
not anticipate problems'.   As *A* did in fact formulate the
issue, he is providing for the ability to anticipate problems or
courses of events as being constitutive of a director's work.

We said earlier that this formulation could be heard as, in fact, being equivocal as to whether *A* is talking of his present performance in his professional slot or of the criteria by which he became a director in the first place. It does not alter the issue, however - if *A* is talking from the latter perspective, he is then formulating 'the ability to anticipate problems' as having been an *eligibility requirement*, and thus a category-constitutive, rather than a category-bound, ability. In other words, it gets formulated as not being simply a category-relevant but a category-required skill.

We can now locate yet a further parameter of use (and of open texture) for these categorizations. Not only are they normatively organized with respect to standards of competence, and with respect to a culturally locatable (situatedly specifiable) set of category-relevant competences, but they are also morally organized with respect to sets of duties and rights that are oriented to as bound to specific social slots. For example, a doctor has the duty to save lives where she can this is a category-bound duty in the strongest sense of the term; it is also a required commitment on her part. If a doctor *could have* saved a life with her skills and resources and did not, she may be seen to have purposely caused the patient's death, or to be a *callous* person, or to have had some ulterior motive in not acting. This obligation and commitment is so strongly required that it may come to be formulated as constitutive of the categorization 'doctor' as a moral categorization and situatedly criterial for one's right to carry it, i.e., one's eligibility *to practise*. Let us try to clarify the issue further. Take the following (S.T. Data A3):

Q:  No doubt it occurred to you, Doctor, when you went home for a social evening that this was a very extraordinary thing to happen?

A:  No, because they know I am always available and that it is my job to correlate any problem or issue that arises in the Order and I would be first to be told.

A number of divisions seem to be implied or embedded in this exchange - particularly in *Q*'s utterance. Firstly, the division between the *domains of action*: work/pleasure. The intrusion or intercutting between such domains of action, it would seem, requires some serious warrant. This carries with it the second possible division - that between the domains of duties/obligations on the one hand and rights/entitlements on the other. (Think here of the uses of the slogans 'A fair day's work for a fair day's pay' and 'From each according to his capacity, to each according to his needs'.) The third division is between *time domains* - the notion of *private time* is displayed as being distinct from that of *public time*. For

some categories of persons, e.g. doctors, this crosscutting
between time domains is an expectable and routine matter, and
their ability and willingness to allow it is part of their observable commitment level, as well as being implicative for assessments of their sense of responsibility, dedication and, crucially, of their *performance* as a discharge of duties and obligations. These are qualities of performance seen as critical
to the making of a *good* doctor: a *bad doctor is routinely as
good as, or worse than, no doctor at all.* They are critical
qualities and indeed can get constituted as *criterial* for the
application of the category-concept to some member. In other
words, what is seen to make a good doctor is often taken to
be synonymous with *what makes a doctor,* although not with
respect to competences alone, but clearly also with regards to
the moral features of the category (duties, commitments).

To sum up: we now find, then, that for some categories X,
not only does the displayed lack of certain competences provide grounds for saying that a person is either not an X or
not a good X (competences already formulated with respect to
a standard of performance), *but further that some categorizations are usable in explicitly moral ways, so that the fulfill-
ment of moral duties and commitments is basic for the assessment of the performance of category tasks* and thus for a
person's being constituted as a *good* X, which is itself central
to the notion of being a *genuine* X, e.g. a good mother, a
good doctor, a good policeman. Clearly, such an utterance
as 'You're not a surgeon - you're a butcher!' may be seen to
be formulating a performance at some operation as having been
badly bungled. 'Surgeon' here is being used as a competence categorization. On the other hand, one may come
across the following: 'You're not a doctor, you're just into
money making/you're a profiteer', etc. 'Doctor' is here
being used as a *moral performance* categorization, where the
concern to help and treat sick people is being provided for as
overriding that of profit and as central to what constitutes a
'doctor'. Categorizations may be used in different language
games, but in such ways as are embedded in the nature of
the particular category-concept and its social and moral organizational character. Both the above utterances come off as
complaints, but the first is a complaint with regard to compet-
ence/ability/skill and makes a judgment with respect to these
issues, whereas the second is a complaint with respect to a
performance as not displaying a proper discharge of responsibilities and expected commitments: it is thus a complaint that
is morally implicative for the character of the *person as a
whole* and not only in his/her categorial capacity. Both
sorts of complaint are embedded in and trade off the nature
of the categorization 'doctor' as a membership categorization
that operates within a social, practical and moral geography.
We have such possible utterances as 'You're not a mother at

all!', 'You're not a real father', 'You're not a policeman,
you're a gangster', etc. What we can observe in such instances is *the intertwining of description and judgment in an
integral manner* – it is not that one provides (or is provided
by) a description on which one can then build a judgment of
the phenomena presented in the particulars of that description; rather it is the case that the very way that a set of
specifics or a single specific (here a person) gets described
is embedded in and displays judgmental work, and *moral-
judgmental work. Categorizations can be made to function at
once as inferences, descriptions and judgments.*

Let us return momentarily here to the data – we find a
further distinction embedded in the interchange; in reply to
$Q$'s formulation of $A$'s having been called back from a social
evening as an 'extraordinary thing to happen', $A$ incorporates
that event into the normal body of his duties:

1 He is always available (this may simply be a commendable
  character trait on his part, a mark of dedication).

2a It is his job to correlate any problem or issue arising
   within the specific community of relevance – this would
   mark out his domain of work and practice (and implicitly
   delivers an appropriate categorization).

 b He would be first to be told – this demarcates a right
   bound to his job and his categorial incumbency.

Points 1 to 2(b) deliver *a commitment, an obligation* and *a
right* all bound to the slot that $A$ occupies, his relevant category incumbency which $A$ provides later on as being 'director'.
In fact, 2(a) is hearable as a formulation of a work-constitu-
tive feature, and therefore, in an occasioned manner, a category-constitutive feature. Note too that 2(a) and 2(b) are
reflexively tied in their production; the three features thus
together provide a very strong warrant for the action in
question, but one that is perceivable as being category-
generated.

The distinction I indicated as being embedded here is that
between an institutional/categorial set of relevances, duties,
rights, interests and practices and the individual/personal
ones traded on by $Q$ in his formulation. This distinction may
be mapped on the three previous ones in various ways; so
instead of accepting $Q$'s formulation implying a violation of
domain divisions (a moral-judgmental matter) and implying an
intrusion or crosscutting between two sets of markedly divis-
ible, distinct domains (the institutional/public-time/work/obli-
gations domain on the one hand and the individual/private-
time/pleasure/rights on the other), we have $A$ formulating the

event in question as being within the *normal discharge of
duty/work, therefore, within the ordinary course of procedure.*
The notion of 'commitment' here is central. *A* has not provid-
ded for what happened as having been an extraordinary circumstance (indeed he tries to resist this account, and the
consequent inferential trajectory), for which an account by
obligation would have sufficed.  Rather he has attempted to
provide for the ordinariness and normalcy of what happened.
However, the distinctions between time domains, institutional
obligations and personal rights, as well as work/pleasure, are
stubborn and resist *general* dismissal.  They are not only
available in the culture, but are issues that members orient
to, and by which they expectably organize their lives. *A*'s
provision of a 'commitment' here provides a 'bridge' between
the two sets of domains (hearable as oriented to in *Q*'s question) to allow for and 'normalize' what could otherwise come
off as an 'extraordinary' circumstance.  Indeed, the 'division'
is thus provided as being of reduced relevance for the
speaker, and so displays the defeasibility, in situ, of such
culturally available distinctions.  So this interchange is very
finely organized with respect to the practical organizational
and moral features of descriptive work (which may both
deliver and trade off a categorization).  What we have dia-
grammatically for that sequence is the following:

| Instead of Q's focus on | We get A's focus on |
|---|---|
| individual | category/individual incum-<br>bent of category |
| violation of right | right/duty/commitment |
| break | continuity |
| attribution of specificity | reincorporation into pattern |

All the four domain 'divisions' indicated above are intertwined
and embedded in each other and work within a moral context,
as well as exhibit a moral organization.  Furthermore, they
provide some of the tools by which members orient to and re-
solve issues of the relationship between individual and collectivity in occasioned and varied ways.  These are issues that
social scientists have long, and largely to little avail, been
concerned to solve;  they turn out to be members' issues that
are organized in fine-grained and complex ways.  Now, the
very notion of 'intrusion', which we introduced as being relevant to our analysis, cannot work apart from a moral context
and without a context of assessment.  Yet it is not a notion
that is at odds with the nature of the work analysed as being
involved in the interchange.  For instance, the division of
'private' and 'public' time is organized in a specific way - the
former with respect to some notion of rights (of the individual), the latter with respect to some notion of obligations

(generated by a collective framework). Most people, for
example, 'own' part of their time, which is their 'private'
time. Doctors and policemen, however, do not completely
'own' it – they are routinely expected to give some of it up
when called to do so in their work ('in the course of duty')
*as* incumbents of these categories. It is part and parcel of
their oriented-to responsibilities and the perceived demands of
their work. So we get the notion of 'off-duty' and 'on-duty'
to characterize such a relationship to their categorial responsibilities in their ostensibly 'private' time. (23) One does not
routinely get an 'on-duty' painter, or an 'off-duty' architect.
On the other hand, for a categorization such as mother, 'on-
duty' and 'off-duty' are not conventionally available characterizations – an 'off-duty' mother? To conclude briefly: duties,
commitments and rights regarding a person's time economy are
bound up with the categorizations relevant for the description
of such persons; such categorizational work is, of course, an
occasioned accomplishment. It is in the very ways that such
categorizations are made or traded on that the attributions of
rights and responsibilities get made and reflexively 'fix' or
constitute that categorization for the relevance at hand, and
accomplish, in and through this, that local and particular purpose. Such divisions and distinctions as we indicated above
are routine and pervasive features of a moral geography within
which such category-concepts operate and over which they may
be mapped. They are thus also a routine and pervasive
feature of members' work in assembling and making sense of
social structures and transforming collective matters into
issues for the individual and vice versa.


ASPECTS OF COLLECTIVITY CATEGORIZATION

Some of the features we have analysed earlier with respect to
the use of 'type' categorizations are more strongly available
in the use of identifiable 'group' or 'organization' categorizations (e.g. Hell's Angels, Irish Republican Army, Vietcong,
etc.), namely, the transitivity of attributes. Take the following sequence of data (H.A. Data):

128 R: Er ... you get young girls going missing from
home.

129 A: Yeh.

130 R: I mean to say we've got one of 'em er one of them
charged with an offence against a young girl.

131 A: Have you?

132 R: Mm.

133   A :   One of the Hell's Angels?

134   R :   Yeh.

135   A :   Oh, mm.

136   R :   That's the kind. They're certainly not angels.

That a Hell's Angel is *charged* with an offence against a young
girl is not here being treated as something arising uniquely
from that person's individual biography, history, character or
personality, or from a specific situation in which he became
embroiled (the use of 'one of them' does not provide for
hearers whether it is one of a *specific* bunch of Hell's Angels
or just a member of the Hell's Angels group - see data Appendix).   Rather, his supposed action is, in a sense, made to
*represent* the character and activities of the other members of
the group.   It is incorporated into what may be thought of
as the 'record' and the history of the group rather than
simply and only being incorporated. into the individual's own
record or biography.   As an event in the group's history it
becomes a kind of action (or involvement, where the action's
*nature* is not clear as in the case of a 'charge') projectable
onto other members of the group irrespective of their own
actual involvement or personal history.

Could that work routinely with all types of groups?   I suggest not.   The Hell's Angels are seeable and treatable as a
*morally* organized group (indeed, morally self-organized).   It
is a group specifically constituted by its members round some
set of moral-practical beliefs, commitments, codes, values,
interests, concerns, etc.   This is important.   With morally
organized groups this transpersonal projection of attributes
and activities is a routine practice.   Indeed, one might say
that morally organized groups are those groups where the
responsibility for the action of one member is morally, if not
legally, ascribable to the group as a whole (and thereby ex-
tendably to the other individual members within it):   where
that individual's action can be made out or seen to be performed under the auspices of that group's membership, or
where in some way that membership within the group can be
accountably made relevant to the understanding of the person's action.   Thus the characterization of both individual
and group are mutually reconstituting.   But the reflexive
character of this relationship goes even further - in the data
it is by virtue of the fact that the premised action (the other
face of the *charge*) of 'one of 'em' (some collection of people)
*is projected back into a determination of the character of the
group as a whole* ('That's the kind. They're certainly not
angels') that the group or collection of persons are achieved
in the talk as indeed being a morally organized group.   In

other words, *the collectivity's existence as such is made out to be an integral matter with regard to the issue at hand, and not an incidental matter.* The operation of a transitivity of attributes depends, in the first place, on this: whether, for some course of action or activity by a person who is a member of some collectivity, that 'collectivity' can be produced as an endogenous feature to that course of action. It is *in* such work that the moral organization of some collectivity with respect to the action/issue at hand is provided for (whether by a self-professed collectivity member, or another). Such work displays the moral-organizational character attributed to some group or collectivity.

One way of accomplishing the defeasibility of such work, then, is to provide that the 'collectivity' (in whatever relevant specifics) was an exogenous or incidental feature to that course of action, i.e. to provide that it is not morally organized with respect to the issue at hand.

There is a further point worth making. Look at the following extract of data (S.T. Data A5 and A7-9):

Q: Did you ask from anybody why they thought this was necessary?

A: If the personnel on the spot thought it was necessary, I would be quite happy to go along with it.

and later

Q: What I am trying to get from you, Doctor, is whether this problem on the Wednesday, that is on the 13th, could not have been dealt with by the ordinary hospital services; why was it necessary to set up this quite exceptional, as it were, clearing station?

A: I think if there is a problem people are not going to go from the Falls to the Royal because you get a scratch with a stone or something like that, and this chap who belonged to the area - he did not live there actually but his mother lives there and he was visiting and saw that there was the necessity, that these things were necessary, that treatment on the spot could be given instead of going to the hospital.

Q: Why was it necessary? Did you enquire from anybody why it was necessary? Did you ask anybody?

A: If they thought it was necessary I was quite happy to accept their judgment and they were on the spot.

The Chairman:   Just a moment - who are 'they'?

A:   Well, first of all Allison and his unit who belonged
around there, who live there, my Lord.   He was visiting his mother who lives right in the centre of the
problem when the problem arose.

What is being provided for by *A* here and relied on is the
transpersonal extension of *warrant*, the transferability of perception and judgment across individual members - a feature of
morally organized collectivities.   The Chairman's question as
to who 'they' were reproduces this feature as one displayed
in the talk.   *A*, however, provides a further warrant for the
group members' having come to some judgment in the first
place - 'they were on the spot'.   Thus, *A* has provided the
warrant for his own response and action, as well as for the
decision and judgment by other group members.   This brings
to view another feature of morally organized groups - that
they need not be spatially bounded or localized in their operations.   The operation of the transitivity convention allows
them to extend their operations and concerns spatially (and
temporally so that they 'reproduce' their character and work
across time), as it is indeed this which may be used to provide for their character as morally organized.

Here we must clarify a distinction that has already been
alluded to in the text - that between a morally *self*-organized
collectivity (a political party, religious organization, charitable
institution, etc.) and a collectivity which can get treated by
members as morally organized with respect to certain issues
and for situated practical purposes, but which is not self-
organized for such.

The difference may be highlighted by the difference between
the kind of collectivity that the Ku Klux Klan may be said to
be and the kind of collectivity, for instance, that 'Americans'
may be said to be.   Although in talk both may be produced
and treated as being morally organized groups for some purposes and with respect to certain issues, we know that the
former is *self*-organized and constituted through rule-bound
elective membership.   And the rules governing this membership inclusion are organized with respect to specific kinds of
beliefs and commitments.   'Americans', on the other hand, is,
as a collectivity categorization, organized in the first place
quite differently: it is not treatable as *self*-organized and
*who* may be said to be American depends not necessarily on a
specific set of beliefs and membership rites (the issue of
naturalization procedures would provide an interesting case
study in this respect), but on such diverse relevancies as
ancestry, place of birth, language, cultural background and
various cultural commitments.   It involves a more complex
(and different) cluster of interrelated practical criteria.

We have already discussed the issue of the multiplicity of criteria. Here again, the difference is in what we have called the parameters of open texture. *For members, the difference is, in the first instance*, that with a morally self-organized collectivity (and we know and can recognize these by virtue of culturally available resources) members may unproblematically orient to the fact or existence (or discovery) of features by which the collectivity *is* (explicitly) morally organized. Disagreements may arise as to *which* features are central, *how* to interpret them, *whether* some member's specific action is, or is not, conducted under the auspices of collectivity membership and *who* can properly be counted as a member or as a *genuine* member.

With collectivities such as 'Americans', on the other hand, it is possible for members to disagree in the first instance on whether *any* specific can be located by which that collectivity as *a whole* is morally organized and for which, therefore, a transitivity across *all* individual members of the collectivity is operable. Rather the collectivity can get reformulated as itself constituted of collectivities which are morally self-organized and *morally organized by that feature*. Examples here might be the Roman Catholic Church, and the Roman Catholic community, respectively. Of course, in the latter we encounter a collectivity not self-organized but one that is nevertheless taken by members to be morally organized with respect to a bounded and locatable set of beliefs and practices. Here one can reproduce the same sort of possible disagreements and members' practical issues as for the morally self-organized groups above.

In other words, one of the interesting differences in the parameters of open texture between different kinds of collectivity is given by the kinds of *disjunctions* that members may encounter in the course of treating and accomplishing such different collectivities as morally organized.

One upshot of these considerations may be that, although for morally self-organized collectivities and collectivities organized by locatable moral beliefs and practices, some 'moral' features may be provided in situated and routinely warranted ways as category-*constitutive* (much as 'doctor', 'mother', etc. can be treated); for ethnic collectivities the provision of certain 'moral' features (e.g. specific sorts of beliefs, practices, commitments, etc.) as category-constitutive rather than as category-bound may be a warrantable basis, for members, for the attribution of 'prejudice', 'fanaticism', 'totalitarianism', etc. Some interesting examples of this might be in the use of expressions such as 'a good German' (in Nazi Germany), 'un-American activities', 'self-hating Jew', etc.

It would seem from this that a member's preference might
be that 'moral' features be treated as category-bound rather
than category-constitutive where ethnic collectivities are concerned.

Much of members' social theorizing is organized through the
production and provision for collectivities in talk as morally
organized groups and the characterization and description of
individuals and their actions as relative to, and accountable
in terms of, their membership in such groups.   Such work –
of producing, displaying or invoking the morally organized
character of collectivities, or the turning of collections of
persons into collectivities – consists, then, of devices for
*making sense of social structures*, of finding explanations for
'social events', locating responsibility (in its widest context),
predicting, ratifying accounts, clarifying domains of expectation, formulating courses of action and the like.   The concept of 'hegemonic' class, for instance, in the Marxist tradition is routinely made to work by constituting, through its
situated use, a collectivity morally organized with respect to
the ideas, values, commitments, etc. that are said to be hegemonic.   It can also thus constitute *another* collectivity (the
'hegemonized' one) as one which is morally organized in a
subordinate way, but which could be organized differently.

Wes Sharrock has written on collectivities and the relationship they may be said to have to a corpus of knowledge attributed to them. (24)   His work on this may be used to bring
out further differences in *classes of collectivity*, a set of
distinctions that could be of great use in elaborating on some
of the distinctions we made above.   Sharrock takes as an
example the category locution 'Baka medicine'.   The name
Baka, he suggests, is not intended to describe the persons
who subscribe to the corpus of knowledge (the particular form
of medical practice and set of ideas) but rather specifies a
relationship of 'ownership' between that corpus and the collectivity named:   'it does not imply that the medicine is known
only to the Baka, but rather, that such medicine in some
sense "belongs" to them, can be seen to be "owned" by
them.' (25)   The consequences of this for both lay and professional theorizing are drawn out by Sharrock and are
indeed powerful.   He gives a list of examples to elucidate his
point:   Chinese geomancy, Russian populism, Azande witchcraft, Cheyenne law, Aboriginal kinship rules, etc.   Sharrock
says that the idea of 'ownership' may be applied to the study
of the relationship between a corpus and a collectivity without
giving concern to the determination of *which persons* subscribe
to the corpus and 'whether in the light of its constituency we
might have to revise the name'. (26)   If some people from the
Azande engage in the practice of Baka medicine, in other
words, it does not become *Azande* medicine.   However, there

are some points that may be raised here in order to provide some further useful distinctions:

1 Not only does the medicine in Sharrock's example not come to be known as Azande medicine, but neither do its Azande practitioners come to be known as Baka persons.  This indicates the following distinction which Sharrock overlooks (in part because all the examples he gives derive from one class of collectivities, namely ethnic ones).

2 The practice of Baka medicine (or thought, law, religion) by non-Bakas does *not* expand the constituency of that collectivity - but for collectivities such as Christians, Marxists, etc. as in Christian ritual, Marxist materialism, the *practice of* or *subscription to* the corpus of knowledge *constitutes* the membership of that collectivity.  The collectivity is expanded if and when non-Christians or non-Marxists take up, come to believe or subscribe to Christian or Marxist thought and/or practice.  Note that the relationship of 'ownership' still holds, but there is a consequential difference that is displayed in the way these different sort of category-concepts may be said to behave.

3 Having knowledge of a corpus of knowledge must be kept distinct from applying it, practising it or subscribing to it. In the former case, of course, persons may have *knowledge of* Marxist or Christian thought, but if they are not subscribers to it or practitioners of it that collectivity's constituency may not be said to have been expanded.

4 If, instead of looking at the first pair part of what is a compound categorization (*Baka* medicine, *Chinese* geomancy, *Marxist* theory), we look at the *second* pair part (Cheyenne *law*, Western *medicine*, Greek *geometry*, Russian *populism*), we notice something further.  There are differences in the way that medicine, geometry, etc. are seen to operate as a 'corpus of knowledge' and the way that laws, rules, etc. are seen to operate.  The former are practices - lay or theoretic (medicine, geometry) - and some collection of items constituted thus as 'facts';  the latter *organize practices* - indeed, they organize the collectivity's *life*.  Consequently, where the former are adopted widely by persons not in that named collectivity from which they are seen to have originally emanated or to whom they are initially tied, the first pair part of that compound categorization may be entirely *dropped* in usage so that we get 'medicine' or 'geometry' instead of Western medicine and Greek geometry - the practices and collection of facts are here seen as universally relevant - and their 'names' are employed only for *contrastive purposes*.  Western medicine becomes then a contrast for ethnic or folk medicine, where the two may be seen to offer *alternative* or *competing* solutions

to practical problems (e.g. anaesthesia or acupuncture).
And the first pair part becomes usable as an origin- or
source-locating categorization.   For *laws* and *rules*, on the
other hand, where they are adopted by other persons, *two*
compound categorizations emerge - one that is source-locating
and the new one.   An example of this is Roman law, which
becomes British law when adopted by the British.   Although
it remains categorizable as Roman law (in its origin and historical context), it none the less *is also* British law now.
And when British law is adopted in Jordan, that system of
laws can be known by both terms, British law and Jordanian
law (and even for some as Roman law), *depending on the
user's purposes*.   Islamic law is still also, in local contexts,
Egyptian law, Pakistani law or Saudi law, etc.   And in so
far as one sometimes talks of, say, British law being *based*
on Roman law it is in recognition of the fact that aspects of it
continue to be developed, and were developed, independently
of the adoption of Roman laws.

5  Some of the differences relate to whether *individuals* or
collectivities adopt and practise a named 'corpus of knowledge'
(which I take it is used as a gloss for such things as beliefs,
rules, practices, concepts and ideas).   An individual cannot
sensibly be said to adopt or practise a law independently of
some collectivity, for 'law' is primarily a concept connected
with collective life (when used in contexts outside the scientific study of natural phenomena).   But an individual may be
said to adopt Azande witchcraft practices alone among his
people, and thus be said to have become a 'witch' (but not an
Azande).   Again, if Western medicine is practised only by
one Indian, for example (or even one Indian, three Chinese
and five Africans), it would still be *Western* medicine they are
practising, and that stands *in contrast* to the kind of medicine practised by their community.   But if a *collectivity*
adopts the practice, the situation becomes different.   The
examples Sharrock gives may be analysed for the *contrast
work embedded in them* (I shall not quote them in full):

> He told everyone that his magic was not the old Zande
> magic of witch-doctors, *bondoku*, but more powerful magic
> he had learned among the Baka people from a man whose
> name, *Bogwozu*, he had taken for his professional cogno-
> men. (27)

and

> There were nevertheless, certain small differences between
> their medicines, and it was on account of these that they
> made him presents and listened to his talk.   His was the
> medicine of the Baka people.... Well, he [Babodo] was
> anxious to add Baka medicine to his own stock of Zande
> medicines. (28)

Nevertheless, as Sharrock indicates, *even if* another collectivity is seen to have adopted the named corpus of knowledge (named after another collectivity), the name provides for a relationship between that corpus and the collectivity after which it is named, namely, that of 'ownership' (where the name is maintained). He gives an example of 'ruling-class ideology'. The use in context of the expression 'cultural imperialism' trades on the same notion of a relationship between a national collectivity and a corpus of knowledge. But again it is clear that in such contexts some *contrastive work* is implicated or embedded. This contrast turns on the contrast in perceived or attributed *interests* between two *collectivities* (or the work that the use of a certain corpus of knowledge does, or the consequences of such work, as between them). This brings to mind, again, the use of the concept of 'hegemony' which we alluded to earlier; such work clearly provides for the character of collectivities as being morally organized with respect to the issue at hand.

6 Another way of putting the difference is like this: it is not the case that *any* materialism which Marxists may subscribe to becomes Marxist. This would be a fundamentally misconceived notion to work with. Rather it is by virtue of adopting/believing/practising a particular sort of materialism (*this* materialism, Marxist materialism) that persons may be said to be or have become Marxists (at least in this, since one *can* have hybrid categorizations such as Islamic Marxists, Christian Marxists, self-avowed or otherwise, despite the protestations of other self-avowed Marxists, Christians or Moslems). On the other hand, *any* law by which, say, Italians organize their lives is or becomes Italian law, unless it is seen to have been imposed. Notice, for instance, that Nazi law imposed on the Italians during World War II remained *Nazi* law. Again, the assignation has an embedded contrast and the various collectivities are seen as being differentially morally organized with respect to that corpus of law. On the other hand, had the Nazis adopted certain old Roman laws about the rights and obligations of slaves and applied them, such laws would have come to be called Nazi laws.

7 Groups such as the Hell's Angels, the Irish Republican Army, etc. are seen, as we mentioned earlier, not only to be morally organized, but to be *self*-organized; in other words, they are organizations. Membership in its strictest sense is the basis for inclusion in the group and provides the mode of categorial incumbency. Adopting that collectivity's beliefs or practices, therefore, will not constitute a person as a Hell's Angel or an IRA member, because for the latter to occur specific actions have to be taken by both prospective member and organization. Such persons, however, may be describable as the Hell's Angels type, or an IRA man, etc.

8  Some categorizations, such as 'Roman Catholic' applied to a church, may be treatable, as we indicated earlier, as designating either a morally organized group (a religious category) or a morally *self*-organized group, an *organization*.  See here Watson's distinction between the use of such a term as a category *within* a device (religion) and its use as a duplicatively organized device itself. (29)

9  Finally, and very briefly, some organizational categorizations, such as 'Nazi', can come to be used descriptively *and* thus, simultaneously, *ascriptively* of other individuals or groups (where the ascription made or displayed is of category-bound features).   But we will leave this issue aside for another time.

Chapter 2

# The social organization of categorial incumbency

Our analysis so far serves to show not only that there are
different language games (1) played with different category-
concepts but that these different games display and depend
on the fact that these membership categories fall into *different classes relative to various tasks* and thus have a systematically different logic in use.  We have already discussed
one set of parameters of categorizational work and category-
concepts - namely, what sort of features are taken to be tied
up with or constitutive of various categories in use and the
methodic character by which such features are displayed,
accomplished as category-constitutive or category-bound,
traded on in inferences, relied on, used in account constructions, etc.  In this chapter we shall take up two further
dimensions:  (a) the varying modes of category incumbency
(and the varying modes of incumbency entry) that members
are perceived as holding with respect to various category
identities and (b) the related question of the public availability of categorial incumbency.  But first let us deal with some
preliminary matters.

If we look at some examples of different categories, we will
see that while, for instance, the category 'victim' is ascribable, the category 'woman' or 'child' is *perceptually applicable*
(or discoverable in the absence of the so-categorizable
person);  the category 'policeman' is discoverable and expectably *disclosable* by the incumbent or perceptually applicable
(in the case of uniformed persons);  the categorization 'friend'
is achievable/ascribable.  What I am indicating here are the
commonsense conventionalities of the procedures for categorization that members employ in their everyday interaction.
To say of these (as well as of all other) categorizations that
they are all *ascribed* - that the procedures for category application and use are basically ascriptive procedures - whilst it
can be seen as an attempt to capture some real feature of such
procedures, nevertheless obscures a lot of differences in their
*ordinary logic of use.*

Now the concept of ascription has been used in conventional
sociology to distinguish *ascribed* status from *achieved* status,
where the former is a status conferred on a member by others,
e.g. sex on birth, and achieved status is that acquired
through the member's own efforts, such as professional status.

Linton, for instance, who defines status as 'a collection of
rights and duties', says:

> Societies have met the dilemma by developing two types of
> statuses, the *ascribed* and the *achieved*.  Ascribed statuses
> are those which are assigned to individuals without refer-
> ence to their innate differences and abilities.   They can be
> predicted and trained for from the moment of birth.   The
> *achieved* statuses are, as a minimum, those requiring special
> qualities, although they are not necessarily limited to these.
> They are not assigned to individuals from birth but are left
> open to be filled through competition and individual
> effort. (2)

The difficulties with this account are clear;  apart from the
problem of treating category incumbency purely in terms of
the notion of 'status', the idea of ascription (of actions, or
categorial incumbencies or 'statuses', of intention or ownership) properly works where there is some *question*, *alternative or choice* either as to *whom* it is proper to relate the
ascribable object (action, category, etc.) or as to *which* item
of a specific class of ascribable properties to relate to some
specific person.   Ascription involves *appraisal* and is conducted in a context of assessment.   Now in what sense can it be
said that  *gender* is routinely or commonly an appraisable
matter?   Or that members are normally involved in a selection
from alternatives when dealing with gender incumbency?   It
is true that if one is told a story of a person whose gender is
not given, and where no conventionally gender-specific attributes or actions are included in the account, one may make an
inference as to gender, based on some sort of appraisal of the
particulars of the account given.   It may also be true that
one may come face to face with a person whose gender is unclear, in the first instance, for some reason, and therefore
some appraisal of various contextual particulars is necessary
in order to arrive at some 'correct' inference as to gender.
But these are clearly 'problem' cases, which are parasitic on
the ordinary range of case;  they are systematically perceivable as problematic precisely by virtue of the orderly, conventionally presumed and available features of gender incumbency.
The very question repeatedly recounted in childbirth stories,
of a father asking:   'Is it a boy or a girl?', reveals the culturally given features of gender categorizability (and, indeed,
an aspect of the normative organization of 'natural' phenomena)
- the doctor answering with one or other gender category is
not normally in the business of *deciding* whether the child is
a boy or a girl, only in *seeing and telling that it is*.

However, the issue of achievement is no less important.
Although gender is oriented to as a *perceptually available*
matter, as we have already noted, it is still an accomplishment

on the part of members that it is sustained and given as just
such a perceptually available matter. Children are members
of a normative order within which they are taught gender-
based behaviour. Add to this the complex issue of constitutive and preferential features of categorial incumbency (which
we discussed earlier; e.g. how feminine is a woman; how
masculine is a man; 'real' man and 'real' woman issues) and
we can see that the matter is by no means as simple or as
black-and-white as traditional sociologists have made it out to
be.

Ethnomethodologists have rescued the concepts of ascription
and achievement of categorial incumbency (role, status, identity) from the schismatic opposing poles they were placed in
by conventional sociology and have treated them as two faces
of the same *analytic*. (3)  In that social structure is a systematic orderly accomplishment of members within a cultural
and natural language community, an accomplishment of members on each and every occasion, the notions of both ascription and achievement are designed to capture the sense of
the procedural activities undertaken by members in the production of oriented-to features of social settings (of which
categorial incumbency of various parties to a setting is such
a feature).  Thus, not only are ethnomethodologists emphasizing the *produced* character of social structures and social
settings, etc., but *as analysts* they do not take anything as
unexplicatedly *given*.  However, there remain problems.
For members of a culture, there are indeed *givens*.  What is
culturally and procedurally treated by members as 'given' must
be differentiated analytically from that which is not.  This
uncovers a vast complexity of members' methods, procedures
and devices for producing and making sense of the social
world, as well as of various specific features of that world in
specific settings.  An interesting question would be, for
example, how such phenomena as are for members naturally
occurring 'givens' are employed as a resource, achieved and
dealt with by members;  what classes of phenomena are systematically treated as not being 'given' in the first place, and
what their features are.  In terms of categorization work,
then, to talk of all socially organized categorial incumbencies
as *ascribed* is to gloss their everyday features and their logic
of use in everyday members' interactional work, and to gloss
their *specific* character and features as *various* occasioned
productions.  Secondly, to say of all socially organized categorial incumbencies that they are achieved, is equally to provide a gloss for the oriented-to, produced character of such
incumbency by 'incumbents'.  Although, for instance, one
may say that one's being categorizable as a 'friend' is an
achieved matter on the part of the categorized person, is it in
the same sense that one's being categorizable as a 'victim' or a
'murderer' is describable as an achievement?  Or a 'cheat',

'swindler' or 'rapist'? Clearly there are significant differences. Conventionally, members orient to a preference for
producing a category ascription for themselves as a 'friend',
at least in relation to some persons, but are conventionally
expected to work to mask the grounds for, and to prevent,
their being called or categorized as 'swindler' or 'rapist'.
So the notion of achievement cannot intelligibly be applied
analytically to both sorts of 'incumbency work' in the same
way, even though it remains a methodological sensitizing
device. In both these cases, however, the categorizability
of persons in a certain manner is an achievement on the part
of members doing/applying/using the categorizations and on
the part of other parties to the setting. (Here we are
already making a distinction between various parties to a setting that is a grounded, but constantly shifting and open-
ended, distinction between actor and respondent, or speaker
and hearer.)

Alan Blum, in his paper The Sociology of Mental Illness,
discusses issues of categorization and category incumbency in
terms of collectivities and collectivity membership; his starting point being the judgment of one person by others as being
mentally ill.

From a sociological perspective, the concept of membership
implies that there are rules which persons so classified respect as maxims of conduct and for the non-observance of
which they can be sanctioned. Thus a sociological description of membership requires some depiction of the rules
which persons so classified respect as maxims of conduct
and which they feel morally compelled to follow under pain
of being redefined as inadequate members. (4)

Blum moves from talking of membership in this sense (he is
referring here to the cultural community) to talking of *membership within a category*. Apart from the conceptual problem
of talking of persons as members of a *category* rather than of
a collectivity, not all categorizations by which persons can be
categorized describe collectivities, or groups. So not all
category incumbents can be seen as members of groups provided for by a category. Blum says, 'We say that age and sex
are membership categorizations, but hair color, eye color, and
weight are not.' (5) Membership categorization devices
(MCDs) is a term coined by Sacks to refer to categorizations
which are used by members of a natural language community
to describe (or otherwise refer to) other members of that community, as distinct from categorizations, for example, which
would describe or refer to objects in the natural world.
Therefore, hair colour categorizations are indeed applicable to
persons and may constitute membership categorizations according to Sacks's version, although the relationship of incumbent

to category is not isomorphic with that of *collectivity member-ship*, since the category would not describe a morally organized group or a normatively ordered collectivity. Blum then moves on to distinguish between the elements of a category (e.g. Element: redhead; Category: hair colour) and members of a category (e.g. Member: child; Category: age), the distinction resting on the nature of membership conditions (see his quote above): 'Members as compared to elements respect the rules governing category placement as maxims of conduct, as conditions and sanctions, and react to performance failures as moral failures.' (6)

Now, firstly, it is clear that 'redhead', like 'child', is itself a *category* - the logical status of the notion of *element* here is unclear. Note that for Sacks, both 'redhead' and 'child' are treated as membership categories, and 'hair colour' and 'age' as *devices* which organize sets of membership categories. The notion of 'device' in Sacks is an *analytic* one whose logical status derives from the very sense of the individual category-concepts. Secondly, although Blum is making a useful point about collectivity membership, his distinction between members and elements of a category remains at best a gloss. Two points here:

1 Membership in the sense in which Blum uses the term is a methodologically useful notion, but it obscures the everyday difference for members of a cultural community between a category-incumbent relationship of actual group membership (e.g. in organized groups such as the IRA, the Roman Catholic Church, Hell's Angels, the Republican Party, the Boy Scouts, the Newton Sports Club, the Steel Workers Union, etc.) and the category-incumbent relationship for such category classes as 'doctor', 'intellectual', 'politician', 'lesbian', etc., which is not one of actual membership, but is also and nevertheless normatively organized through and through. Blum's problem here is precisely that he is not treating these concepts as categories themselves and reserves this treatment for what Sacks would call an MCD, although even then not consistently. So presumably 'doctor' would be a member of the medical profession. But the very procedure of categorizing a person as a doctor or of using the category 'doctor' of a particular person is thus obscured.

2 How would categories such as 'victim', 'offender' or 'aggressor' fit Blum's notion of members and elements? On the one hand, in what sense can incumbents be said to 'respect the rules governing category placement as maxims of conduct'? On the other hand, in what sense can they be grouped together with 'redhead', 'blonde' and 'tall man' as elements, when they are differentiated from the latter set by their character as moral concepts? Moreover, as we shall see

later, they may be used as accounting categorizations that are
event-specific, but they may be expectably and routinely dis-
avowed, distinctions unavailable within Blum's scheme.

How, for a category such as 'rapist', would a person 'react
to performance failures as moral failures'?   The only moral
failure relevant in this context would be the failure to be a
'good person', 'a decent citizen', 'a law-abiding man', etc.,
that is, a failure implicated in some faultable performance conventionally and normatively tied to *another* category, and
moreover one which is an amorphous category-concept – an
umbrella descriptor that can have diverse particularizations.
Whilst looking at categorizations in terms of *alternative* ones
is useful, it by no means provides for an adequate understanding of specific categorization work.   For some categories
(that are not at the same time moral concepts) a failure of
performance is simply *that*: a failure of performance.   Such
a failure is translatable on many occasions into a judgment of
incompetence rather than of a *moral* failure, as, for example,
for a lawyer – although such a judgment may or may not be
morally implicative.

It is clear, then, that the *different classes* of category-
concepts have shifting lines that are task-dependent, and that
this variety and complexity is concealed by Blum's scheme.

Every category-concept carries, as we saw earlier, a *cluster*
of features both substantive (possible actions, traits, preferences, haunts, appearances, etc.) and formal (morally implicative, event-specific, collectivity-related, etc.).   It is these
latter features that provide for the discourse domains within
which the category-concept operates and which provide the
criteria for its behaviour within the limits of a domain.   Situatedly, it is the task at hand which provides the relevance
(for use) of any one feature of the category-concept and it is
in terms of that task that this feature is accountably displayed
or traded on.   Among some of the different membership category-concepts one finds various *family resemblances* locatable
in there being one or more cluster features in common between
some of them.   This is what prevents category-concepts from
fitting into *fixed classes*, but allocates them to various
classes or overlapping sets contingent on what formal feature
is being used as a way of organizing such class domains *for a
particular task at hand*.

Let us now look in closer detail at the two related sets of
formal features of membership categories with respect to the
issue of category incumbency that we indicated earlier:   the
mode of category incumbency or the category-incumbent relationship and the social or public availability of category incumbency.   A cautionary note is in order here:   the *incumbency*

of a category cannot be taken for granted by the analyst. *That* X is an incumbent of Y category is co-produced or displayed by parties to a setting. What that incumbency consists in for those parties and how it is made a feature of that setting, i.e. displayed, accomplished, ascribed, perceived, avowed and/or recognized, is different for different settinged categorizations and is in part contingent on the conventional category-incumbent relationship known in common by members.

## THE CATEGORY-INCUMBENT RELATIONSHIP

Let us take two examples of categorizations and make a few preliminary comments on them in line with the above concerns: the category 'doctor' and the categorization 'vandal'. To begin with, let us start with a possible utterance such as 'There was a doctor at the scene of the accident'. For a doctor to perform 'doctor-type' activity in an ostensibly nonmedical setting, he has to avow that he is a doctor (or a nurse that he is a nurse, a first-aider that she is a firstaider). The activity involved requires a certain set of abilities, and it is the possession of such abilities that entitles (and practically enables) a person to perform. The activity performed is only selectively permissible – it is categoryrestricted – and the avowal in such contexts, therefore, is a form of permission-seeking or entitlement-claiming via a declaration of *eligibility*. On the other hand, should one discover after an accident that one of the persons who had been at the scene was a doctor and had not declared himself or offered much-needed help, that person's discovered category incumbency is used to characterize his action as a withholding and to provide for an obligation which in the context of the withholding is seen to have been broken. Thus, the category incumbency is transformed into a moral matter. Take, however, an utterance such as 'The vandal walked up to the car and kicked it'. One does not usually ask permission to kick a car, for it is not the sort of action for which permission is routinely giveable; nor is the destruction of a phone booth, the ripping of bus seats, or the smashing of windows, etc. Such actions have the (moral) *character* of not being routinely acceptable or permitted. Secondly, the categorization 'vandal' is not one that could be generated separately from some specific action (whether observed in the performance or in its results). One would not routinely be hearable as giving a rational intelligible story if one were to say, 'A vandal came to see me yesterday'. (Compare this with 'A doctor came to see me yesterday.'/'Yeah? What did he want?') It is *in* giving the co-selected description 'walked up to the car and kicked it' that the speaker can accountably use the descriptor categorization 'vandal'. 'Vandal' is an action-consequent categorization, and moreover one that is

negatively morally implicative, i.e. it carries with it, as an
action-bound feature, a negative moral judgment. (7)

It is clear, then, that the two categorizations 'doctor' and
'vandal' are different - the latter not only does not depend on
self-avowal but is the sort of category whose use would be
disjunctive routinely as between category user and categorized person.   In the case of 'doctor', the category incumbency
is supposed to be pre-present to the actual occasion of category use, so that 'identification' of category incumbency may
be an issue for members and is accomplished either through
self-avowal, inference, recognition, documentation or question-
answer.   For 'vandal', on the other hand, 'identification' of
category incumbency is not involved, and thus category incumbency is ascribed or attributed in appropriate contexts,
since a *judgment of the person* is involved, as well as of his
action.   It is on each and every occasion of action which can
warrant the description of 'vandalism' that category ascription
is made and thus category incumbency decided, and it is
decided and established *for that occasion*.   One can say that
one 'identifies' X as *a* doctor (or as *the* doctor) but one only
identifies X as '*the* vandal' and *not* as 'a vandal'.   In other
words, one may *recognize* that X is a doctor without knowing
him personally.   One may recognize or identify some stranger
as *a doctor* (through his talk, title, costume, car sticker, display of knowledge, behaviour, etc. - one can also *guess* this
from such features).   One does not, on the other hand,
identify or recognize some stranger *as a vandal*; one would
*categorize* that person as a vandal on seeing him engaged in
some appropriate action or activity, or if there were reason to
attribute some observable consequence of a presumed act of
vandalism to him (e.g. a smashed phone booth).   One *can*,
however, recognize that a person (whom one has seen before)
is *the* 'vandal' (who did Y) and thus possibly attribute to
him some other actions of vandalism on that basis, or simply
call him a vandal.   (An utterance such as 'He's a bloody
vandal!   Everytime I go to London to watch the match, he
and his cronies are ripping up seats in the coach!' in this
context is intelligible.)

In the difference between the logic of use of the two sorts
of categorization one can locate a distinction between different
*communities of categorizers*.   For 'doctor' (in this culture),
membership in the profession or category incumbency is awar-
ded by a specific community (members of which alone can
award it) when a judgment is made that this person has
acquired the skills and knowledge enabling him/her to perform
appropriate activity properly.   Only other doctors can confer
this incumbency, or withdraw it *formally*, although members
of the lay community may use the categorization and apply it
in a gamut of ways, including the denial of *right* to that

categorization. Yet a 'doctor' who is not practising does not cease entirely to be a doctor, though people may be reluctant to submit to treatment at his/her hands. Even for a person to say of someone that 'He's not a doctor at all really' may not stand as a challenge to *actual* category incumbency but only to its appropriateness or the person's moral right to practise, etc.

For 'vandal', any community of categorizers (even if it only has a population of one) is in principle equal to any other. If there is a disagreement as to whether someone may be called or is a 'vandal', it is resolvable by inspection of the particulars of the case and not by who the various categorizers are; or it is left as a disagreement. And *any* member can engage in all aspects of such categorization work, although the community of categorizers here may be stratified by local contingencies, e.g. 'the eye-witness', and accorded differential rights of account ratification. (8)

Vandals themselves have no rights, obligations, expectables, etc. as doctors do. The person categorized as 'vandal' may have such rights and obligations – the 'vandal' does not. The category functions in this respect like the category 'criminal', where it is men *despite* their criminal status that have these rights. This is clearly in sharp contrast to such a category as 'President', where it is the category itself that is the organizational locus of obligations and rights.

We can see now that Blum's scheme is less than adequate – we may locate a variety of incumbent-category relationships. Firstly, there is membership incumbency proper, e.g. in the Boy Scouts, the Republican Party, the Lawyers' Guild, etc. There are other instances, where we might talk of membership that bears some family resemblance to this usage; we might, for example, talk of persons as being members of the medical profession, of the opposite sex, of an age group, of a congregation. Note that they are not talked about in terms of their being members of 'doctors', 'women' or 'thirty-year-olds', whereas a Boy Scout is a member of the Boy Scouts, a Republican Party man may be a member of the Republican Party, etc., i.e. the relationship of individual incumbent to the social organization constituted as that category is one of membership. One may say that the lay notion of membership can imply a community of members organized internally and recognizably with respect to moral rules, norms and values of conduct which are community-specific/relevant and/or demarcative.

Another parameter of the category-incumbent relationship is that some incumbencies are expectably and routinely disavowable by the person categorized. *'Incumbency' itself is not a non-disjunctively decidable matter*; indeed, some categori-

zations are essentially disjunctive ones.   Examples of this
are 'criminal', 'vandal', 'rapist', 'coward', etc.   These are
categorizations that persons do not routinely or expectably
avow of themselves, and where such categorizations are seriously made of them they would be expected to disavow them.
In a different way, categorizations such as 'good man', 'Good
Samaritan', 'hero', 'genius', etc. are also not seriously and
routinely self-avowable or self-ascribable (and may in occasioned ways involve a preference for public disavowal).
However, these latter are expectably *solicited* or solicitable
categorizations whereas the former are routinely not so.   One
may dream of being, aspire to being or imagine that one is a
Good Samaritan, a hero or a genius, but not that one is a
criminal, a vandal or a rapist, without being a candidate for
the categorization 'unbalanced', 'psychotic', 'insane', etc. (or
for some lesser 'evils', eccentric, weird, odd, etc.).   In all
these cases there may be an oriented-to organizational disjunction between perceivable warrant for incumbency and actual
categorization work.

Another parameter of incumbency is *transience*.   People
categorized as 'vandal' are seen as transient incumbents of the
category – it is a transient categorization.   Although somewhat differently, 'child' may also be used as a transient categorization.   Further, some category incumbencies are event-
consequent ('victim', 'injured person', 'widower') or event-
specific (e.g. 'bride' (9)), some are action-consequent or
activity-consequent ('thief', 'vandal', 'murderer'), some are
behaviourally implicative ('saint') and some are belief-depen-
dent ('Marxist', 'atheist').   Others are ability/competence
categorizations – blacksmith, doctor.   And yet others are
categories whose incumbency by persons is seen to be a naturally occurring one – 'woman', 'child', 'black', 'tall person'.
These last ones are also treatable as *stable* incumbencies.

It is clear, then, that one dimension of the category-incumbent relationship is the mode of incumbency entry and indeed
the *trajectory of incumbency*.   I have no wish here to indicate exhaustively the dimensions along which category-concepts
may behave; rather I am simply indicating some parameters
by which they are interactionally organized.   It is important
to note again that the category classes I am indicating thus
are not mutually exclusive with respect to every feature or
parameter but provide for shifting avenues of categorizational
work and use.   Such conventional properties of various
category-concepts and the clusters of features (both formal
and substantive) bound up with them provide members with a
rich mosaic of normatively organized inferential, ascriptive and
judgmental procedures.

## THE PUBLIC AVAILABILITY OF CATEGORIAL INCUMBENCY

Take the following extract (S.T. Data B6-8):

1  Q: The situation is that you have no idea who these
      people were or where they came from?

2  A: I have not: I would not know one person.

3  Q: They could have been Roman Catholics, could have
      been Protestants, could have been any religion at
      all; is that what you are saying?

4  A: That is true.

5  Q: And they could have come from the Falls Road,
      could have come from outside Belfast, anywhere at
      all?

6  A: Any place.

7  Q: Roughly what were the ages of the people who were
      treated?

8  A: Again there is not a fixed age group; it was a
      general age group.

9  Q: You do not have to ask embarrassing questions
      about this in order to see whether they are young
      people or old people or teenagers?

10 A: I am trying to think. Remember this is a year ago.

Q's utterance 1 provides a formulation of the course of the
conversation just prior to it to the effect that A has 'no idea'
who the people he had treated at a first-aid centre on a particular night had been. (10)    The just-prior conversation
turns on the fact that A and his co-workers did not ask for
the names of those they had treated because questions of that
nature would have been embarrassing and would have hindered
the execution of the charitable function of the Order under
whose auspices they had been working (see Appendix 2).    In
utterances 1 to 5 the 'upshot' of A's account is formulated:
that as a result of that policy A has no knowledge of the identity of the people treated - neither *who* they were, nor *where*
they came from nor *what religion* they were affiliated to.
Utterance  9 (Q) You do not have to ask embarrassing questions ... to see whether they are young people or old people
or teenagers? displays an orientation to a feature of one class
of membership categorizations, which is that 'stage-of-life'
categorizations (Sacks) may be available to persons *on looking.*

They are not the only categorizations to be so available. Gender categorizations are also glance-available, as we earlier indicated. Here, then, we have a feature that may turn out to mark an important distinction between various classes of category-concepts in their situated uses. If some categorial incumbencies are commonsensically available on sight, then one cannot properly be said to be involved in *ascribing* them to persons when they are accountably used in discourse or in the course of interaction.

When I say that these categorial incumbencies are available *commonsensically* on sight, I mean that they are routinely and accountably taken to be not concealed in the first instance, but rather expectably available on first inspection, and that once incumbency is read off at first look, then that perception is (as a rule) presumed correct *at its face value*. Gender and stage-of-life category incumbency (among others of which more will be said presently) have thus the character of public availability for the looking. That, and in such ways as, such category perceptions are situatedly defeasible (11) systematically sustains this commonsensically oriented-to feature. For instance, the production of equivocality in a certain setting as to the correct category incumbency routinely carries with it an account for such equivocality or ambiguity which displays the expectably *seen and seeable* character of gender and stage-of-life categorizations. (A possible example might be: A: Was it a man or a woman? B: I couldn't tell, the sun was in my face.)

Now, although the stage-of-life category incumbency of a person may be taken to be available on sight, his or her precise age *is not*. Age is assignable or disclosable. But the methods, therefore, by which age is topicalized in a conversation turn on the very on-sight availability of stage-of-life category incumbency.

As compared with gender and stage-of-life category incumbencies, other categorial incumbencies are not so available on sight. Political beliefs, religious affiliations, etc. may be displayable in talk and action or through other *interactionally available matters* such as known-in-common persons' names, but are not naively taken to be available for the looking. They are essentially *revelatory* matters - objects for revelation - through first-person avowal, third-person report, discovery or close inspection of a variety of 'objects' (talk, action, names, biography, residential location, records, profession, etc.). It may be, for instance, that in inquiring about the names of persons treated by A, Q, in our data above, was in fact not seeking a search procedure for any particular person's identity, but a *key* whereby a name could deliver to a hearer whether a named person was a Protestant

or a Roman Catholic (for example, as could a named location (12)).   The non-availability of a name here does not
simply mean the non-availability of a *specific* identity but it
also. warrants the non-availability of a *search procedure*
where the search is not only for a specific individual but for
various possible items such as collectivities, accounts, descriptions of relevant events, etc.   That is to say that the
particular names provide procedures for finding out, for
example, whether there were more or less Catholics injured at
any event than Protestants.   The search direction here may
be different from that involved in instances of individual
crime, where a police investigation seeks to pick up clues to
a specific individual's identity (clues that may include such
things as religious affiliation).   On the other hand, if you
have a *name*, you have a way of finding out an extensive
amount of relevant information.   In the data, A's not having
the names of the persons treated is used by Q as grounds for
concluding that A has no knowledge of a whole number of
things regarding these people.   Although, of course, there
are all sorts of other ways (besides knowing a person's name
and taking down personal particulars), of finding out or
getting to know an individual's residential location or religious
affiliation.

In as much as political beliefs, religious affiliations and the
like are revelatory matters, they are thus *also* matters for
concealment.   Some people may intentionally display such
affiliations as in the wearing of a cross, a Star of David or a
Koran miniature;  i.e. they display their affiliation not
through the implicative, presuppositional or discursive structure of their talk, and display it thus as a natural feature of
that talk, but rather display it in a *beforehand* manner, as an
announcement.   During the Lebanese civil war, for example,
it became a practice for some persons to sport big crosses.
This was taken to be a display not only of religious affiliation
but also of a *political* one (affiliation with the Phalange or
extreme Right), since the categorization of 'Christian' was
made of dominant relevance by those also advocating certain
political ideas and practices.   Thus it is that photographers
attempting to produce 'snapshots' of the troubles in Lebanon
could accountably caption a photograph showing a young
woman wearing a huge cross in Beirut as 'Phalangist' and be
seen to have captured the real sense of the photograph (and
the slice of life from which it had originally been generated),
and to have provided a proper description for it.   The use
of 'photography' to produce and exhibit seen-at-a-glance
features of the social world provides an important and useful
methodological device, as well as a topic of research in its
own right. (13)   In that certain categorial incumbencies are
(or may be) available at a glance, captions underneath photographs can presuppose and trade off the availability of such

incumbencies and can provide crisp, brief descriptions of the
photographs, which may nevertheless say much.   The photograph and its caption may then together stand as a brief *text*
(e.g., photograph of soldiers;   *caption*:   'The Shah wields a
strong arm' - the category 'soldier' is available at a glance
from the uniform worn by the incumbent).

Thus, profession is also made available at a glance, in some
instances, in the same way as religious affiliation.   The
wearing of a habit by a nun or a priest functions in an interesting manner given that the 'habit' here may display simultaneously *two* categorial incumbencies - religious affiliation
(Christian-Catholic) and profession.   In other words, in
wearing a habit one is providing not only for a religious affiliation, but also for a professional pursuit of it.   And in thus
making it publicly available one is providing for the relevance
of the categorization '*religious person*'.   In other words,
the *categorization 'professional Christian' may situatedly
generate the use of the categorization 'religious person'*. (14)

In making publicly and routinely available at a glance what
is not conventionally thus available one may be thereby providing for a strong relationship to the revealed category incumbency.   It may display and provide for an unequivocal,
overriding category incumbency and affiliation to a set of
beliefs and practices:   a display, in other words, of what is
(or should) *take precedence* in terms of categorial identification.   This is not to say that such situated displays of relevance (or readings of relevance) are not also, in occasioned
ways, defeasible.   Indeed they are.   But they are defeasible in orderly ways that preserve and trade on the oriented-
to, seen-at-a-glance character of certain features of the social
world.   Now consider the use of the 'wedding ring' as a
symbol of commitment (and a display of a category incumbency)
and the possible implications of a married person's not wearing a ring.   In wearing a ring, one is making publicly available for the looking what is not necessarily so available:   the
fact of a marriage, and the actual categorial incumbency of
*another* in a position of expected precedence for the ring
wearer, in terms of rights and duties.   Thus, this practice
is bound up with the conventional (and normative) expectation
of commitment to the marriage tie (and possibly the marriage
institution itself, in some form or other).   It *may* be taken
routinely as a display of such commitment.   So where a
person does not wear a ring and is discovered to be married,
we may take it that the person not only is not making available publicly and for the looking that she is married, but also
that she is *withholding* such information from the looking and
telling of others.   One is *withholding* a display of commitment, or a display of relevant rights and duties tied up with
a third party's categorial incumbency.   Here we can observe

one of a class of cases in which a discrepancy between a
known category incumbency (i.e. married person) and a
category-bound display (i.e. wearing a wedding ring) can
entitle observers to ascribe an *action* ('withholding') on the
basis of the noticed absence of the category-bound display.
Consider here too the example of a man in wartime, wearing
ordinary clothes and discovered to be a soldier (but not on
leave) - the categorization 'deserter' becomes immediately
relevant since wearing civilian clothes in such circumstances
may be seen as 'having discarded one's uniform', 'trying to
conceal one's identity', 'not wanting to be taken for a soldier',
'being an undercover agent', etc. What is interesting here
is the tie between *tradition* (established institutional practice) and the formulation of certain *absences* in terms of *with-*
*holding*, i.e. not simply as omissions but as the *commission*
*of omission*, so to speak. Given that the *practice* of
wearing a wedding ring is a *tradition*, a ritual, then *despite*
the fact that it embodies and displays a person's place within
the organization of certain social rights and obligations, the
particular individual's actual commitment to the particular
marriage (or the marriage institution) remains equivocal.
That is to say, *once a practice is conventionally oriented-to*
*as a tradition, its application by an individual member is not*
*necessarily as implicative of her commitment as its omission.*

Where there is a 'tradition', provisions for a 'rule', conventions whose violation is publicly implicative, practices enforced
by an 'authority' (e.g. the wearing of a uniform for certain
jobs), there may then be an orientation on the part of members to the possibility of a 'split', a 'dichotomy' or disparity
between the 'public' and 'private' character of behaviour (an
issue over which the notions of a reality/appearance dichotomy
may be articulated). However, this is not a programmatically
relevant dichotomy for *any* situation and *any* member, but one
that may situatedly arise in occasioned and orderly ways.

To recapitulate briefly, then: for a whole host of identities
(categorial incumbencies) that are not naively and routinely
taken to be available or seeable at a glance (affiliations, certain memberships, ties, commitments, professional pursuits,
etc.) there is a host of ways of making them so, turning them
inside out, so to speak - marriage (rings), the clergy (habit),
party membership (buttons, IDs), the army (uniforms), the
police (uniform), the Hell's Angels (dress), the medical profession (stickers on the car, robe), etc. Imagine, for
instance, talking of a police force without any visible means of
identification - entire aspects of the social order would be different and the 'functions' of such a police force would be correspondingly different and would be oriented to differently.
The significance of this is clear in the context of such available categorizations as 'informers', 'agents', 'plain-clothes

men', 'spies', etc., as well as in the context of situations
wherein the ostensible work of 'preserving law and order',
'keeping the peace', etc. is carried out increasingly by non-
uniformed rather than uniformed persons or where, at any
rate, the ranks of that group of persons are swelled. Such
situations have two consequences, at least in terms of members' orientations and the organization of their activities:

1 Any member can programmatically turn out to be a 'policeman' (further generating the categorizations 'agent' or 'spy').
Thus, the problem of the appearance/reality dichotomy of a
person's categorial incumbency becomes programmatically relevant: the uncertainty or equivocality of this categorial incumbency would become a routine practical problem, but one
which also routinely and practically would not be resolved.

2 The attribution of responsibility for certain sorts of actions
or activities, as well as the situated assignation of rights and
obligations, may become problematic, thus also obscuring the
*character* of such actions for members. (15)  One very nice
example of this is available from the reporting on the wave of
kidnappings and murders in Argentina. (16)

> Buenos Aires, Jan. 9 - Two weeks after the seizure by
> armed men of Roberto Quieto, a leftist Peronist guerilla
> leader, his whereabouts and the identity of his captors
> remain a mystery....
>
> The armed forces and the Federal police are conducting
> an intensive campaign of arrests and investigations of sus-
> pected leftist subversives but spokesmen say that they know
> nothing about Mr. Quieto's seizure.
>
> Armed men, usually identifying themselves as policemen,
> have been seizing leftist politicians, union activists, law-
> yers, doctors, students and teachers almost daily. In
> many cases, the bodies of the kidnapped persons are later
> found riddled with bullets. ('New York Times', January 11
> 1976)

Hence we have a whole series of social practices - insignia,
habits, uniforms, signs and markers that *visually* describe a
connection or tie between some person and some membership
category. They are visual descriptors or announcements and
are oriented to as such by members. How this is displayed
and topicalized in talk, or used as a resource in the construction of inferences and descriptions, remains to be analysed
further. What I have tried to do so far is to indicate, mini-
mally, a feature of certain sorts of categorial incumbency -
those that are in the first instance commonsensically available
at a glance and those that are not but are nevertheless made

so available for various practical tasks and relevances in a variety of ways. That this distinction and this perceived orderliness has interactional consequences and a methodic outcome may be fully appreciated by looking at Garfinkel's work on the case of Agnes's sex change; (17) one of the things that sex-change persons try to accomplish is that their 'correct' (chosen) gender should be tellable at a glance, where if it is not so tellable *that* would be a problem for them (recall the importance of electrolysis in the Johanssen case). Of course, such a telling is defeasible and may be defeated by other features of the person's appearance, talk or conduct which may become available only through the course of an interaction. And there are various ways of discovering, ascribing, displaying or accomplishing features of categorial incumbency that for category kinds such as 'gender' or stage-of-life categorizations are expected and produced in such a way that they 'fit' with what is tellable at a glance, some of which, moreover, may be produced so that they get constituted as *part of* what is tellable at a glance (for example, the *way* a person walks). Disguises are constructed in such a way that their users minimize the need to engage in talk, especially in question/answer sequences which increase the possibility of 'discovery' of the relevant (hidden) categorial incumbency under whose auspices the person is in fact doing what she is doing. So 'disguises' may get constructed in such a way, for instance, that the tie between a person's categorial incumbency (which has to be made tellable at a glance) and her location/conduct/context is self-evident and accountable.

Given these various features we can say that the social or public availability of category incumbency is organized in the following various ways:

1 *Perceptual availability*: a) natural, e.g. gender, age bracket; b) emblematic (uniforms, emblems, etc.); c) scenic.

2 *Behavioural availability*: display through talk and action.

3 *First-person avowal*: where for some categories the avowal comes off as an *admission* (e.g. 'I'm a thief').

4 *Third-person declaration*: of which authoritative declarations figure prominently and are related to.

5 *Credential presentations*.

The achievement, production, display or discovery of a 'fit' or a 'disjunction' between these various modes of category incumbency availability (where relevant) is a rich area for

analytic interest. One sort of disjunction between some of
these various modes of category incumbency availability is
particularly interesting. Consider, for example, the category
'*policeman*' and take an incumbent in uniform - a circumstance
that makes the incumbency *perceptually available*. Suppose
this person is seen, for example, stabbing another person in
a side-street, or in the back room of a bar passing drugs to
a dealer; the behavioural availability of the categorization
'criminal', 'killer', 'dealer' or 'crook' does not in these instances defeat the former available categorization (so as to
produce also 'masquerader'), nor is it defeated by it.
Rather it modifies the description of the person as an incumbent of the category that is perceptually available, so that
what we find normally is that such a person gets described
as a 'corrupt policeman'. Take a man seen crying - he is
clearly not easily seeable as a disguised child or a disguised
woman, but, possibly depending on local views, as a childish
or effeminate man. A priest, seen in habit and discovered
having sexual relations with a woman or shoplifting, is again
not in the first instance seeable as a person *pretending to be*
*a priest*, but rather as a corrupt priest or a kleptomaniac
(thus preserving the relevance or applicability of the category
'priest'). It would seem, then, that a category incumbency
that is perceptually available is stronger than one that is
behaviourally available where there is a disjunction between
them. It remains the dominant one although it is modified by
the other. (18)

In Chapter 5 we shall deal with further and different issues
of categorizational disjunction and asymmetry.

Chapter 3

# Lists, categorizations and descriptions

## CATEGORIZATION-RELEVANT LISTS

In Chapter 1 we looked at the following piece of data:

> R: Well, there's not much happening yet as far as I know,
> ... the only thing we know is that the place is being
> used by er all these er dropouts and er Hell's Angels
> and they're prepared to have a battle royal complete
> with er weapons and goodness knows what with a load
> of skinheads.

In noting the equivocality of identification here ('dropouts'
and 'Hell's Angels') we indicated that the first categorization
is a descriptor concept and an individual designator while the
second is an organizational designator (a collective categorization).  We also noted that the utterance part 'dropouts and
Hell's Angels' seems to have the character of a short list.
The two issues are related.  In this section we shall try to
locate some of the features of lists on the one hand and categorizations on the other that provide for this equivocality.
We shall mainly be dealing with two sorts of list structures -
category lists and lists that deliver categorizations (or categories) and/or elaborate on them.  What we will find is that
such lists provide different ways of 'describing' aspects of the
social world - descriptions that do more than merely describe.
In the process of our investigation we shall look at some general features of lists, and in the second section of this chapter
(The Practical Translation Problem), we shall look more closely
at how descriptions can be built through the concerted co-
selection of items.

  One facet of lists is that the items in them have some kind
of relationship to each other.  Roughly speaking, they seem
to have 'something to tie them together', some organizational
principle that can accountably be seen as having informed the
selection of the different items for *this* list.  For a particular
purpose, whatever it may be, not any set of items can be seen
to constitute a *proper* list - and even where they may be seen
to make up a *list*, not any set of items be seen to form
a practicable, reasonable, appropriate or intelligible list.
The principle that organizes the list may be internal to the
items in the list and/or external to them.  That is to say,

the items may 'fit' together because of some family resemblance, some common denominator or some normative tolerance, or because they all relate to a person or thing external to the list by virtue of which alone the list was organized; we may call the latter kind of list an instrumental or task-related list. An example of the former would be a list of monarchs who ruled France; an example of the latter would be a shopping list, or a list of 'things to be done today'. A list that combines both features would be a food shopping list, for example. Now let us consider that there are at least two features that may be expected to characterize a proper list for some purpose: differentiation and adequacy. The first ('differentiation') means that the list cannot (sensibly) be constituted of items that are totally interchangeable for *all* purposes (although they may be interchangeable for this one); that is to say, at least some of the items in the list must add something to the character of the list, unless the list were specifically intended as one whose purpose was to provide possible items (different ones) usable for the same purpose (e.g. a list of items that one could buy from the store in which to keep food fresh). Such lists are lists of *alternatives*. The second feature ('adequacy') is a practical assessment matter; lists are produced for particular practical tasks (even when such tasks are the playing of games), for example, as descriptions or instructions geared to some purpose. If a list is found to be purportedly a description or set of instructions that miss out certain *relevant* or necessary items, then that is a trouble.

In view of the above one might ask why then is there any sense of equivocality about the components 'dropouts and er Hell's Angels' with respect to whether these two categorizations refer to the same persons? We do not wish to be stipulative here and say that this would not then constitute a 'proper list' - the data does not provide for such a hearing even on the part of A, and the equivocality seems to be of a systematic kind logically embedded in and contextually generatable by the nature of that form of double categorization. (Moreover, claims about the 'improper' or 'inadequate' character of lists are matters for practical resolution by members in a setting.) Nor do the above-mentioned list features provide adequately for this sense of equivocality - we would like here to analyse the orderly way by which this equivocality is hearable, produceable and, indeed, a routine feature of certain sorts of lists. Let us look at some further instances of data (H.A. Data):

(I) R: I mean to say, I went in one night when there was erm half a dozen of them there er ... the place was open, the lock was broken on the door, there were tools lying all over the place, on the floor, round about er screwdrivers, er, saws, pincers, hammers, ... everything.

A: Mmm.

(II) R: Er the Hell's Angels types are the people who er *don't* stop at home ... they sleep out, they sleep rough, they're a dirty, scruffy idle shower, they live off social security er plus er thieving er things here and there.

(III) R: Breakers, housebreakers, shop breakers, thieves, goodness knows what....

One thing to notice about (I) is that the entire utterance has the character of a list of 'findings' (that they may be complaints emerges from the nature of that sequence) and what this list of 'findings' on R's part amounts to is a description of a scene. Descriptions may and often do get produced in the character of a list of items/features. One thing about descriptions is that they are, in principle, open-textured (i.e. further items may be added), repairable and, in Hart's terms, defeasible. That is to say, there is an indefinite number of ways of organizing and producing descriptions of scenes (people, places, events, etc.). Descriptions that *do* get produced, therefore, are produced through a process of *selection of items*. They are essentially selectively ordered, and ordered so as to accomplish that task for which, in the first place, they were produced. In data list (I) the organizing principles of that list are: (a) items selected are those which are descriptive elements of scene A (of which R is thus producing an accountable description); (b) items are selected by virtue of the task which that description accomplished – the provision of the grounds for and the features of *a complaint*. That description of a scene, through its being constructed with a *specific* set of items, is organized so as to produce the grounds for a previously articulated complaint, and thus the features of a complainable: 'these Hell's Angels people have actually been breaking into the Planet workshops'. It is clear here how the organization of a list of items can be assembled by reference to the task which that list is intended to accomplish, whether or not those items also have, or do not have, some conceptual or logical category linkage, some common property or some *obvious* family resemblances between them. List (II) can be seen to be structured in a similar way – it is a description of a 'type' – more specifically, it is a description that is achieved through the production of a list of items selected to *deliver* a 'type', and in that a complainable. The items selected are each 'complainables' in and of themselves. The list works as a list of features that 'belong to' or characterize Hell's Angels behaviour, a list that is thus organized

round 'real' features of the world external to the list's production.   It is organized and assembled, however, *so as to
produce* a 'complainable' type, methodically and accountably.

We said earlier that one of the features of lists was differentiation between list items for the task at hand - we can
thus have a set of items that are *alternates* (we are not
interested in this kind for the purpose of the present analysis) or a set of items some at least of which *add* to the list's
features.   But here again we can locate a difference - in
data list (III) the items stand 'discretely', as simple additions
to a list.   But in lists (I) and (II), as we have seen, *the
set* of items comprises a description of a scene or a 'type' of
person.   The items are co-selected *to stand together.   They
exhibit cumulativity*, so that what we get, through the set of
items, is a *gestalt*.   They *thus* have the character of *descriptions*, rather than *itemizations*.   The items stand
together, both as descriptions (of scenes/persons) and as
certain *sorts* of descriptions (delivering complainables - that
the Hell's Angels had been breaking into the Planet workshop;
what the Hell's Angels types are like, i.e. a categorization).
Consider here, for instance, another kind of cumulative list
description, one constructed to provide for the local recognition of the described person:

Subject is white male, 6'2", 157 lbs., black hair, receding
hair-line, wearing a tweed jacket, last seen driving a white
Chevy sedan.

We can also find lists that deliver a category, where the co-
selected items work as class-recognition procedures.   Suppose
we are asked (in a general knowledge quiz, for instance),
'What is something that is black and has a two-segmented body,
eight thin legs and spinnerets?'   Such a listing of features
might enable us to provide a category that answers to this
description, e.g. 'spider'. (1)   In contrast to these two
examples, stock-taking, on the other hand, might include the
production of *itemized lists*.

A feature of some cumulative lists is the following:   for some
of them, the *order* by which items are presented is critical for
the *gestalt delivery* of a description, or for the delivery of
the description's sense.   In our data, while it is not absolutely important for the sense of the description in which
order the items of list (II) are produced (although this may
remain interactionally consequential, as we shall see presently),
we find that in list (I) the case is different.   Here, the
*order* of the list items projects the possible order in which the
set of 'problems' or complainables are encountered by R, in
what is a beautiful example of scene-setting (and a temporally
organized description).   Another example where the *order* of

item delivery is criterial for the delivery of the description is the following list of items: red, orange, yellow, green, blue, indigo, violet - this order conventionally delivers the *rainbow*, or the colour spectrum.

A further property to note here is that all three data extracts have, as part of their produced character as lists, elaborations within those lists on certain items. And in each case the elaborations produced are in the form of a *sub-set list*. So that, it seems, lists may be produced embedded within other lists. In each case the sub-list elaborates on an item by specification of what that item concretely consists in (or *how* it fits) as a feature of that part of the world being described; such sub-lists are concretizing or exemplifying lists. So, in (I) we have (a) 'tools': 'screwdrivers, saws, pincers, hammers, everything'; and (b) 'lying all over the place': 'on the floor', 'round about'. In (II) we have an elaboration on (a) 'don't stop at home', with 'they sleep out', 'they sleep rough', and on (b) 'idle shower', with 'they live off social security' and 'thieving'. And in (III) 'breakers' is specified as 'housebreakers' and 'shop breakers'. Now, specification of what a list item consists in can situatedly achieve various tasks in the course of a conversational sequence from a display of the grounds for one's inference, the basis for one's knowledge or the authentication of one's description to the achievement of disambiguation. The point I wish to indicate here is that within a produced list there is a latitude for the elaboration and specification of list items which is routinely and methodically oriented to by speakers as well as hearers in the course of accomplishing the facticity of one's account. The problem can be formulated as one of *'practical translation'*. What does 'don't stop at home' amount to? What does 'idle' consist in for the speaker? What does it take for things to be properly describable as 'lying all over the place'? Such descriptions *mask their specifics* and in doing so may situatedly produce as a practical problem the issues of agreement and precision. *In masking their specifics, and thus their origins, they mask the standards and criteria employed in their production.* They may also thus mask their essentially moral character. We shall deal with this issue in the next section.

We are now in a position to return to our initial problem and to account for it: 'the place is being used by er all these er dropouts and er Hell's Angels'. Are both the dropouts *and* Hell's Angels using the place, or is it that the *same* persons are being characterized as *both* dropouts *and* Hell's Angels? I want to suggest that the equivocality here has a systematic basis and one, moreover, that does not *routinely* produce practical problems for speaker/hearers. It is clear from the earlier discussion that, although lists are produced so that there is differentiation between *some* of the items, other items in the list provide elaborations and specifications on prior items in the list.　That 'dropouts and Hell's Angels' may be heard not only as a straightforwardly simple list comprising two items, but equivocally as an item plus elaboration is given by a number of overlaid features of the utterance design.　To begin with, as a reference pronoun, 'these' may be said to 'collect' items together.　Secondly, 'dropouts' is a category, we said earlier, that designates the *property* or *feature* of incumbents of that category, whereas 'Hell's Angels' is an organizational category by which members of that organization are designated as incumbents.　Given substantive cultural knowledge that the Hell's Angels is a group organized by specific principles and codes of behaviour that are, at the very least, *congruent* with the constitutive property/feature of the category 'dropout', then 'dropout' may be hearable as displaying that property of the Hell's Angels which is relevant to the talk, to the speaker's interests.　Alternatively, given such knowledge, 'Hell's Angels' may provide for what kind of 'dropouts' the speaker is referring to.　Indeed, given the list format, the category 'dropout', in providing a named property, may be a first instruction for discerning the organizational principle of the list – both in constituting or indicating by implication what the task may be for which the list is organized, and thus also reflexively indicating by what principle 'Hell's Angels' was selected as a next item.　On the other hand, however, the two categories 'dropout' and 'Hell's Angels' are not totally interchangeable.　Significantly, therefore, such equivocality is hearable for certain kinds of lists of *two* items;　it is this which allows for the possible elaborative role of the descriptor category. (2)

It is in these points that the equivocality of the categorizational dual reference in 'dropouts' and 'Hell's Angels' is embedded.　And, as we can now see, it is an equivocality built into the very organization of that utterance and the sort of concepts (categories) situatedly used as its building blocks.

Equivocality, then, is itself neither accidental, nor a mistake in understanding, nor evidence of an inability to understand or reason competently.　Rather, it is methodic, being grounded in members' methodic practices for the production of descriptions of persons and events out of selected and variously describable items;　it is a possible consequence of utterance design (although often some feature of an utterance is only retrospectively constitutable by hearers as being equivocal).　Equivocality is also not always, and not necessarily, an issue for members or a problem for them in understanding the *practical* import of talk. (3)

So, according to one possible hearing, then, what we have

in constructions of the above kind are cases in which the
descriptor category may serve to elaborate that property (not
available in the c; anization's name) of the organizational
category that is relevant to the list and the task at hand and
by which that category was selected as the next item.   By
virtue of that, the organizational category is constituted *or*
characterized by that property or one congruent with it.
Let us look at this another way using Sacks's notion of 'membership categorization device' (4) as a tool.

One of the rules that Sacks proposes for the organization of
membership categorization devices in discourse is the *consistency rule*:  If you can hear a second category to be drawn
from the same device as the first, then hear it that way.
An example of this would be 'The baby cried.   The mommy
picked it up', where the device from which the categories
'baby' and 'mommy' are both hearable as being co-selected is
that of 'family'.   (This is in part by virtue of the notion of
'category-bound' actions.)   Another example would be an
introductory round, such as:   A: What do you do?   B: I'm
an engineer. You?   A: I'm a doctor.   Both categories here
can be heard as being drawn from the device Profession /
Occupation.   The rule can be reformulated for the latter
example as follows:  If the hearable task or concern at hand
can be fulfilled or accomplished by following a first category
with a second drawn from the same device, then do so.
This is *a relevance version of the consistency rule*.   It also
is one that is applicable for symmetrical formulations and displays of relevance as between speaker and hearer.

We begin now to see the immense complexity of conversational structure and the tasks of accomplishing interactional concerns.   If we try to apply the consistency rule mechanistic-
ally to the data, we have the following problem:  'dropouts'
is a different *sort* of category from 'Hell's Angels'.   We
cannot immediately see what device they could both come from.
One might, for instance, proffer such constructs as 'irresponsible persons', 'trouble-makers', 'deviants', etc., but this is
essentially a *constructivist* enterprise since we have no way
of choosing between these different but cognate categories,
and the candidate device-category implicated for one person
by the hearing of the category items in the data may not be
the same for another hearer.   The issue of psychological
reality emerges forcefully for such an attempt.   One may
avoid this issue by modifying one's analysis and formulating it
in terms of *implication*, but this still has, of course, to be
properly grounded in the data.   We will treat this issue
presently.   If it is seen as a list, then 'dropouts and Hell's
Angels', as we have argued, is organized to produce a component of a *complaint* about persons who use the Planet playground (dropouts and Hell's Angels), the complaint turning on

the feature-description 'dropout'.  The category 'Hell's
Angels', second to the first category 'dropout', can be seen
to be selected by the very property delivered in that first
category.  One can say, therefore, that, rather than looking
for an exogenous device from which both 'dropout' and 'Hell's
Angels' are drawn, *the category 'dropout' itself functions
as the device from which the second category is drawn.*
'Hell's Angels' is thus treatable as a variant of 'dropout' - it
specifies a 'species' of 'dropout' and in that sense the structure is akin to 'tools lying all over the place ... screwdrivers, er saws, pincers, hammers' and to 'Breakers, housebreakers, shop breakers'.

There are at least three methods by which we can analytically and legitimately locate the use (production, invocation,
display, implication, etc.) of categorization *devices* in talk
(i.e. of device-categories):

1 Where the device is provided for by the semantic-taxonomic
sense of the category-concepts on the one hand and the talk's
relevances on the other, such that there is a 'fit' between the
two, i.e. the operation of a relevance version of the consistency rule.  This is Sacks's usage.  What is involved here
is a strict implication which provides for the task and relevances at hand, whilst reflexively it is that task and those
concerns which provide for the relevance of that device, as
an outcome of categorial co-selection.  Such devices or collections may be observably used as *resources* by members in the
organization of their category-selection procedures, e.g.
'family', 'occupation', 'religion', 'nationality', etc.

One simple way of seeing that two categories are not from
the same device is to see that the two categories are not
mutually exclusive.  And one way to see that they are from
the same device is to see that they are mutually exclusive.
One example might be in a list structure such as 'nationalists
and communists' or 'Palestinians and Israelis'.  In each case,
the two categories are seeable as mutually exclusive in their
constituency;  as such they are *alternative categorizations*
in their routine contexts of use - one, but not the other, is
appropriate (where it is) to describe any one person. (5)

2 Where the device is hearable as explicitly provided *in* the
talk, as in the example above of 'dropouts and Hell's Angels'.

3 By conventional or pragmatic implication - where the device
is hearable as part of the upshot of the talk or the task to be
accomplished or work intended by the speaker, and hearable
thus through the local and topical production of 'fit' between
certain features of the category-concepts.  Indexically implicated devices would include 'enemies', 'friends', 'strangers',
'guilty parties'. (6)

It is important to note, however, that in many contexts of talk, the location or 'hearing' of a device-category at use by members is not in itself relevant for the practical purposes of understanding; the context of the talk itself provides a self-explicating character to the list of items/categories used.
For example, take the sentence 'Communists, Catholics and women came out in large numbers today to vote on the Abortion Bill.' In Sacks's terms, the three items here do not come from the same device (or collection); but neither need we look further than the details of that particular utterance - what we could have there is simply an *itemization of membership categories* for which the abortion issue is important.
The various categories are thus locally produced as standing for collectivities that are morally organized around the issue of abortion, an issue for which *these* membership categorizations are relevance-providing identities. One cannot, and need not, therefore, locate some exogenous single device-category to provide for such an utterance.

An interesting example where a device-category may be located by hearers is the following:

> While on the hunt for communists, Jews, and other 'enemies', the S.A. flying squads did not find housebreaking, robbery, looting, violence, kidnapping or blackmail for ransom to be beneath their national dignity. (7)

While the two categories 'communists' and 'Jews' are provided syntactically as being from the device 'enemies', (8) the inverted commas round the last category actually provide for their being co-selected as categories *whose incumbents are considered to be enemies by the S.A.* (Nazi storm troopers). The context of the talk further provides here for the *relevance* of 'victims of the S.A.' or, possibly, 'opposition groups', etc., but these are only made relevant *implicatively*, as available descriptions that would include Jews and communists (and others). What provides for the co-selection here of these membership categorizations, then, is the task and relevances of the talk. In inspecting this one may see what sort of features (activities, relationships, etc.) are being invoked of, or attributed to, the incumbents of these two membership categories, either as category-bound, category-relevant, category-embedded or category-specific, and whether locally, or through trading on members' conventional knowledge, or both.

The issue, then, is not a mechanical application of the consistency rule where one *decides* what device these two categorizations (or any co-selected categories) *are drawn from*, but rather to see what device-category they could, strictly or conventionally, imply *for the task or relevance at hand* that is

displayed in the talk within which this category list is embedded.   And it is not always or necessarily the case that the
talk's relevances include the implication or generation of a
further category (a device) which could thus help achieve
that relevance for what it is.   Take, for example, the following sort of exchange at the scene of some shoot-out:

A:  Who are you?

B:  I'm the doctor.   And you?

A:  My son's in there!

Clearly, what is being provided here is a relevant reason for
being at the scene - the organization of the exchange involves
the production and reliance on the relevance of some category
incumbency to the scene, which then becomes available as the
reason for being at the scene, and a self-explicating one in
the context of the category-scene tie displayed.

In other words, what should be of interest to the analyst is
the *implicative logic of categorizations*.   How would the
locating of a device-category appear warrantable and intelligible?   The concern here is not to locate the device as the
organizing principle for the choice of categories by the
speaker, but the tools or basis by which this device is made
relevant and the methods by which it can be assembled *in
situ*.   The 'device', then, is not so much *presupposed* as
*implicated* by the selections.

The point holds not only for category lists but for any *co-
selection of categories* for some purpose;   it is the task that
provides for the relevant category features by which these
categories were selected and it is these features that provide
for the practical interests at hand and the relevance of some
device or other.   A speaker may be seen to be (and may
indeed be) starting with a device 'in mind', in other words,
some categorization whose relevance is to be established as
part of the particular task at hand, and therein to choose the
categorizations that would provide for this device/task.   But
this 'device' is in the first place only accessible through the
*in-situ* organization of category-relevant knowledge.   The
implicated device-category works as an implicit or in-built
*accounting scheme* for whatever the topic at hand may be.

Compare, for example, the following extracts of data ('News-
week', June 21, 1976):

(I)  it appeared that Syria might succeed in its attempt to
     put an end to the *political* and *religious* warfare that
     has racked Lebanon for fourteen bloody months.   The

fighting between the country's *Christian* and *Muslim* armies had ground to a halt. [Emphasis added]

(II)  Although the *leftists* blocked the *Syrians'* drive on Beirut, that did not end the suffering in the capital. Pro-Syrian forces controlled both the airport and the important cross-roads at Khalde to the South ... and *right-wing Christian* troops held the territory to the North. [Emphasis added]

Extract (II) is taken from the very same article as (I), yet the various parties in conflict are categorized differently in each.  Whereas in (I) the co-selection of categorizations provides the warrant for the use of a 'religious' account (in this case one provided *before* the use of the categorizations), in (II) it is another sort of account that is made available, a 'political' one - embedded in the use of both the categories 'leftists' and 'Syrians'.  The use of the third categorization, 'right-wing Christian troops', maps both 'religious' and 'political' identities onto the same collectivity and makes possible the use of both sorts of accounts, accounts that have already been proffered earlier on (in I, which much precedes II) and thus are warranted by those categorizations whilst, reflexively, providing their warrant.

As competent members of the culture within which such categorizations and concepts operate and make sense, we can see just what sort of ties there are (real or projected) between such co-selected categorizations and the task or concern at hand.  Alternatively, and further, one may inspect the world to see if such a tie or fit pertains (and/or to what extent it pertains).  If one looks at the world and sees that a category-list, for example, does not fit the world for the *particulars* of the task at hand (apportioning blame for a specific event, predicting a certain course of action, describing particular events or actions in a specific way, etc.), i.e. that it is not the proper *mapping procedure*, then that list may be faulted, and then it is the whole *ascriptive* or *accounting* enterprise that is faulted.  How this is done (and what inferences are consequently drawn regarding the speaker) depends on the sort of task attempted and its specifics, and is situatedly decidable.  For some tasks (specific descriptions, action attributions, inferences) the most unlikely list may be seen to 'fit' the world.  Such membership categorization lists (and other category co-selections) may thus be seen as *social structural mapping procedures* - they are *procedures that make transparent, or provide a version of, the social structure of collectivities*.  Their negotiation, elaboration, specification and defeasance display the morally organized character of knowledge and of members' procedures in assembling and making sense of social structure.

## THE PRACTICAL TRANSLATION PROBLEM

In the previous section we discussed category lists, as well as
lists that members routinely construct and use that *deliver* a
category.   Routinely, such a category (or categorization) may
be provided by the speaker before or after the list of features
which are hearable as *amounting to* that categorization (or as
providing a description of category features and incumbents).
One of the extracts of data we looked at went like this
(H.A. Data):

> R:   er the Hell's Angels types are the people who er *don't*
> stop at home ... they sleep out, they sleep rough,
> they're a dirty, scruffy idle shower, they live off social
> security er plus er thieving er things here and there.

We have the category first, and then a list of attributes and
features that are made out to be those characteristic (or constitutive) of that category – this enables the category to be
used later on in a predictive or generative capacity.   We
noted that embedded in this is another structure:  not only,
as we indicated earlier, is a second list embedded in the primary list, but it is a sub-list of features whose character as
a sub-list *depends* on the prior provision of a categorization
(or some other formulation of descriptive items):  'idle shower,
they live off social security er plus er thieving'.   We described the sub-list here as an elaboration or specification of
one of the items of the primary list, and thus as providing
some resolution to what we called the 'practical translation
problem'.   What is displayed here is the procedure for category ascription in this particular case and the warrant for it.

Let us further explicate in some detail what we mean by the
'practical translation problem' and its relevance for the analysis of talk.   As should become clear, the sense of 'problem'
we intend is that given by Sacks.

> we want to find problems;  we want means to get us prob-
> lems (where such problems are not in the first instance
> known to be 'problems' that members occupy themselves
> with).... Also, and in some way separately, the character
> of the problem we construct is delimited in this way:  We
> construct only such problems as the actions we have are
> methodical solutions for, or, the actions we have can be
> analyzed to evidence the employment of methods, which are
> methodical by virtue of producing solutions to those prob-
> lems.   We construct only such problems because our scien-
> tific commitment to constructing methods as the only sorts of
> descriptions of behavior which are acceptable, requires that
> our constructed problems be such as the actions can be
> seen *rationally* to achieve solutions to. (9)

Let us then proceed with our explication.  The hearer of a
conversational utterance has the dual task of (or licence to):

1  Understand(ing) the speaker's utterance.

2  Respond(ing) to it;  tak(ing) some kind of position on it.
For this, there are *normatively* available *preferences* – questions prefer answers (to evasions, clarifying questions, etc.);
proposals prefer acceptances;  descriptions and inferences
prefer assent;  assertions prefer agreements;  complaints and
explanations prefer acceptances, etc. (10)

To understand a speaker's prior turn, i.e. to accomplish
(1), a hearer has to understand the (intended) illocutionary
force of that utterance and make sense of the (intended) work
of the speaker in providing for that force through the specifics (particulars) of her speech.   This is a normative pre-
requisite for (2).

Let us confine ourselves to descriptions, whether intended
simply as descriptions or used to make complaints, furnish
inferences, provide accounts, deliver categorizations (and
characterizations/assessments) or otherwise accomplish a
variety of practical tasks.   Note here the following:  suppose
a description is used to make a complaint (as in much of our
Hell's Angels data);  we have the situation then of a double
requirement/preference for assent.   Firstly, the description
itself prefers assent;  secondly, the complaint prefers acceptance.   But for the latter to be accomplished requires and
presupposes the accomplishment of the former, i.e. assent to
the description from which the complaint is constructed.   The
assent would here perform a double duty, and we can say that
what happens in such conversational contexts is that *a double-
duty preference is operable*.

If a description's first preference as a next turn at talk is
assent to it, then that assent or agreement with it has to be
produced as agreement *about the world* as it is, and not just
agreement with *a speaker*;  the agreement has to be produced
as agreement that is objectively grounded and morally accountable, and not simply as a voluntaristic/arbitrary agreement
with some version of the world.

The hearer's agreement (where it is with a description) provides that the world (or some feature of it) is as described by
X, and not that whatever X says or whatever description X
produces will capture those features, nor that whatever description X produces is only up to X.

Acceptance of a description (where the hearer has no independent knowledge as to the particulars of that description)

is acceptance that the world (or some features of it) is describ*able* in the way X has described it, both empirically and morally, and not that whatever way X describes it will do for the hearer and others as well.

An earlier extract of data demonstrates well the distinction for members between agreeing with some speaker or accepting his account where it is only the speaker's person that provides the warrant for agreement and having grounds or a good reason for that agreement (where such reason may be the demonstrable good character or honesty, competence, know-how, reliability, etc. of the speaker):

Jay:        Wuhdidju think of, when Romney came out with
            his statement that he w'ss um. ... thet 'e w'z
            brain//wash//ed

George:     I *think* he *wa*:s
            (pause ca. 5.0 sec.)

Jay:        IN - in uhm, what
            (pause ca. 2.0)

George:     I don'kno:w, b't if he says he w'z *brain*-washed,
            (pause ca. 7.0)

→ Sy.:      He's one a' these'Rom//ney c'do no wro:ng.'
            -types. hh

→ George:   *He*'s en honest *ma:n*

→ George:   This much I *do* know.

The above data indicates the importance of *demonstrable grounds* for agreements, inferences, beliefs, descriptions, etc. when faced with a challenge.

If we reformulate a hearer's tasks here, then we will have the following:

1  a  Analysing the communicative intention of the utterance/
      speaker.  Understanding what X's utterance amounts
      to:  both what he is trying to say, and what he is
      trying to do *in saying* that;  both the intended sub-
      stance of the description (its sense and reference)
      and its intended illocutionary force.

   b  Analysing and making sense, for oneself, of the par-
      ticulars of that utterance, as it proceeds, and inspect-
      ing its grounds, thus analysing what *can be said* of/
      with those particulars (and what can be done with

them for practical purposes), thus checking on and
ratifying the speaker's 'proposal' and making one's
own conclusions about the topic and issue at hand.

2 Taking a stance vis-à-vis the description and the work
that description (or account) may be intended to accomplish, e.g. agreeing to a judgment or inference, the
agreement having in the first place and essentially to be
fashioned out of agreement with the description and a
perceived 'fit' between the description and the work it is
put to.

In other words, then, there must be a 'fit' between the
description as a gestalt, the account's sense, and the items
out of which that account is constructed.    Task 1 (b) is a
way of finding/testing the warrant of the descriptions provided, as well as locating the grounds and warrant for the
hearer's own response – it is not that (a) and (b) are two
*separate* steps that a hearer makes;   rather (b) is embedded
in (a), for to understand what the speaker intends is already
to have checked through the items by which his utterance is
constructed for the task at hand.    However, they can be
*analytically* distinguished.    In certain interactional contexts,
moreover, (a) may not be fully available whilst (b) is, or (b)
may not be fully available whilst (a) is, so that (2) becomes a
problematic next step.    We will presently exemplify this.
Before we go on, I should stress a point of importance.    (1a)
and (2) are not intended necessarily to describe either the
*actual* intentions of the speaker or the actual (psychologically
accurate) stance of the hearer vis-à-vis the speaker's prior
turn at talk or proffered account.    Rather they are meant to
capture the *displayed* intention and the *displayed* stance made
available through the talk (the *public* character of the talk)
regardless of whether the speaker/hearers actually do feel or
think or intend what they provide for through their talk.
Hunter puts the case for this analytic position clearly:

4 The game can develop only in terms of the moves that
have been made.  By this I mean two things:
i What anyone says in the language-game *is* the move
he is making.  We can no more ask whether he has
made the move than, if someone puts his piece on a
certain square in a game of chess, we can so ask.
There *is* a question, that scarcely arises in most
games, as to just *what* move has been made (this, I
suggested, is what is going on when we ask 'Do you
mean it?' or 'Do you mean such-and-such?'), but once
that is clearly answered, the game can only proceed
from there.  If you say something and I do not
believe you, the game may end there;  but it need
not;  it may take a new turn, in which I devise a

strategy based on my scepticism, perhaps saying just
the things you will not want me to say if you are
insincere in what you have said.

ii Just as in chess, for example, I may make a powerful
move by accident or with some other strategy in
mind, so the moves we make in language-games have
their power, so to speak, independently of whether
we mean them.    (If for devious reasons I tell my
wife that I will quit tomorrow if she encourages me,
and she does, I have as much commitment to quit as
if I had meant it.    And if she encouraged me *just
because* she suspected I was not in earnest, and to
call my bluff, when in fact I was in earnest, she
could not complain if next day I did quit.)

5 Because moves in the language-game may be hard to
make, because there are things that, except for devious
purposes, we cannot make ourselves say, developments in
the language-game will often show more clearly than anything else, and even in the face of other biographical
evidence, what our attitude is, for example how seriously
we have been thinking something. (11)

Where there is a disjunction between (a) and (b) (a disjunction between speaker and hearer), inference as to the
speaker's motives/competence/knowledge is made possible *as
an accounting procedure* for the discrepancy.    Where this disjunction arises, then, it makes procedurally possible an asymmetry between (1a) and (2).

The 'practical translation problem' can be located then in (1)
- it is that problem for which accomplishing (1) properly is
the solution and is a solution requisite for the/an appropriate
response to be made, i.e. for (2) to be properly accomplished.

If we look at (1) closely, we will see it has a number of
parameters.    I shall not try to deal with them all.    But it
becomes clear from this that the practical translation problem
can have many versions - I shall only look at some of them.

The data extract we looked at earlier has an interesting
structure (H.A. Data):

32 R:  er the Hell's Angels types are the people who er
       *don't* stop at home ... they sleep out, they sleep
       rough, they're a dirty, scruffy idle shower, they
       live off social security er plus er thieving er things
       here and there.

Specifically, we have seen that it consists of a list of items in
which sub-lists are embedded, both list and sub-list of items

consisting in some elaboration on (or specification of) a
categorization:  the Hell's Angels types.

For the hearer to respond on the basis of some perceived
'fit' between description and work (task), she must also
secure some concrete understanding both of what the describing items consist in and what they amount to, such that
she may be able to *paraphrase and report on them* if necessary.  In other words, the hearer has to secure some sense
for what the speaker intends to say and what the produced
'description' really amounts to:  for example, a proper description of the world, or an unintended display of prejudice.

Suppose our data had gone:  'er the Hell's Angels types are
the people who er *don't* stop at home ... they're a dirty,
scruffy idle shower'.  Here (call it case I), most of the
concrete particulars have been eliminated, and only those descriptive items remain which are *umbrella descriptors* or which
are referentially polymorphous by virtue of being *excluders*. (12)

Such 'descriptions' routinely come off as displays of 'prejudice', 'idle complaining', 'abuse', and the like.  And it is not
difficult to see why.  There is no provision of warrant here,
no display of ascriptive procedures (and the descriptions are
negatively morally implicative), no grounds furnished, etc.
A hearer has to take it at face value, 'on faith' so to speak
(unless she had independently available particulars).  What
practices do 'dirty', 'idle' and 'scruffy' consist in such that
those are proper descriptions for them?  This is one version
of the translation problem.  'Scruffy', 'idle' and 'dirty' are
generic descriptions for which the follow-up (or inferential)
options conventionally taken up by hearers concern what the
grounds for these descriptions are, what the warrant for
producing them was and further relevant or tied matters -
they are *treatable as candidate tokens of judgmental closure
on the part of the speaker*, for the practical purposes at hand.
How such a closure might have been achieved is, however, not
available to the hearer.  In that a hearer may be expected to
employ in his/her hearing and response a variety of procedures and resources for making sense of and coming to an
'understanding' of an utterance, and of the course of the
conversation within which it is embedded, from local knowledge to categorial knowledge, the first speaker may then, in
producing his/her descriptions, tailor them so that they provide the accountability of the provided description.

Suppose, on the other hand, the data had gone:

R:  er the Hell's Angels types are the people who sleep out,
    they sleep rough, they live off social security er plus
    thieving er things here and there.

Let us call this case II;   here we can locate another possible version of the practical translation problem:   there is no utterance-provided decisive practical indication as to what the speaker intends these descriptive items to amount to and what the illocutionary force of his description is to be (there may be, of course, some such indications from the prior course of the conversation, from the context, prior knowledge of speaker's beliefs, views, etc.).   The strongest implicative item here (in that possible available implications are more circumscribed, and in that it is *negatively* morally implicative), is 'live off ... thieving', the *last* item.   This is significant.

Thus, where such particulars are given first (or given alone), *what they are to amount to* is not always or necessarily unequivocal or clear for members, for the same particulars can be collected under different descriptions, and the *timed* character of speech becomes a possible feature of (or factor in) an asymmetric understanding (a disjunction between (a) and (b) above).   The 'translation' of the particulars into a categorization (description/device) that they could amount to is a task that the hearer faces, but one for which the speaker may routinely provide a resolution - thus also displaying the auspices under which he speaks.

In case (I) what we would have is (1a) provided for and (1b) missing, so that the proper move to (2) is made difficult.   In case (II) what we would have is (1b) available, but (1a) equivocal or ambiguous.   This makes the move to (2) risky for both speaker and hearer.

The speaker, in other words, in providing for a proper response (or the preferred one) from the hearer routinely orients to the 'practical translation problem' and designs her utterance/description so as to provide in the selection of descriptive items both the solution and the puzzle for which that is a proper solution.

We can see, then, that the description actually provided in the data has an immensely complex and fine organization to it.

The speaker might have said, 'idle shower, they lie around all day in the park and sit in the pub all night'.   'Idle shower' would have remained an accountably used categorization and its *sense* would still be the same (for it delivers its property constituent in its very name, and in this context also works to deliver a complaint).   But the criteria for having ascribed it to those persons would have been displayably different.   Thus, the description of 'idle' in the data is provided its accountable grounds:   'live off social security plus thieving'.   The speaker resolves the possible practical translation problem so that 'don't stop at home' is provided as consisting in 'sleeping out' and 'sleeping rough' (and not, for example, in 'spending one's evening at the pub'), in such a way that 'don't stop at home' can be seen as a proper item in a list of (a certain kind of) complainables regarding the behaviour of the Hell's Angels types. But equally, then, 'sleeping out' and 'sleeping rough' are provided with their intended sense (their formulation or normatively built redescription) as 'don't stop at home' and as a 'dirty, scruffy idle shower' rather than, say, 'an energetic nature-loving lot' or 'an outdoor bunch', etc. (13)

At this point let us briefly note some further features and parameters of the problem: multiple description embedding, formulation frames and the 'particular'/'general' dimension of practical descriptions. Let us take these in reverse order.

We said earlier that membership categorizations (and other descriptions) carry with them a cluster of features that go together (implied, presupposed, category-bound, category-relevant, etc.) - properties, activities, practices, moral features, inclinations, beliefs, etc. Action categories also carry such a cluster of features (implied, presupposed, action-tied, action-consequent, etc.) - character, moral judgments, consequences, grounds, locales, states of being, etc. It is in this complexity that the three features above are embedded. Given the above network, and given the relevance for selection of items of the practical task of any occasioned description, the ways that such descriptive work handles and provides solutions to the 'practical translation problem' in the course of accomplishing that task are complex, varied and very finely organized.

If we look at a number of descriptions (and accounts), we can notice that they routinely and massively exhibit an organization of descriptive items that is articulated at both the 'particular' and the 'general' levels. But 'particular' and 'general' here derive their character from the nature of their mutually elaborative relation in situ, and not from some rigid a priori conception of what a 'particular' (or 'concrete') item looks like and what a 'general' item looks like. We may indeed have some commonsense conceptions of this which we employ (14) in our activities but what specific item will do as a 'particular' or 'instance' of some 'general' one, and what 'general' item will do as a formulation of the 'particular' at hand is ultimately a situatedly practical judgmental matter for members in some interaction. Let us look at some examples of data: (15)

   I  Kenneth's stepfather, who was known to me, was at least as unsatisfactory. A lazy man and a gambler, he made little secret of his dislike for Kenneth, and

was responsible for a great deal of unhappiness and
poverty. He finally left home two years ago, after
taking the contents of the electricity and gas meters.

II　Mr K's family are well-known to the Social Agencies in
O, but he himself is an honest, quiet and sober man
who normally holds a good job, and is currently employed by Grasswell and Taylor.

III　At the time that he was placed on Probation 2½ years
ago he was resentful, cheeky and unpopular with other
boys: his way of trying to get the admiration of his
colleagues was to indulge in stealing and other unlawful activity.

IV　He has had frequent disputes with his mother which
have resulted in him leaving home on several occasions,
his behaviour generally has deteriorated and he has
been drinking.

The four examples above exhibit a diversity of ways of
articulating both the 'particular' and the 'general' dimensions
of description work and various methods of meeting the practical translation problem. They are all taken from Probation
Officer reports, which are designed to present assessments of
each person's case and make recommendations for a course of
action on that basis. Given the textual character of these
reports, then, and the task they are designed to accomplish,
they are particularly well suited for an analysis in terms of
the issues we have been discussing in this section, but such
an analysis requires detailed work of a scope that would take
us far beyond the concerns of the present study. However,
two points must be indicated: firstly, texts of this kind have
to provide their materials in 'one go', so to speak - they are
not embedded in, or immediately open to, speaker/hearer
interchanges, question/answer sequences, solicited clarifica-
tions, collaborative formulations, etc. The descriptive items'
sense and reference have to be as fully and self-explicatively
provided for as possible within the framework of the text.
Secondly, the descriptions are produced in an essentially contrastive design. Much of the descriptive work of the report
(see Appendix 4) gets produced in contrastive sequences
where each contrast pair part provides for the feature that
achieves the contrast, maintaining a displayed sensitivity to
the textual context. At the same time, the contrast pair part
itself is composed of a set of items, and in order for the contrast to work, the cumulative sense of those items in conjunction has to provide for the contrast feature. Such cumulative
work is complex and we have already seen some of its features
in the previous discussion of (cumulative) lists.

Now S.E. Data extracts I and IV seem to provide solutions to the practical translation problem at the level of *implication* (a solution to 1a). Data extracts II and III deal with the practical translation problem through providing elaborative particularizations of items that thus get constituted as more 'general'. In III, for instance, the descriptive item 'his way of trying to get the admiration of his colleagues was to indulge in stealing and other unlawful activity' provides the grounds for his coming to be (characterized as) 'unpopular' - its explanation, so to speak. In II, the item 'who normally holds a good job' provides for a possible description that is cognate with the ones already provided: 'honest ... sober' (and may even be seen to be a specification on 'sober') - it is treatable as a particularization then that provides a warrant for a description embedded in the cumulative work of that contrast pair part, where the upshot of that part may implicatively be something like 'decent man' or 'straight guy' (in contrast to the implication of the first contrast pair part: that his family are often in some sort of trouble). Even in this case, some work is being done at the level of implication. Further, the item 'is currently employed by Grasswell and Taylor' provides a simple and direct instantiation of the item 'who normally holds a good job' albeit the full force of this instantiation depends on local knowledge.

We can see, then, that the methodic practices of descriptive (and accounting) work as organizationally produced around some version of the 'practical translation problem' are complex and many-layered. (16) We cannot hope to deal with them all adequately here; we shall therefore look more closely at some of the practices operating at the level of implication, since this issue is emerging as one which is of particular concern to this work and which has not, despite its pervasive relevance, been generally dealt with elsewhere in any real detail. But before we proceed with that we have a few remaining points to consider.

If we look at S.E. Data extract I, we see that it starts with a prospectively oriented summary of the sense and upshot of the subsequent items: 'at least as unsatisfactory'. But in the items that follow there is another summing up, this time retrospectively oriented, of the sense and upshot of some preceding items: 'responsible for a great deal of unhappiness and poverty' sums up the sense and implications of 'A lazy man and a gambler, he made little secret of his dislike for Kenneth'. But this second summing up is still, itself, a specification of the first summary: 'unsatisfactory', whilst the item that follows, 'He finally left home', etc., is a further instantiation (and retrospective justification) of that second summing up. What we then have is that the items 'A lazy man and a gambler, he made little secret of his dislike for

Kenneth' is bounded by two summings up (or 'formulations' of sense and implication (17)) on either side.

In our first example of Hell's Angels data we saw that 'don't stop at home' translated into 'they sleep out, they sleep rough'.   But 'they sleep out, they sleep rough' also translated into 'they're a dirty, scruffy (idle) shower'.   Thus, the same set of items, or 'particulars', can serve as the instantiation of a first item (a 'general' one) and the displayed warrant for the ascription of another set of 'general' items (in this case a categorization).   Such *'formulation frames'* are common features of extended descriptions and accounts.

In the H.A. Data extract the two formulation frames may be said to be *symmetrical*:   they formulate the same sets of items, but not each other.   In S.E. Data I the two formulation frames may be said to be *asymmetrical*, since the first one collects all the subsequent items under its rubric, *including* the second formulation itself, which may be seen as embedded in the first.   It might be interesting to look for instances of talk where there is a displayed or oriented-to disjunction between two formulation frames.

In the S.E. Data, extracts I and II display prospective-retrospective embedding of item within item.   In the H.A. Data extract, 'idle' is embedded in the last set of formulations; at this point it has not yet been provided for in the 'particulars' but now gets its elaboration and instantiation in 'they live off social security plus thieving things here and there'. This kind of *multiple embedding* is another feature of the organization of descriptions and accounts.

Both the formulation frames and such multiple embedding can work in a sequence, across turns, so that a highly complex organization of description is collaboratively produced and thus economically co-produced.   A beautiful example of this comes from our Hell's Angels data (H.A. Data):

58   R:   Well, I mean there's nothing there now, is there?

59   A:   Well, there are some workshops, yes, which have quite a lot of tools and equipment and things....

→ 60   R:   Well, er that's been one of the troubles, you see, er, they've er ... er ... a lot of the things have been left there relatively insecure.

61   A:   Yeah.

62   R:   er, screwdrivers, saws, goodness knows what - wonderful breaking instruments.

63 A: Oh ... I see.

→ 64 R: I mean it's no good just putting a padlock on a building and saying well it's locked up, it's secure, that er that doesn't stop these people....

→ 65 A: No - what you're saying these Hell's Angels people have actually been breaking into the Planet workshops...

→ 66 R: That's what I mm consider myself - my own personal opinion.

67 A: Yeah.

68 R: I mean to say, I went in one night when there was erm half a dozen of them there er ... the place was open, the lock was broken on the door, there were tools lying all over the place, on the floor, round about er screwdrivers, er, saws, pincers, hammers, everything.

69 A: Mm.

70 R: It's just asking for, er, trouble.

Any solution to the 'practical translation problem' provided by a speaker/hearer is defeasible. Moreover, any version of the problem for which the speaker/hearer offers a solution may not situatedly be treated as adequate, relevant or exhaustive for present concerns. A speaker/hearer may still continue to provide or seek *further* solutions that constitute different versions of the problem as the puzzle to which these are the proper solution. Formulation framing and multiple embedding are ways of doing that: they are ways of ramifying the problem and its methodic solutions for the practical purposes and concerns at hand. Any such ramification, however, will be subject to *practical* closure. (18)

Let us now turn to the issue of implication we indicated earlier.

In addition to the S.E. Data extracts I and IV, we can look at:

V Unfortunately, however, the root of the trouble seems to lie not only in the environment, but also in John's relationship with his mother. *She has told me that he was not 'planned' but that in any case she wanted a girl* and I believe he experienced almost a total rejection at birth. (Emphasis added)

VI  Since his release from Realey, however (where he spent
a week after telling a lie to the court about his age),
he has shown small signs of a change of heart.  *He has
indicated his regret at the way his conduct has affected his mother's health, has been prepared to spend
time talking about his life, and has gone out and got
himself a job.* (Emphasis added)

If we look at these various S.E. Data, extracts I and IV to
VI, we will see that a number of the descriptive items are
*conventionally and normatively consistent* with one another.
Each item taken by itself provides for a cluster of possible
inferences and implications;  each data extract is constructed
such that there is a congruence between the cluster of possible inferences and implications for each 'particular' item (we
will see in the next chapter a further example of congruence
between some category-bound features in the case of 'women'
and 'children').   In other words, there is what we can call
an *implicative fit* between them.   It is this implicative fit
that provides in part for the sense and intelligibility of the
descriptions in each contrast pair part as well as of the contrastive work itself.   But it is a feature of various descriptions, and not only those embedded in contrastive work, as
we can see when we look back at our data describing the
Hell's Angels types earlier.   (Both *that* description and the
ones above are constructed for some specific task, however,
and are not general discursive descriptions where the work
being done is simply that of *describing*.   The latter work
may present a different case.)

The *implicative fit* we indicated may provide for *implicative deletion* in the process of sense assembly, where both
implicative fit and implicative deletion may be conceived of as
*discourse-sense assembly procedures*.   For example, 'he drinks
a lot' could provide for (or be a prelude to) 'he's unhappy',
'he's spending all his money', 'he's often in a bad temper',
'he's going to cause the breakup of his marriage', 'he has a
bad character' or any number of other descriptions, inferences and implications.   If you further get 'he gambles', most
of the implications above are still inferentially intact, although
'he's often in a bad temper' is not *conventionally* implicated
by, or bound up with, the notion of 'gambling' as it is with
that of 'drinking' – the same holds for 'he's unhappy'.   Conventionally, where these are tied into 'gambling', it is by way
of yet *another implication*, and that is 'he's going bankrupt',
for example.   Here we are dealing with the realm of convention and not strict entailment.   The cumulative work of 'he
drinks a lot, he gambles', then, is the achievement of implicative fit between the two contextually available sets of items
(e.g. 'he's spending all his money', 'he's a bad lot', 'he's
causing the breakup of his marriage', etc.) and a *candidate*

*implicative deletion* (of e.g. 'he's unhappy', 'he's often in a
bad temper'). Suppose that for a third item one had 'and
he's chasing women all the time' - then 'he's unhappy' and
'he's often in a bad temper' would be deletable as an implication of such talk (although not a logical impossibility). Now
it is clear that the other possible implications (available inferential alternatives) would still be relevant through the implicative fit between the three items. (19) The speaker of
such an utterance may stop there, giving rise to a version of
the 'practical translation problem' - what does the selection of
descriptive items amount to for the speaker? The *hearer*
may provide a *formulation* here as a solution to this; such
a formulation may be, for example, 'he's a bad lot'. This
formulation is *a selection of a particular implication* as
being what it is that the speaker's talk is intendedly providing for. Alternatively, the *speaker* may, and routinely does,
provide such a formulation selected from the co-implications
in his/her description. So what we could have is 'he drinks
a lot, he gambles and he's chasing women all the time, he's a
bad lot'.

It may be noted that implicative fit and implicative deletion
as sense assembly procedures comprise a specification of some
methods of prospective-retrospective understanding of and
within talk. The sense of the description being provided
(and its work) which is delivered as a solution to a version of
the 'practical translation problem' is extracted from the set of
relevant implications of the 'particulars'. The context of the
discourse and the setting routinely provide, of course, for the
relevance of the topic and practical task at hand and therefore may be systematically relied on as a resource, both in
the work of implicative deletion and in formulations that are
provided as solutions to a version of the translation problem.

Now take S.E. Data extract IV. 'He has had frequent disputes with his mother' does not clearly provide *who* is to
blame; it may therefore imply, among other things, contextually available, that 'his character is bad', 'he is behaving
badly', 'he has an unhappy home life', or 'he is a victim of
parental oppression', etc. 'He has been drinking' may also
imply 'he's unhappy', 'he has a bad character', 'he's behaving
badly', etc. The latter implication is actually selected in 'his
behaviour generally has deteriorated'. The work of deletion
provides that such a formulation does indeed make sense and
is a 'proper' one for the descriptions provided, since it is the
formulation that provides for the deletion work's sense of
accountability. *The solution to the translation problem provided here is basically a solution to what the speaker's description is intended to amount to so that the 'problem' oriented to here is the practical induction problem.* The formulation is a formulation of what, in other words, the speaker is

*trying to say*, having provided resources for the hearer,
however, with implicative force, by which she could make her
own formulations of what the 'problem' is, or the 'issue', the
'case', the 'truth', or what the description may *really* amount
to for any one.   The speaker's solution to the problem,
then, establishes which solution is appropriate and has to do
that by being accountable as a solution (formulation of the
description) that is observably grounded in its details as
well as in those details provided.   Such details then turn out
to be resources used (observably) in the construction of the
formulation, and resources provided to the hearer for such
construction and ratification.

We can return to the two-fold practical hearership task we
earlier indicated and reformulate it for the speaker in the
following way, using Austin's distinction between illocutionary
acts and perlocutionary effects. (20)   The speaker has to
make the hearer not only understand what in fact the speaker
*is saying*, but concur in it as something *sayable* of such
details (which thus get constituted as members' *data*);   to
provide for its authenticity, accountability and observability
and secure the hearer's agreement to that.   The two-fold
task revealed by the practical translation problem may then be
describable for the speaker as (1) providing for the illocutionary force of one's description/talk and (2) eliminating the possible difference (asymmetry) between the illocutionary force
and the perlocutionary effect of one's utterance(s), or at least
of crucial aspects of them (given that perlocutionary effects
may be many and connected).

The way 'hinting' works is to trade on the above features.
One way, of course, of talking about or characterizing some
turn at talk as 'hinting' is to say that the speaker is 'implying
something'.   One way of 'hinting' is to provide a description
without a formulation, i.e. not to provide, as the speaker, for
a solution to the practical translation problem but to leave it
to the hearer to make the required sense of that description
through the use of the procedures of implicative fit and implicative deletion.   'Discretion', 'tact' and 'snideness', for
example, are located by members in such practices (although
not only in these).   The speaker, however, may choose
another method and one that is designed to shield her from
attributions of specific intent, which indeed allows her to disavow such attributions.   This is achieved by way of providing a formulation selected from among the possible implications
(left available through the operations of implicative fit and
deletion) but one that is *weaker* – such an assessment is a
situated matter and tied in to what is contextually made relevant by the parties to the talk.   An example of this would
be, say, the following talk about a couple: 'He's never at
home and never seems to have any money on him.   His wife

must be unhappy.'   'Never at home' can provide for the inference that he's spending a lot of his time outside, either at
work or at play.   For this, depending on contextual appropriateness a number of possible inferences are available (it is
systematically available and contextually relevant inferences
that may be heard as the implications of talk) – another
woman/women, doesn't care for his wife, 'work is his priority',
etc.   'Not having any money' may provide for the inferences
'not earning enough', 'not managing properly', 'spending it on
other things:  women, gambling, drinking'.   The latter
hearing 'fits' this item to the prior one (although situatedly it
may indeed *not* be the speaker's actual intention to provide
for this, and it may be that, in fact, one of the other inferences would be the correct one).   The formulation 'his wife
must be unhappy' is selected out of an implication that
depends for its articulation on *another* implication of the first
two items (where the former may be seen as a *second-order*
and the latter as a *first-order* implication); the two items
provide, given the standardized relational pair formed by the
two categories, 'husband/wife', that the person talked about
is breaching his category-bound obligations to his wife, i.e.
'not doing the right thing by her'.   Instead of doing what
his relationship to his wife normatively requires him to do, he
is doing something *else*.   It is through *this* that his wife
may come to be expected to be 'unhappy'.   On the other
hand, it is *what* his not being 'at home' and not having any
money *consists in*, i.e. what these items express *in themselves*, that constitutes the implicativeness of expensive play
such as women, gambling or drinking.   Austin's distinction
comes again to mind here.

Keeping in mind Austin's point about the redescribability of
actions in such a way that the description may incorporate
more or less of the action's context/consequences, we can see
that the distinction he made not only holds for utterances and
speech acts, but is also applicable to reports on, and descriptions of, non-verbally performed or 'embodied' actions.   So,
*in doing* Y and Z a person may be said to be doing/being X;
and *by doing* Y and Z he may be said to be accomplishing W.
This distinction is preserved in the *reportability* of both
speech acts and nonverbal activities.   A formulation in terms
of such a second-order implication (one that articulates an
available inference within a perlocutionary framework) then
may be seen in situ as being somewhat 'weaker' than first-
order ones – or at least as *not* superseding or deleting the
relevance of first-order implications where both are available
through implicative fit.   The first-order implication may still
be heard strongly, then, although disavowal of intention to
provide for such an implication is in such instances conventionally available for the speaker, and strongly so available
since she may be seen to have provided explicitly for an

available implication and a solution to the practical translation problem.

Chapter 4

# Category-occasioned transformations

## CATEGORY-TRANSFORMABLE FEATURES/ACCOUNTS

We have seen how certain features may be seen as bound to specific categories (e.g. actions, attitudes, rights, obligations, concerns, beliefs, etc.) in various occasioned ways. We also saw that some features may be found to be constitutive of specific categories in methodic and occasioned ways. Furthermore, we noted that certain category-concepts are open-ended in specific ways, so that for different tasks at hand, and within the context of various language games, what may be for some occasions treatable as a category-*bound* feature may, for *that* particular task, get formulated as a category-*constitutive* feature, in an orderly and accountable manner. This is the *task-transformability* aspect of such features of the social world, which is grounded in the logic of language use.

We will now look at another aspect of the practical transformability of features of the social world - their category-relative transformability on the practical occasions of their production within natural conversational contexts. Take the following extract (S.T. Data B8-10):

1 Q: Roughly, what were the ages of the people who were treated?

2 A: Again there is not a fixed age group; it was a general age group.

3 Q: You do not have to ask embarrassing questions about this in order to see whether they are young people or old people or teenagers?

4 A: I am trying to think. Remember this is a year ago.

5 Q: I understand.

6 A: I suppose the bulk ---

7 The Chairman: The old men came in with heart attacks, the young men with bloody noses, is that not right?

8 A: It is.

9   Mr Chambers:   Is that the situation?

10   A:   It is, yes.

11   Q:   The people who had what one might describe as
          wounds caused by violence were young men, is that
          right?

12   A:   And young women and young children.

13   Q:   But by and large were those who had sustained
          injuries caused by violence young men?

14   A:   Not necessarily.

We will first concentrate on utterances 7 to 10.   In that
sequence there is a sensitivity being displayed to the different methods by which the 'problems' (bloody noses, heart
attacks) routinely come about - this sensitivity, or relied-on
commonsense knowledge, is displayed in the differentiation
between the old men's 'problem' and the young men's problem;
the former is an *ailment* or rooted in one, the latter is an
*injury*.   At a very simple level, then, one may say that in
'disease' or 'physical-problem' contexts, 'heart attack' is a
problem description embedded in the knowledge domains that
are bound up with the category 'old man', whilst 'bloody
noses' is embedded in the knowledge domain bound up with
the category 'young men'.   In other words, 'heart attack'
and 'bloody noses' are category-embedded physical problems.
They are category-relevant, and I say category-relevant
rather than category-bound advisedly.   Now 'heart attack' is
a description of an event or 'happening', whereas a 'bloody
nose' is an injury which sustains (from routine contexts of
use) the possibility of *active participation* in its making by
the injured party.   Whether this is actually seen to have
been the case is a situated matter - but the distinction here
is one that is *relevant* to the sort of social organization of
responsibility conventionally available, i.e. our moral syntax.
One may in fact participate in the production of an occasion,
or in an activity, which brings about one's own heart attack.
But heart attacks conventionally provide for the description
of the person in question *as a victim*.   On the other hand,
although many bloody noses may be given to innocent parties
or may be the result of an unprovoked attack (where the
injured party may thus be seen as a victim), the problem
'bloody nose' conventionally accepts and sustains with itself
the description of the injured party as having possibly called
it upon him/herself, i.e. as having been an *agent* of its production.   The distinction is between *victims* and *agents*
here.   It is a *contrast* that is made operable and hearable
precisely through the presuppositional structure of the utter-

ance and its contrastive design ('old men'/'young men', 'heart attacks'/'bloody noses'). Furthermore, the utterance through its structure, projects a candidate origin for the complaints - fear, shock, in the case of the old men; skirmishing, fighting, in the case of the young men. By playing on our category knowledge of youth and age and constructing that utterance as a category-fitted account, we are provided with *possible* reasons for the respective complaints and thus a candidate solution to the nature of the events being talked about which is the concern of the conversation. That is to say, not only does this utterance display a sensitivity to the different methods by which such complaints may come about, but an equal sensitivity to the sorts of things that members of the two age categories may be involved in. By inspecting, for example, the category 'old men', the hearer may discover how it is that 'heart attacks' may have been selected, given the sorts of things that 'old men's' experiences may involve, and thus find the description/inference given in the utterance to be warranted (expectable, reasonable, accountable). But given our knowledge of the contexts in which heart attacks often come about, this then provides for what it is indeed that these old men could have been up to that night. That is, the description of some of the events of the night in question, provided in the utterance, is in the nature of an account whose features are conventionally co-selected and co-fitted together and work therein to provide reflexively for each other's sense and warrant. It is through and through a normatively organized account but one that can be defeated empirically since it is also an account that makes empirical claims. What we then have is the following.

In the first part of the exchange, the issue of 'age' has been introduced by the questioner in his attempt to arrive, jointly with A, at some characterization of the events of the night in question. The answer given by A provides that there was no fixed age group among the people who received treatment at the first-aid centre. The questioner then persists in his use of age-grouping as a framework relevant to the description of the persons treated and indeed uses specific categorizations as methods for organizing the descriptions of persons: 'young people', 'old people' and 'teenagers'. What then happens is that the chairman intervenes with an utterance which attempts to provide a possible description of some of the events of that night fashioned out of the tools provided by the first questioner (age categorization) and *in terms of them*. The age categorizations made relevant in an earlier turn by another speaker are now used to generate a description whose character is intelligible in terms of those categorizations and which works as an account for the distribution of problems (heart attacks, bloody noses) - a distribution by age. But, as we have seen already, such an account is implicative of a deeper one (embedded in it) regarding the *nature* of the proceedings of the night's events and actions.

The chairman does not simply use the categorizations provided by the earlier speaker - he effects a transformation on them; instead of 'young people' and 'old people' we now get 'young men' and 'old men'.   This uses a specific *gender* to organize the account and cuts out the relevance, not only of 'women' (the female gender) for the description of the night's events, but also of 'children' as a relevant age category. Although the prior questioner had not specifically used 'children' as a stage-of-life categorization ('old people', 'young people', 'teenagers'), nevertheless it is a categorization which could be *made relevant*, since it could be included in 'people', which includes both various age groups and the two genders, the device actually used by Q in the data, initially, to organize his question and his subsequent selection of items.   In the choice of 'old men' and 'young men', however, we have not only a set of age categorizations, but also and *conjointly a set of gender categorizations*.   In the way that *gender* has been specifically made relevant, 'children' or 'child' as a purely stage-of-life categorization has been excluded from the focus of relevance.   Now one important difference between gender categorizations and stage-of-life categorizations is the following:  looking at examples of the former (man, old woman, youth, girl), we see that *gender categorizations* (excluding the generic male/female) *are sensitive to stage-of-life discriminations*.   If we look at some stage-of-life categorizations (old person, teenager, child, young man, baby), we find that although they *may* provide for gender, *they need not*. Indeed, it turns out that this is not the case for persons only, but applies also to animal categorizations, as evidenced by the analysis of animal taxonomies in Tyler's introduction to his 'Cognitive Anthropology'. (1)

In providing male-gender categorizations to describe the persons hurt and in need of treatment, the chairman is providing a description not only constructed by reference to stage-of-life discriminations, but one that is critically dependent on gender-bound features and generative of gender-bound accounts.   Now, if it had been 'young women' coming in with 'bloody noses', or even 'young people', the account for this possibly would have been different;  the 'bloody nose' (treatment-requiring condition) would have had to be seen as produced in a context that was congruent with members' knowledge of categories and category-bound features regarding women and mixed populations.   So where, for example, a 'bloody nose' in conjunction with the category 'young man' may operate to produce the relevance of another category such as 'unruly youth', 'gang member', etc., depending specifically on the occasion of practical use, within that self-same context that description, 'a bloody nose', in conjunction with the category 'young woman' would conventionally provide for a hearing of 'victim'.  The categories relevantly generated would thus be different - in other words, what the 'bloody nose' may be seen to amount to (and this may be provided in ways such as the generation of further categories or the provision of full-scale accounts, reasons, speculations) is conventionally, inferentially dependent on the category whose incumbent it describes.  The appropriate or relevant category provides the sense of the description, and a reformulation of category relevance would effect a *transformation* on that sense, i.e. on what a specific feature of the described scene or events 'comes to': what, in other words, *it is*. This property of features of social settings is what we mean to indicate in our term *category-transformable features* - the features involved here being *substantive ones*, it is clear how this property is analytically a feature of descriptions, accounts and inferences about social matters.

Category transformability is a pervasive feature of social settings as well as the descriptions that both constitute accounts of and are themselves a feature of those settings. It is observably oriented to in our data extract - following the chairman's formulation, Mr Chambers retrieves his turn at talk by providing a questioning formulation of the chairman's account, which is answered in the affirmative.  He then does a further transformation on the sense of the prior talk, as we have seen, but one that is grounded in it - where in the chairman's utterance we have 'old men' and 'young men' selected as the relevant categories in such a way that the relevance of 'women' and 'children' is implicitly deleted, in Q's question we have 'young men' being *explicitly* provided as the only categorization from the device-category 'people' (inclusive of both genders and all age groups) whose incumbents had 'wounds caused by violence'.  It is a stronger formulation that makes explicit and categorical what was implicit and relevant - what was available as an inferential possibility. If wounds inflicted by violence were sustained only by incumbents of the category 'young men', then that violence and those wounds could assume a certain character for members embedded in their category knowledge with respect to young men and to violence.  Were the categories 'young women' and 'young children' to be made relevant to the description, the character of that violence and those wounds, as well as the events and actions leading to them, would be alternatively constitutable; they could be transformable from something that provides grounds for a characterization of the events as, for example, 'street fighting' into one such as, say, 'attack on a community'.  This is not a logical necessity, but one that is a possibility built into the informal logic of the conversational resources and interactional methods available to interactants, resources that include the logic of the concepts involved and our commonsense knowledge of the social world.   If 'young women' and 'young children' are made relevant categorizations for the reporting or description of the events in question, then the categorization 'victim' may be generatable with respect to the issue of 'violence', whereas 'victim' *or* 'agent' are conventionally generatable for the category 'young men'. Note that the categories 'women' and 'children' routinely and accountably go together, although the former is a gender and stage-of-life categorization and the latter is purely a stage-of-life categorization.   What we find is that both categories 'women' and 'children' conventionally have congruent or even similar *category-bound features* with respect to the issue of 'violence'.   Where they are co-selected, it is these congruent features that hearably provide for their 'fit' and thus for the relevant sense and implications of the talk.   Imagine, for example, the different sorts of accounts that might get implicated by the following descriptions of some 'conflict':

There were men fighting them.

There were men and women fighting them.

There were men, women and children fighting them.

There were women and children fighting them.

In our data, for example, once we have 'women' and 'children' appended to 'young men' as categories whose incumbents received 'wounds caused by violence', we have the device-category 'community' or 'civilian population' made relevant as a possible accounting framework for what sorts of things could have been happening on the night in question.

In the following piece of data (S.T. Data, C5):

Q: Just think carefully because we want to be clear about this:  is this the only incident involving any of your ambulances that you heard of?

→ A: You mean by civilian armed people?

→ Q: By civilian armed men, yes.

A: It is, yes, that I can remember.

Q's transformation on A's question is hearably informed by considerations of the category transformability of accounts and descriptions, which I have just been discussing.

Let us look at some more instances of oriented-to category

transformability. The following extract is from the Hell's Angels data:

138 R: I, I mean to say the cult that they have I mean to say they arrange their own wedding ceremonies.

139 A: Yeh ... do they?

140 R: They have this weird and wonderful er system of one leader.

141 A: Yeh.

142 R: And he has his one woman.

143 A: Yeh, oh.

144 R: It's, it's, er contrary to anyone's idea of a decent way of life.

145 A: Yes, mm ... okay.

146 R: You see, it's not just a childish er er....

147 A: Do you know what ages they are ... do you know what ages these lads are?

148 R: Anything from seventeen up to twenty odd.

149 A: Yeh, I see, what about ... do ... do you have I mean do you have any contact with the, the er Boris and Jim who er are supposed to be working down there?

'Childish' can be said of an adult who is seen to behave like a child: the latter perception turns on the tie between certain activities, behaviours and beliefs to the category 'child'. When said of an adult, it is a judgment of deficiency, for inasmuch as children cannot behave like adults except by first going through a process of learning and growing up, adults who behave like children may be seen to be regressive or deficient or not acting as 'they should do'. (2)    Age is a category of transition along which one travels but one that is *normatively organized in one direction*. To say 'childish' of some adult activity, then, is to *downgrade it* - since what children do is not conventionally conceptualized as properly serious, aware, consequential, etc. So it is a condemnation of a specific sort, one which implicates a conception of 'immaturity' rather than, say, 'wrongdoing' or 'malevolence', of 'irresponsibility' rather than 'criminality'. Therefore, too, where there is a 'trouble' concerning some adult's behaviour

or actions, the term 'childish' may be used to delimit the
extent of that 'trouble' and its nature, and to formulate it as
not meriting very serious consideration, in the face of a third
party's complaint.   When R in our data complains that 'it's
not just a childish ...' (matter, problem), he is providing
*both* that it is not children who are involved *and* that the
matter is of some consequentiality and seriousness.   This
hearing is also built into his sequence of complaints:   'they
arrange their own wedding ceremonies', 'the system of one
leader' and 'his one woman', 'contrary to anyone's idea of a
decent way of life'.   All these are adult-relevant ways of
talking and are formulations of what are taken to be routinely
consequential matters.   So what R has provided, in the form
of a complaint, is a set of serious adult-relevant issues (where
the category 'adult' is implicated in the presentation of the
issues:   cult, weddings, systems, leaders, women, way of
life).   Should either the relevance of 'adulthood' or the consequentiality of the pertinent matters be modifiable, then the
assessment of 'not childish' could be changed.   'Consequentiality' is itself an assessable matter.   But in the provision
for the relevance of implicit or explicit adult categorizations
the work of consequentiality is, in part, reflexively accomplished.   If, however, A's question to R ('what ages these
lads are?') in response to R's 'it's not just a childish' had
been answered with, say, 'about fourteen or fifteen' (instead
of 'seventeen up to twenty odd', in utterance 148), it would
become possible to argue with R's characterization of the
nature of these activities – the categorization 'boys' might be
invoked and, although it does not clearly function the way
the category 'child' would, it does not work properly as
'adult' either, without some other work being done.   'Kids'
would work appropriately here.   The serious nature of wedding ceremonies is not, in itself, enough to defeat a recharac-
terization attempt, for fourteen and fifteen is below the age of
consent, and for kids of that age to arrange their own wedding ceremonies does not make for calling their activity 'a
cult' without some further provision.   The very descriptions
and assessments R provides are transformable by making
another membership categorization relevant, and the very same
activities and events can be recharacterized depending on the
categorization made relevant.   R displays an orientation to
this when he specifically says later, 'they're certainly not
children' (i.e. they do not have the right or the excuse of
young age).

The redescribability in the above data, the possible *transformation*, rests on the selection of *alternative* characterizations (which may be seen as coming from the same device in
Sacks's sense).   But the character of such a transformation
rests on category-bound features.   The above instance displays and trades on what could be formulated as category-

exclusive and category-proscribed activities. That is to say, not only is 'marriage' bound to the category 'adult' (normatively for *this* culture) but it is *exclusively* bound to it, so that if non-adults are perceived as engaging in it, not only may they be said to be 'copying adults', 'pretending' or 'playing', but may yet be seen to be engaged in a breach - witness the way child marriage conducted in other cultures is talked of in *this* culture. But further, not only is it the case that adults alone can do marriage, but also the case that, therefore, adults are supposed to do marriage seriously, since it is a serious issue (being something which marks out or divides adults from children). In that children do not 'marry', any 'marriage' ceremony or 'wedding' they are perceivedly engaging in is 'play' and 'play-acting'. So, in saying 'they're certainly not children', R is providing among other things that they cannot be seen to be playing. Whether an activity gets constituted as 'play' or something else depends, then, on the assignable/observable membership category of those who engage in it and which is made relevant. Let us turn to another extract of data (H.A. Data):

158 R: I've just been down there and seen them at night and they just get some old wood together, sleep down on the ground on the deck and er light the fire and er things like that.

159 A: Yeh.

                                                             [X]
160 R: I mean to say if er [if an African came and built a hut in the middle of town and er lived like that],
                                   [Y]
[there'd be a real outcry].

161 A: Yeah.
                  [Z]                          [W]
162 R: [But if a white man does it] [...]
(Bracketing indicates lettered components only.)

The utterances 160 and 162 are hearably producing a contrast, although utterance 162 is not completed and the second contrast feature is not provided. Nevertheless, such contrast work is routinely understood. In the contrast structure 'if X then Y, but if Z then W' we have a routine and pervasive form for the doing of contrast work - it rests firstly on a difference (often heard contrastively) between X and Z and projects a contrastive difference between Y and W. Routinely the latter is a difference which is either *gradable* (where the W is a downgrading or upgrading on Y) or *polar* (a difference of degree or kind). The relationship between X and Z is an *analogic* one, where the contrast is thus an analogical contrast (in which all but one feature of the two items are

hearably the same). Now although W is *not* provided in our
data it does not matter for our hearing of the contrast work;
the contrast might have worked as well if R had concluded
with 'but if a white man does it, it would be OK' as with 'but
if a white man does it there would be an outright rebellion!'.
The fact that 'there'd be a real outcry' [Y] is a strongly
formulated assessment sets up an expectation that W would
either be the polar opposite or a downgrading of the contrast
feature of Y. But it could intelligibly be an upgrading, and
this latter sort of structure is one on which many jokes trade
and which is constitutive of many 'surprise sequences'. In
this data, a particular hearing (i.e. if a white man does it, it
would be OK) is also locatable in *contextually attributable
beliefs* – namely, in that R disapproves of the sleeping and
living practices of the Hell's Angels and has been correspondingly engaged in extended complaints about them. At any
rate, whichever *way* one fills in the W slot, whether it is
heard to operate an upgrading or a downgrading on [Y], the
two utterances are hearable *contrastively*. And the contrast
is built around the following issue: that the way in which
some activity gets assessed and responded to depends on *who*
is doing it. (Sharrock and Turner make a similar point. (3))
Here we can further break down [X] and [Z] and the contrast: if A does [O], then [Y], but if B does [O] then [W],
where A = 'an African', O = 'came and built a hut in the
middle of town and ... lived like that', Y = 'there'd be a
real outcry', B = 'a white man', and W = a second contrast
feature (e.g. 'it would be okay'). Thus if O [A] then [Y],
but O [B] then [W].

It is clear that not only is the assessment of the same action
or activity category-dependent, but also what that activity is
perceived to amount to, or be, is category-dependent,
although it may not be explicitly articulated in the formulation
of the activity – e.g. 'building a hut in the middle of town'
may be 'bringing down the neighbourhood', or 'spoiling the
cityscape' or it may just be 'doing one's own thing'. In
Sharrock and Turner's data, (4) 'banging cars all day' may
be constitutable as 'being mad on cars', or 'being inconsider-
ate to the neighbours', or 'working', depending on whether it
is adults or kids involved, although there are a lot of other
things that could also provide for transformations of what that
(or any activity) amounts to, some of which we shall look at
below. Now from the structure of the contrast 'If O [A]
then Y, but if O [B], then W', it is clear that the contrast
between Y and W rests on that between A and B, or is bound
up with the imputedly contrastive nature of membership category A and membership category B. One of the strongest
and most routinely available contrasts between categories is
where two or more categories are hearable as coming from the
same collection and are thus treatable as totally *alternative*

categorizations rather than simply different ones (obtained in
a minimal contrast form). (5)   If we look at the data examples
provided so far in this section we will see that indeed all of
them are of this kind.   Such contrasts orient to and display
the category transformability of actions and activities (whether
the specific transformation made or oriented to in situ is subscribed to or not by all the parties concerned) and reveal the
category-bound and category-restricted or proscribed features
usable as resources, both for the generation of the contrast
and the operation of a transformation on the perceived and
described character of an act or activity.

Such transformabilities recurrently generate issues and
material which novelists and dramatists use to develop a major
or secondary problematic in their stories or narratives.   An
example of this may be found in E. Gaskell's 'North and
South', (6) where the main character (Margaret) is seen alone
with a young man one evening in a distant part of town, and
she has occasion later to conceal the fact.   This is misinter-
preted by Mr Thornton, the man she loves, who does not
know that the young man in question was her brother (whose
presence it would have been dangerous for her to reveal).
This issue is a central source of problems for Margaret in the
later stages of the novel, and it is not till much later that
Margaret grasps its full implications.   Let me quote a section
of the work:

'Will you tell me what you refer to about "reservations" in
his manner of speaking of me?'
'Oh!   Simply he has annoyed me by not joining in my
praises of you.   Like an old fool, I thought that everyone
would have the same opinions as I had;   and he evidently
could not agree with me.   I was puzzled at the time.   But
he must be perplexed, if the affair has never been in the
least explained.   There was first your walking out with a
young man in the dark'-
'But it was my brother!' said Margaret surprised.
'True.   But how was he to know that?'
'I don't know.   I never thought of anything of that kind,'
said Margaret, reddening, and looking hurt and offended.
'And perhaps he never would, but for the lie - which
under the circumstances, I maintain, was necessary.' (7)

The identity of the man Margaret was with ('brother' or
'lover') constitutes what she could have been up to that evening, with its attendant implications for assessments of her
character.

The equivocality of the situation, whether the young man in
question is a 'lover' or someone whose presence with Margaret
in that setting can be legitimized by some other relationship,

is resolved in favour of the former when Margaret's lie as to
her presence at that station provides for a motivational scheme
consistent with that option.   Note here that the suspension
of a final problem resolution in favour of the preferred option
is a typical structure of novels but is not necessarily the
course of daily life.   The suspension of such resolutions in
novels comes by way of continuously providing accountable
obstacles to, amongst other things, the acquisition of appropriate knowledge, or getting to know 'in time', or through
other devices such as the provision of competing moral frame-
works for a character's selection of options, or the provision
of hierarchical solutions to dilemmas in favour of the dispre-
ferred option.   More on such issues as members' matters
later on.   The above sort of transformability is available
from the category-bound and exclusive set of rights/expecta-
tions/duties located in standardized relational pairs:   brother/
sister, lover/lover, single man/single woman.   We will turn
in the next section to look at further sorts of transformations,
and in a later chapter we will deal with more issues raised by
members' contrastive work.

## CATEGORY ACCRETION

Let us begin here by noting that a person may be a Roman
Catholic, a man, an Irishman, a doctor, a husband, a father,
a friend, an IRA member, a communist, an intellectual, a quiet
man and a music lover all at once.   He may further but only
within a *specific* period and on *particular* occasions in his
life be a 'victim', a 'defendant', a 'fool', an 'injured person',
a 'member of the audience', 'the cook' (for an evening), 'the
driver', etc.   Here the complex nature of members' categorizations work begins to surface clearly.   Furthermore, the
complex *network* of members' categorization procedures begins
to be available.   Let us make three initial points:

1   If we look at the above categorizations we find that some
of them *presuppose* others, while some may at least *implicate*
others as possibly relevant.   For example, 'husband' presupposes 'man', while 'father' implicates 'husband'.   'Roman
Catholic' *also* means 'Christian', while 'Irish' implicates
'Roman Catholic', and 'IRA man' conventionally presupposes
'Roman Catholic' (which is a defeasible presupposition rooted
in local knowledge).

2   Another distinction we can find in the above categorizations
is that some are taken to be lifelong or at least stable categorizations for any member (man, Irish, doctor) and where they
are *changed* that change involves some specific and elaborate
work by both the member and others.   Even then, the *prior*
status remains, *as prior status*, a locus of generative implica-

tions.   Other categorizations, on the other hand, are locally
occasioned categorizations in a specific sense.   They are
seeable as temporary, e.g. 'defendant', 'victim', etc. - one is
expected to pass from those statuses, indeed even to be able
to enter some opposing status, at other points, i.e. enter the
incumbency of alternative categorizations.   Moreover, some of
those categorizations, such as a 'victim' or a 'member of the
audience', are event-specific or event-tied.

3  Categorizations may be used attributively, as well as
referentially, (8) - which is to say that the primary use in
situated contexts is tied up with how these categorizations
may be working in ascriptions, accounts, descriptions or
judgments.

These three initial points should enable us to see further
some of the work involved in categorizations.   Let us look
again at a piece of data which we analysed before (S.T. Data
B 9-10):

1  The Chairman:  The old men came in with heart attacks,
the young men with bloody noses, is
that not right?

2              A:  It is.

3  Mr Chambers:  Is that the situation?

4              A:  It is, yes.

5              Q:  The people who had what one might describe as wounds caused by violence were
young men, is that right?

6              A:  And young women and young children.

7              Q:  But by and large were those who had
sustained injuries caused by violence
young men?

8              A:  Not necessarily.

We said earlier that the importance of specifying *who* it was
that had had 'wounds caused by violence' has to do with the
fact that the very description of the events of that night, and
the accounts produced for such a description, hinges on what
categorization is made relevant to that description.   Where,
in utterance 5, Q is constructing the basis and implication
for a plausible rational account that what had been happening
was some kind of a straight fight (political/religious/ethnic,
etc.) rooted in the category-bound features of 'young men', A

in utterance 6 *transforms* that basis, and therefore the possibly plausible description of what happened, by introducing
'young women and young children', thereby implicating or
generating the relevance of the notion 'attack on a civilian
population'. We also mentioned that in this transformation,
instead of the notion of 'agent' of an event being implicated
where the category 'young men' is made relevant, the notion
'victim' gets implicated with the categories 'young women and
young children', with respect to the issue of violence.

Another way of putting this is the following: where you
have someone with 'wounds caused by violence' you have the
relevant and appropriate categorization 'injured party'. This
categorization may be transformed into another one - 'victim'
or 'agent' (or 'offender'), the transformation being contingent
on, among other things, the selection from the categorizations
'young man' or 'young woman' or 'young child'. In other
words, rather than simply locating the characterization of the
situation or providing a discursive account of it, what may be
done is the recategorization of the person involved - here, for
example, from 'injured party' to 'victim' - by the relevant provision of *another* category such as 'young woman/young child'.
In this case the *transformation* operable on the first categorization (implicit or extractable from the talk) by the relevant
provision of the second categorization can produce an *accounting* third categorization - 'victim'. Secondly, the first categorization is event-specific, while the second is a *stable*
categorization, and the third one is an event-specific *accounting* categorization. One may note too that the second categorization here is used in an attributive sense. We can thus
see the orderliness of this categorization work. It is this
sort of transformability that I call category accretion.

It seems sensible to say that concepts/notions such as
'victim', for example, are embedded (or implicated) in the
informal logic of use of other morally implicative concepts and
morally organized assessments even though they are *not explicitly* negotiated and assigned in interaction. It is conventionally, contextually and logically embedded in the very
way that responsibility and blame get attributed and produced
and that moral accounting work is done. As a concept not
explicitly used, then, it may nevertheless be enthymematically
available as a *resource* in the context of morally organized
work and talk and as an *implication* of such talk. D.R.
Watson, in his paper on victims and offenders, (9) provides
a formulation of H. Sacks's economy rule: (10)

one membership categorization is 'referentially adequate' for
practical purposes, for the identification of persons. Which
category is chosen is fundamentally an 'occasioned' matter
(Adato, forthcoming), i.e., depends upon the context in

which reference is being made. Thus, a person cast as a 'victim' may be an incumbent of a vast number of other membership categories, but the single category 'victim' is, in a given context, an adequate reference. (11)

Although it is indeed true that, in many contexts, a single category may be 'referentially adequate', if reference is the *prime task* of the categorizational use (which it routinely is not), what I should like to propose is the following: that, in the first place, a categorization's being seen as 'referentially adequate' depends itself, in many contexts, on the perceivable relevance, display, presumption and implication of *other* categories in context; that certain categories *programmatically make relevant* certain other categories, although such operation or presumption of relevance may situatedly be defeasible; and that these two features of categorizations are tied into their attributive, and not simply their referential, uses. Categorizations may, for some purposes, be treated as definite descriptions that situatedly generate (or defeat) the relevance and production of other definite descriptions (and other categorizations).

Categorizations in context, then, are perceivable as being contingent on other categorizations, or generative of them, where these other categorizations are made either relevant or expectable, as in the following extract (S.T. Data F):

Mr Murray:  Was it in connection with the IRA outrages of the mid-fifties?

A:  That he was interned, yes.

The Chairman:  You are saying yes. You see, Counsel sometimes puts questions that quite unintentionally appear to be vague. I do not know whether you accept that there were IRA outrages between 1956 and 1962. Do you?

A:  I say that my husband was interned at that time because he was a Republican. I am not saying that he is a member of the IRA. I am saying he was interned because he was a Republican.

We saw earlier how the relevant application of the category 'young woman' or 'young child' to a person categorized as someone with 'wounds caused by violence' may transform this categorization into that of 'victim'. Such a transformation and the problem it resolves (what the 'injury' amounts to, what tale lies behind it) is one that is contextually embedded - both problem and resolution are situated matters. In the example we used, the setting is that of an enquiry into events that had happened some time before, and the examiner is seeking to arrive, in co-participation with the witness, at some account.

One can offer further examples. Suppose that at a wedding, at the very moment when the priest asks if anyone knows of any reason why the bride and bridegroom should/ cannot be wed, someone stands up and answers, 'Aye – the bridegroom already has a wife!' The consequent recategoriz- ability of the man from 'bridegroom' to 'already married man' does not end there – rather, a *third* categorization of rele- vance is generatable: 'would-be bigamist'. If the disclosure is made a little later, after the ceremony is complete, the categorial transformation becomes even simpler: the 'bride- groom' becomes 'a twice-married man' and a 'bigamist'; with this, the *relevance*, or future relevance, of other categoriza- tions (or identities) is *activated*: 'law-breaker', 'con man', 'defendant', 'fraud', etc. Their actual activation *in use* is a methodic accomplishment of parties to a setting. In other words, a situated choice of categorizations still is made according to contextual relevances and tasks, but it is not just *any* categorizations that are relevantly available for such selection work. 'Relevance' has a conventional basis in the very logic of use of concepts and members' procedures. It is, in part, the very concealment of identity above that pro- vides for, and displays, its relevance to the task at hand. The problem is context-provided and has to do with the norms and constraints of disclosure. Clearly, one does not and need not disclose all the identities that one may be said to have/carry, but the relevance of specific categorizations (iden- tities) is context-specific and context-generated. As with 'injured person', 'person with wounds caused by violence', etc., 'bridegroom' is an event-specific categorization. The recategorization from 'bridegroom' to 'bigamist' through the operation of 'already married man' does not eliminate the usa- bility of that first categorization entirely, because the event itself (the wedding, injury, etc.) is sustained as an event of a specific character, although it is rendered reappraisable. The transformation simply *elaborates* their sense and character – instead of just an 'injured person', we have a 'victim'. Instead of simply a 'bridegroom', we have a 'bigamist'. The disjunction between the first categorization and the third one, treatable as one of 'appearance/reality' in situations of con- cealment, is one between the 'truth' and the 'whole truth'.

This *elaborative* relationship rests precisely, I suggest, on the fact that the first categorization is event-tied; it is not, therefore, negatable but merely reappraisable. The third categorization is a contexting or *accounting* one. It is not strictly an *alternative* to the first but builds on it. More-

over, the second categorization, which may be used to effect
the transformation on the first, is used *attributively* in both
cases. Now, in the second example, we have a further
point of interest - the categorization 'bridegroom' is conventionally contingent, in its routine contexts of use, on the
assumption of a further operative categorization, 'bachelor'.
In other words, the context of talk and interaction in which
that categorization is routinely produced can display the *conventional* presupposition (12) that the person so categorized
is a bachelor. The latter is not an event-tied categorization.
In the context of the wedding example, that implicit categorization 'bachelor' *is* negated should the categorization 'already
married man' be made relevant, since they mean exactly opposite things. The consequent recategorization 'would-be
bigamist' or 'con man' is one that is an *alternative* to
'bachelor' in practical contexts of use - it *deletes* its applicability or rests on its deletion. If we wanted to talk of applicable categorizations as identities-in-use, then we would say
that it negates or deletes that identity. Instead of an
*elaboration transformation* of category applicability, then, we
would have a *deletion transformation*. The disjunction
between first and third identities here rests on that between
appearance and reality, articulatable as between the 'truth'
and 'not the truth'.

Another example of a categorial deletion transformation
should serve to further illustrate the point: take the case of
a man at the point of settling a drug deal in some 'under-
world' location. As the preliminaries are being engaged in,
a person walks in and identifies the dealer to the other party
as being a policeman. In that context, then, the relevance
of the category 'policeman' operates on the presumed category
'drug dealer' to *delete it* and produce an alternatively relevant category such as 'agent'. Now it is noteworthy that in
both these latter cases not only does the third (or consequent)
categorization work as an alternative to the first, i.e. in opposition to it, but the intermediary transforming categorization is
also perceivable and treatable as an alternative to the first
one. This intermediary categorization, in that it is being
used attributively, may (and does in these two cases) have
category-bound and category-constitutive features that are
seeable as in opposition with the first categorization which is
itself a stable, rather than a locally or event-specific, one,
since it is consequent on an activity (drug dealing) which is
implicative for the characterization of the *person as a whole*.

The discovery of the relevance of a category such as 'policeman' or 'secret service man' to someone, A, with whom a
person, B, has had a relationship of friendship, *may* (depending on the length and strength of that relationship and various other contextual features) produce a locally appropriate

consequent characterization such as 'careful man', 'dark horse', etc., where no locus of interest for that category/ identity of person A is derivable from the identity or life of friend B.  It may be, in such a case, that A simply is not allowed to tell anyone of his work;  it may be simply that he/ she prefers not to tell anyone;  it may be that he expects to face dangers and thinks it better not to involve anyone or cause worry to particular friends, etc.  On the other hand, if friend B has, say, a politically or criminally relevant iden- tity, the discovered identity of friend A would be seeable as transformative of his first one and deleting of it.  Instead of 'friend' one could have 'spy/agent'.  Such a consequent (as well as the intermediary) identity would work situatedly as an *alternative* to the first and *public* one.  The feature that makes the difference may be locatable as follows:  whether the prior categorization is perceivable and treatable as having an *exogenous* relevance or an *endogenous* relevance to the features of the intermediary or discoverable identity/character- ization.  It is clear, for instance, that being an injured person is treatable as exogenous to the *fact* of one's being a woman or a man or a child, although which of these categori- zations is applicable is relevant to the characterization of what the injury amounts to, how it came about, the likelihood of injury in certain places, etc.  Similarly one's being a 'bride- groom' is not conventionally seen as endogenous to the fact of being an already married man;  but on the other hand, clear- ly, having or 'posing in', as it turns out, the identity of a 'drug dealer' is treatable as endogenous to the work of being a policeman (the intermediary covert identity) - although indeed *that* may turn out to be defeasible, and the policeman may get constituted as a 'corrupt policeman' or 'on the make'.

In conclusion, one may perhaps formulate at least two pro- cedures for the operation of a category-occasioned transforma- tion on any member's given identity as shown overleaf.

By 'account-providing', I mean to note that the consequent categorizations for each operation described provide for the relationship between the initial and intermediate categorizations.

These two procedures are characterized by a common prop- erty:  they both culminate in the production of a consequent categorization which is economically account-providing.

| | INITIAL CATEGORIZATION | RELEVANT INTERMEDIATE CATEGORIZATION | CONSEQUENT CATEGORIZATION |
|---|---|---|---|
| 1 Deletion/ Substitution Operation | Stable Categorization(A) | Stable Categorization(B) | Stable Categorization(C) (Account-Providing) |
| 2 Elaboration Operation | Event-Tied/ Locally Specific Categorization(A) | Stable Categorization | Event-Tied/ Stable/ Action-Consequent Categorization(B) (Account Providing) |

# Chapter 5

# Category-generated problems and some solutions

We have so far attempted to elucidate some basic features of membership categorizations. Using some of the explication we have been engaged in, we will now turn our attention to some problems arising in the context of, or through the use of, categorization in discourse and some means available for their resolution.

## CATEGORIZATIONAL ASYMMETRY AND DISJUNCTION

The first kind of problem we will consider under this heading is that arising from *asymmetric category sets*, such as the following: policeman/offender, judge/defendant, probation officer/client, doctor/patient, etc. These asymmetric categorizations involve two actual or candidate category incumbents, one to fit each pair part of the set, and the asymmetry pertains to the relationship between them and describes the *contrastive* organization of rights/duties and/or knowledge and skills as between them. These are organized in terms of a specific practical problem or set of tasks, i.e. each set operates within a *specific practical domain*. Such sets may be treated as a sub-set of what Harvey Sacks called 'standardized relational pairs'. (1) With such asymmetric sets a certain sort of disjunction may arise - our interest is primarily in its method of resolution. Where disjunctive accounts are produced, and where the account producers are contrastively located as incumbents of an asymmetric category set, then the resolution of the account's disjunction is routinely made on the basis of the perceivedly asymmetric organization of rights, duties and/or knowledge in favour of *only one side of the category pair*. Contrast this to the many other instances of disjunctive accounts as between, for example, husband/wife (where it is *not* perceivedly asymmetric), friend/friend, neighbour/neighbour, where the possibility of a middle-ground resolution or a finding of 'misunderstanding' is programmatically relevant and routinely a preference. Similarly, the judgments and assessments produced by the presumed incumbents of each category pair part in an asymmetric set are also treatable asymmetrically where they are in disagreement. In other words, the practical maxim routinely used by members on such occasions is that 'there is only one side to the story', or only one 'proper', 'adequate' or 'full' version. Thus, in the pro-

duction of stories and accounts by third parties, involving
the use of such category sets, this asymmetry is displayed as
an organizational feature of such stories and accounts.

Let us now look at an example of what we will call *disjunctive category sets* (following Coulter (2)), such as madman/
visionary, terrorist/revolutionary, rioter/protester, poet/
versifier, policeman/gangster, doctor/butcher, which involve
the alternative characterization of one and the same person.
These kinds of category disjunction operations routinely
involve a categorization of the kind we earlier identified as
being disavowable or non-solicitable.   They thus involve a
category set, one member of which would be disclaimed by the
categorized person, and may be viewed thence as cases of disjunction between avowed-categorization/ascribed-categorization
(although the disjunction may arise between two persons in
connection with a third party).   Having said this, however,
we must note that the first three sets indicated above are
significantly different from the last three:

(a)   Madman/visionary, terrorist/revolutionary, rioter/pro-
tester:   these represent alternative categorizations by which
if a member is to be thus categorized with respect to some
specific practice or action, then one pair part of the category
set is exclusively usable and so usable contrastively by any
one categorizer.   Let us call this a Type I disjunctive category set.

(b)   The second kind (policeman/gangster, doctor/butcher,
poet/versifier) are sets that represent alternatives that are
not usable exclusively, although they are usable contrastively.
But the contrast trades on and displays an assessment of the
category-related work of the first pair part incumbent.   It
does not altogether defeat the applicability of the first (avowable) categorization, but rather trades on its perceivable
relevance.   What it does is to transform the modality of
relevance.   It is a grading assessment involved here rather
than a qualitative one as we might get for Type I.   Let us
call this a Type II disjunctive category set.

In the case of the asymmetric category sets, the asymmetric
or contrastive assessment of different accounts is routinely
accomplished through inspection of the account-producers'
presumed asymmetrical categorial relationship.   In both Type
I and Type II category disjunction operations, a second and/
or alternative categorization to a first (implicit or explicit) is
produced as a result of a *locally* contrastive assessment of a
member's practices, actions and beliefs.

A word of caution here - we are not engaged in saying that
there is a fixed and rigid set of asymmetric or disjunctive

category sets/pairs. Rather we are pointing out some examples of them and attempting to explicate what their informal logic of use may be. Any list of such category pairs, however, must remain open-ended and indefinitely extendable and cannot be exhaustively specified in advance.

Let us look at the following data extract (S.T. Data D2-3):

Q: Would you agree, Father Mulvey, that there are people, be they calling themselves civil rights workers, or revolutionaries, or anarchists, who have been deliberately placing the people of the Bogside in conflict with the police for the past twelve months?

A: No, I am sure I would not accept that in the sense of the whole community of the Bogside.

Q: Let us amend it to portions of the community of the Bogside.

A: I cannot think of any particular incident where some people have said 'Let us attack the police'.

Q: I am not asking you that. I am not meaning physical conflict, I am meaning where the police have been obliged, on the one hand, to restrain or to take action against the people of the Bogside -

A: There have been situations that have arisen as a result of protests organized by civil rights members, or people saying they were members of the civil rights movement.

What I am interested in first are the categorizations 'police' and 'people of the Bogside'. The hearable asymmetry between these categorizations, produced and displayed through this sequence, is one embedded and operative within an *oppositional* context: 'the police have been obliged ... to take action against the people of the Bogside'. But the character of this oppositional asymmetry, its sense and intelligibility, depends on neither logical nor only conventional grounds, but on local knowledge, belief and practices, and is pragmatically given in the context of the talk as contingent on 'people ... who have been deliberately placing the people of the Bogside in conflict with the police'. We may now begin to locate another set and source of categorizational disjunctions.

We noted earlier that policeman/prisoner is an asymmetric category pair and a specific instance of what Sacks called a standardized relational pair (although to treat it this way is to extend Sacks's point, for he limits his use to examples of *symmetric* pairs). Now Sacks employed another analytic in conjunction with this notion, and that is the notion of the collection K: professional/layperson. (3) One observation about such a collection is that it is Pn-adequate. (4) Moreover, it does not project a specific relationship between the two pair parts; it is a *demarcative* set rather than a relationally constitutive one, in its abstract formulation. Locally, it can be realized in many ways - if we take a realization such as doctor/layperson (thus maintaining the Pn-adequate nature of such a collection), we find that this sort of category set masks the different specific relationships between various possible incumbents of the device-category 'layperson' and the incumbents of the category 'doctor' (or 'policeman', 'judge', etc.). Such sets are, *by definition*, asymmetric category sets with regards to the organization of knowledge/skills/resources and certain kinds of rights/obligations. The two pair parts are also *logically exclusive* categorizations, for 'layperson' works as an excluder category (5) in relation to the first pair part, 'professional' and any of its realizations.

If we provide various realizations of the set 'doctor/layperson' (Sacks's, in his analysis, would be 'SPC - member/client or suicidal person' (SPC meaning Suicide Prevention Centre)), we find doctor/patient, etc. among them. Here we have a few interesting and significant features. Firstly, we can now locate an asymmetric *standardized relational* pair, and not simply an asymmetric (demarcative) set. Secondly, the set stands for a collection that is not Pn-adequate (doctors/patients - cf. medical profession/public). Thirdly, the two categorizations are no longer *logically* exclusive, but are so only conventionally or pragmatically. (A doctor can be another doctor's patient.) The category set is, in other words, descriptively tied to an *occasioned* relationship. The first pair part consists of a *stable* categorization, whilst the second consists of an *event-specific* categorization (or action-consequent one, as in policeman/thief), i.e. a *locally occasioned categorization*. Of course, the patient may be a doctor, the thief may be a policeman (the defendant may be a judge, the lawyer's client may be a lawyer himself); nevertheless, routinely and conventionally, the second-pair-part incumbent is *not* hearable as also being an incumbent of the first-pair-part category (i.e. second-pair-part incumbents are not hearable conventionally as being drawn from the first-pair-part population) unless there is a special accounting or contextual provision. When a policeman arrests a police officer for stealing, the occasioned description is, routinely, something like 'policeman arrested' rather than 'thief arrested'. And when a doctor goes to another doctor for treatment, his category identity as 'doctor' is expectably and conventionally a *relevantly disclosable matter*.

Now, one important point about a category such as 'police-

man' is that it can be turned into a collectivity categorization
which is used in indifference to the specific and actual incumbents.    So we have 'the police' and, similarly, we have 'the
army', 'the civil service', 'the government', etc.    If we try
to provide a formulation of collection K for such categories,
we find that we do not, conventionally, have category sets
such as police/laypersons, army/laypersons, government/lay-
persons, but rather police/people, army/people, government/
people (or citizens, civilians, etc.).    We find, too, that such
category sets are *not*, strictly speaking, sets in the collection
K (demarcative and asymmetric with respect to knowledge,
etc. and rights, etc.), but are immediately asymmetric, standardized collectivity relational pairs.    What they do have in
common with collection K (and perhaps this is a basic feature
of such a collection) is that they are Pn-adequate sets for
practical purposes and are thus conventionally treatable as
pairs with mutually exclusive categories, i.e. 'people' is treatable as an excluder vis-à-vis the first pair part, 'police',
'army', 'government', etc., whichever is relevant.

The hearer's maxim formulated above applies even more
strongly in the case of such collectivity categorizations.    Let
us recast it somewhat.    If we formulate collectivity-related
category sets that are S-R pairs, but not members of the collection K, we find that we not only have category sets such
as police/people, but we can also have sets such as police/
suspect(s), army/rebel(s), government/dissident(s), etc.
Again, conventionally, incumbents of the second pair part are
not hearably *also* incumbents of the first pair part category
where such provision is not made (although, logically, they
could be).    They are also not Pn-adequate sets.    Such hearings are only strengthened by the character of the collectivity
categorization, for such a collectivity is treatable and hearable
as morally organized with respect to category-tied and set-
relational tasks.

So here we have two conventional hearings that do not map
exactly onto *logical* possibilities (and lexical ones):

1    The demarcative and mutually exclusive hearing of the
category set police/people, government/people.    These are
Pn-adequate sets and can thus be treated and used as categories from a Pn-adequate collection such as 'community', etc.

2    The mutually exclusive hearability of category pair parts
such as police/offender, police/suspect, army/rebels, soldier/
insurgent, etc. (6)

We can now map a further feature onto the above.    In that
a category set such as policeman/suspect is a standardized
relational pair, it is an S-R pair of a *specific* type - it is

usable as an adversary or *oppositional* pair. Therefore, incumbents of the second pair part of an oppositional asymmetric category set are conventionally treated as drawn from the population 'people' rather than from 'police'. So we can see that the category set police/people, given an orientation to its locally occasioned realizations, can be treated as generative of a category-related disjunction along with methods for its resolution. The disjunction I mean here is that between a conception and use of the category set police/people in which the category 'police' is used *oppositionally* to the category 'people' and one in which it is used *complementarily*.

Such different usages reproduce for local relevance, and in inferentially generative ways, the various parameters of such category sets as we have been elucidating. We can now formalize certain aspects of our discussion in terms of an *asymmetry convention*: in the use of two categorizations treatable as an asymmetric category set, do not hear the incumbent of the second pair part (the asymmetrically occasioned categorization) as also an incumbent of the first pair part category identity unless special provision is made. Where such disclosure is not provided, then hear the incumbent of the second pair part, the asymmetrically *occasioned* categorization, as *not* being an incumbent of a first pair part category identity (the *stable* categorization).

$$I_O \neq I_S \quad (O = \text{occasioned}; \quad S = \text{stable}; \quad I = \text{incumbent})$$

We can locate, embedded in these points, two generic (more abstractly formulated) disjunctions: the logical/conventional disjunction and the category-feature disjunction. Let us look at some data (S.T. Data E1-3):

Q: You have told us more than once that you think that there was a real risk of strangers coming in to Londonderry from outside and taking advantage of perhaps a comparatively small incident to provoke violence?

A: Yes, that was the fear.

Q: I want to get a good deal of this Londonderry Inquiry into, perhaps, proper perspective. I take it from that answer that you, knowing the people of Londonderry, would have believed them able to live in peace with each other if some sort of external irritation such as you were envisaging had not been applied?

A: I would think so, yes.

Q: And when you give that answer you include, do you not, the police within the term 'people of Londonderry'?

A: Yes, I would.

Q: Therefore - I think this important - and I am sure
   you as a priest will see its importance - you are prepared to ascribe to the police motives as peaceful and
   as good as you would ascribe to your own flock and, in
   particular, to the people of Bogside?

A: I would like to think I would do that.

Q: You would agree?

A: Yes.

Now, in the course of talk, it is routine that speakers employ
not one but a number of analytically formulatable devices, embedded in each other and finely articulated together to accomplish the task at hand.  The foregoing exchange trades on
and displays different devices to defeat the potential disjunction we are concerned with in this instance.  Since 'people'
can also be 'people of Londonderry', 'people of our town',
etc., there is a wide latitude for task-oriented category choice
available to speakers.  In the context of the category use in
this data (see Appendix 2), in addition to the context of local
knowledge, it might be difficult to include 'police' in 'people of
the Bogside' or to use these categorizations complementarily.
So rather than talking of 'police' and 'people of Bogside' (the
categorizations systematically used throughout that inquiry),
another category, treatable as an MCD, (7) is used by the
speaker to cover *both* the 'police' and the 'people of Bogside',
namely, 'people of Londonderry'.  We can note here the tension between logical features and conventional ones:  when *Q*
asks *A* whether he would include the police within the term
'people of Londonderry', he presses on him a logical set of
criteria for response - *of course*, the police in Londonderry
are *also* people of Londonderry.  *A* cannot answer in the
negative without some lengthy justification and explanation
that would involve making substantive points either about 'the
police' in general versus civilian populations (as in, e.g., a
Marxist view) or about how the police in Londonderry are, in
essential ways, at odds with the people.  Moreover, *A* would
have to indicate thus that in his earlier talk of 'the people of
Londonderry' he had explicitly been excluding the police, i.e.
had been using the term 'people' as an excluder (or a demarcative one).

In the data, getting *A* to 'include ... the police within the
term "people of Londonderry"' enables *Q* to get him to concede
that the same 'good' motives can be attributed to the police as
to the rest of the people.  This is a first step towards undercutting the possibility of a category-feature disjunction.

Firstly, he undercuts the oppositional use of the police/people
category set in the Londonderry context.   Secondly, this
undercuts some of the grounds for the oppositional use of the
'police'/'people of the Bogside' category pair through the
attribution of good motives to the police.   Thus, this opposition, already a focus of the talk in that inquiry, can get produced in less implicative ways, as a situated rather than
strategic one.   The importance of motive 'acquittal', achieved
through the use of the logic/convention disjunction device, is
demonstrated in the following sequence (S.T. Data E4-7):

Q:  We know also you would accept, would not you, that
both in July and in August the police action, however
much or however little you may criticize it, was their
reaction to a developing situation of violence?

A:  Yes, my Lord, if ...

Q:  They did not begin it, did they?

A:  No, my Lord.

Q:  And you would accept, would you, that perhaps with
errors of judgment, perhaps not, they, citizens of
Londonderry, eager like all others to live in peace,
were doing the best that they could to contain a situation which was putting them under great strain?

A:  I am sorry, my Lord, I could not accept that entirely.

Q:  How far would you go?

A:  The criticism I would make of the police may be just a
criticism of their judgment.

Q:  Exactly.

A:  But the point at which it became impossible to stop the
disturbance and at which I say something in the nature
of a revolt started, was the point at which the police
led a civilian faction or at least acted in collusion with a
civilian faction coming into the Bogside area.

Q:  But again, you were good enough to indicate that this
is a criticism of their judgment?

A:  I think it may be, yes.

Q:  Not a criticism of their motives?

A:  I would like to think it is not a criticism of their

motives. If I am in order in saying this, unfortunately, the history of relationships with the police over
the past year would lead people in the Bogside area to
feel that the police wanted to get in and punish them in
some way, and this was the reaction, and it was the
reaction to this action in collusion with civilians that I
was afraid of when I at first complained.

Q: We have heard an enormous amount, no doubt rightly,
in criticism of the police. It takes two sides, does not
it, to create the sort of unhappy situation that we have
been considering?

A: Yes.

When *A* blames some of the intensity of the problem under
discussion on the police's acting 'in collusion with a civilian
faction coming into the Bogside area', he is blaming the
police for *partisanship*. In the category set 'police/people',
used complementarily rather than oppositionally, the incumbents of the category 'police' have to be perceived and/or
formulated as being *impartial*. Impartiality in this respect
does not conventionally imply strict neutrality *regardless* of
the substance of the issue, for the 'police' have, in this context, a conventionally formulated task of 'upholding the law',
'fighting crime', etc. These are category-generated tasks
for them and category-bound duties. *Impartiality* is formulated and assessed by reference to a notion of what's fair, true,
lawful, just, in the particulars of the case at hand, and
bounded by what the category-related tasks are seen to be.
It is not that by not taking *any* side on any occasion the
police are seeable as being neutral and impartial - rather
sometimes it is indeed the perceived refusal to take sides that
is seen and seeable as partisan, where one side is perceived/
formulated as being 'in the right', and 'under attack' and the
other as being engaged in 'aggression', 'criminality', etc.
The same holds for such collectivity categorizations as 'army',
'government', etc. So in formulating 'partisanship' on the
part of the police, *A* is here not only further undercutting the
possible complementary usage of the categorizational pair
'police'/'people of the Bogside' (a usage that *Q*, in part, may
have been attempting to maintain as a strategic possibility with
his use of the categorization 'people of Londonderry'), but he
is shifting responsibility for the situatedly produced oppositional relationship *away* from the 'people of the Bogside' *to*
'the police'. However, given his earlier acquittal of the
police's motives, he is here again compelled to characterize
this displayed 'partisanship' as, possibly, a matter of 'judgment' rather than 'motive'. Were 'motive' to have been located as underlying this partisanship, then, by implication, it
might have been possible to provide that it was an intrinsic

feature of the police's relationship to the people of the Bogside, i.e. that it was a *strategic* partisanship.

Let us at this point reconsider an instance of Type II disjunctive category sets, policeman/thug, for example, where
the second pair part involves a (downgrading) assessment of
some performance such that someone may be describing a
policeman as acting like a thug or attributing thuglike behaviour to him/her - a performance-related disjunction.   In
other words, the policeman in such a disjunction operation is
being provided as not really acting like a 'good', 'real',
'proper', 'straight' policeman.   So rather than accepting the
use of the category 'policeman' of that presumed category incumbent, the disjunctive categorization 'thug' is used (where
'policeman' is the category avowable by the categorized
person).   Such assessments, indeed, display the speaker's
perception of the category-bound and category-constitutive
features of 'policeman' in his *contrastive* use of the categorization 'thug'.   Such oriented-to features can also be discur-
sively displayed and produced, as evidenced in both the
above data and the following extract (S.T. Data D7-8):

Q: You see, what I am suggesting to you is this:   you
   have spoken of this deterioration in relationship and I
   am suggesting to you that that is no accident.   Do
   you think it is an accident?

A: I do not think anyone deliberately set out to create
   tension between the police and the people.

Q: I suggest to you, Father Mulvey, that that is exactly
   what happened.

A: I am sorry, I do not agree with you.   I think the
   deterioration resulted because of misuse of authority
   and partisan behaviour on the part of some policemen.

A here talks of the 'misuse of authority' by *some* policemen as
the situation which generated a bad relationship between 'the
people of the Bogside' and 'the police'.   The presumption as
well as implication here is that in routine situations one would
not and does not expect the 'police' to be partisan, but rather
to be 'impartial' or 'fair'.   Here is where another kind of disjunction may, and routinely does, arise;   for some people the
very category 'police' is a category describing (in one of its
uses) an essentially partisan collectivity - a category, for
example, used to designate a collectivity of persons who are
essentially defenders of 'the establishment', 'the ruling class',
etc., i.e. defenders of a sectional interest, a 'repressive
force', etc.   This would be a Marxist view, for instance.
So that, unlike Type I disjunctive category pairs where the

disjunction between avowal and ascription is one about which
of two alternative categories are applicable to some member
with respect to a specific practice/action/problem, here the
disjunction is not about *what category is usable*, but what the
category in use *amounts to*, what work it does, what its
organizational features are, what its conventionally typical and
expectable features are; in other words, what it is *practically* as a resource for understanding and assembling social
structures.   If, however, we look at Type II disjunctions we
may find how these distinctly different ones arise.   Let us
call them Type III.   Routinely it is the case that Type III
disjunctions develop through the disjunctive presumption of a
disavowable category feature, where this feature is one which
routinely is seen to be constitutive (or typical) of a disjunct-
tive category, e.g. 'thug' (in the same sense that 'vandal',
'murderer', etc. are routinely and conventionally disavowable
and disjunctive in their use as between avowal and ascription).
Such a disjunctive category, however, for our purposes here,
is routinely one which is used in disjunctive category operations of Type II, such as policeman/thug.   We may then
specify a Type III disjunction by the assimilation of the dis-
junctive-disavowable category pair part in a Type II disjunctive operation to the first pair part, so that we have something like 'all cops are "legalized" thugs'.   The disjunction
that routinely arises then is a *category-feature disjunction*,
often displayed as a *context-of-use disjunction* between the
use of the category 'police' in a context which employs,
implies or depends on this added disjunctive feature inclusion
and one which denies it.   Or the disjunctive feature may be
explicitly provided for, so that the disjunction arising over
the organization of the category features (and all the implications for category use bound up with this) is explicitly articulated.   Such Type III disjunctions arising at the level of
disjunctions in the perceivedly category-bound or category-
constitutive features may be shown as also arising in relation
to Type I disjunctive category pairs, as, for example, 'revolutionary'/'terrorist'.

A brief analysis of part of a previous extract of data is
interesting with respect to some of the above issues (S.T.
Data D2):

Q: Would you agree, Father Mulvey, that there are people,
   be they calling themselves civil rights workers, or revolutionaries, or anarchists, who have been deliberately
   placing the people of the Bogside in conflict with the
   police for the past twelve months?

A: No, I am sure I would not accept that in the sense of
   the whole community of the Bogside.

What is of particular interest here is the utterance part 'be they calling themselves civil rights workers, or revolution- aries, or anarchists'.  If one looks at the 'or', it might at first glance seem that the speaker is making some distinctions between 'civil rights workers', 'revolutionaries' and 'anar- chists'.  But the 'or' construction turns out to be doing something else here.  'Or' routinely provides for alternatives, but these alternatives may be either *oppositions*, as in 'You can join the Royalists or the Republicans', or *substitutes*, as in 'get me half a pound of butter or margarine'. (8)  What the modality of 'or' is on any specific occasion of its use is provided for by our knowledge of the world (local, categorial, conventional) as well as by its *context* of use.

In this instance, I suggest that the speaker is employing the substitutive sense of 'or'.  He seems to be publicly suppressing any commitment on his part to a specific category choice.  By saying 'be they calling themselves', $Q$ is provid- ing *either* (a) that the three categorizations intrinsically carry a feature *in common*, this feature being the relevant one for the purposes of the present discourse *or* (b) that for practi- cal purposes the distinctive feature difference between the three categorizations is irrelevant.  Now what $Q$ seems to be doing is treating the category-concepts here as *mere labels* and setting up a determinate population $P$, members of which (some or all) might call themselves by *any* of these three labels (and by *which* label all or some members of $P$ choose to call themselves is here observably treated as irrelevant). Supposing, however, that $Q$ had said, 'that there are people, be they civil rights workers, or revolutionaries, or anarchists, who...'.  Had $Q$ said that, dropping the utterance component 'calling themselves', what he would have been doing would have been to set up *three real, separate populations (P1, P2, P3)* (albeit overlapping), some or all of whose members for these practical purposes at hand *can be considered in the same manner*.  That is, they happen to be similar for the purpose at hand.  $Q$ would here be using the category-concepts at a real-world level, as intendedly capturing some real classes in the world, rather than as *labels*.  In the latter case, whilst $Q$ would be implying or saying that the three groups coincide in a certain respect (e.g. 'have been deliberately placing the people of the Bogside in conflict with the police'), he would still be implicitly acknowledging some distinction between them, some *real* distinction, and not only a difference in *the way they categorize themselves*.  When $Q$ says, 'be they calling themselves', it is not hearable that all or some members of this determinate population $P$ call themselves by these three names *alternately* (a possible hearing if the 'be they' is dropped); nor is it hearable that $Q$ does not know *which* of these terms some or all members of $P$ use of themselves (again a possible hearing if 'be they' is dropped).  Rather, what is *conven-*

*tionally* hearable is that *whether* they (all or some) call themselves civil rights workers, revolutionaries or anarchists (i.e.
which of these three names they call themselves) is of no
practical relevance for the present issue, which presumes that
at least *some* of these persons (members of *P* under consideration) call themselves by *one and not another* of these terms.
Indeed, this is in conformity with our conventional knowledge
and practical understanding of the world (and the use of
names) in that these three categorizations may indeed be used
and treated as representing three overlapping classes of
persons, three collectivities some, but not all, of whose members may also be members of one or both of the other collectivities. What *Q* may be heard to be doing is projecting an
implicit categorization of some population of persons (as a
class) that is *more* or *other than* they would use of themselves:
an embedded categorizational disjunction. What is involved
here is that any category-bound features of, or family-resem-
blant features between, the three categorizations are used
(through the method of implicative fit and deletion available to
members) to project a determinate class/category of persons
*unmentioned but mentionable* and grounded in *Q*'s very talk and
*choice* of category terms. To defeat this implicit categorization, and as one available resolution of this explicit-avowal/
implicit-ascription sort of categorizational disjunction, (9) a
relevant distinctive feature may be formulated as being bound
to or constitutive of one or other category – a disagreement is
further generatable thus as to what attributes/features may be
seen as bound or relevant to that category as between the
speaker and others.

In concluding this section, and before going on to related
matters, let us recapitulate on the three major types of categorizational disjunction operations we have outlined:

Type I disjunction operation

This involves a *deletion* of the avowable categorization (actual
or implicit) and a *substitution* of an alternative categorization
which is contrastive in its sense and upshot. An example of
this would be 'sick person'/'hypochondriac'.

Type II disjunction operation

This involves a *downgrading assessment* of the relevant category-bound performance and the ascription of a categorization
that is contrastive to the avowable, and formally applicable,
one *and that amends its relevance*, e.g. policeman/thug.

## Type III disjunction operation

This involves the assimilation to an avowable categorization of
a routinely disjunctive and disavowable categorization, so that
the latter is treated as a bound feature of the former.   This
is displayed in category-feature disjunctions and, implicitly,
in context-of-use disjunction.   An example would be 'the
police' as 'legalized thugs' or as 'keepers of law and order'.

## DILEMMAS

In the last chapter we discussed how various categorizations
can become relevantly implicated in the course of some interaction.   We also indicated Sacks's notion of an economy rule
that, for any situation, one category may be referentially adequate.   Indeed, routinely, we find that one categorization *is*
referentially adequate.   Given, then, our discussion of category accretion and other issues of categorial implication, we
must keep clearly in mind the difference between *categorial
relevance* and *referential adequacy*.   In looking over the
transcripts of natural and other conversational and textual
materials (newspaper reports, etc.) we regularly find that *one*
categorization is used to refer (or attribute some feature) to
any specific person.   One categorization, chosen for its self-
explicating relevance, may perform the practical task at hand
for which a category selection is required and by which *that*
particular selection is warranted.   This does not mean, however, that in every such case one (and this) categorization is
the only one *relevantly available*.   In a conversation of two
people, for instance, where one person *A* is involved in making
a complaint about a person *C* to another person *B*, and *B* is
involved in 'defence work', different categorizations may be
relevant - the ones selected by each co-conversationalist will
be speaker-task-relevant, although there may be recognition
of the settinged relevance of the other speaker's categorizational uses, as well as an orientation *in use* to other possible
categorizations that may be made explicit or left implicit (to
avoid, for example, being seen as a 'gossip', or merely
'abusive').   There is, in other words, an orientation to a
*relevant category environment*.   This is not routinely a problem for co-conversationalists.   Regularly, however, situations
arise in which it *does* become a practical problem. (10)

In the northern Iranian town of Tabriz, a group of soldiers
suddenly found themselves confronting a large but peaceful
group of anti-Shah demonstrators in the local bazaar.   As
the chanting marchers approached, one soldier said he was
going to join them.   He was immediately shot by one of his
comrades, who in turn was attacked by the angry crowd.
The soldier who had fired was saved by the quick interven-

tion of a colonel, who took off his own pistol and offered it
to the demonstrators, shouting: 'We are the same people.
Why do we kill each other?' After that, most of his
soldiers stacked their arms in a truck and joined the
marchers. The protesters urged the soldiers to participate
in the chant of 'Death to the Shah', but they refused.
Some wept.

The incident in Tabriz last week was but one of a number
of symptoms of a growing restiveness within the Shah's army
as its small-scale clashes with the citizenry continue.
('Time', January 1, 1979)

In this report, the accountability and intelligibility of the
conclusion (paragraph 2) hinges precisely on our understanding of the interlocked and simultaneous relevance of different
categorial identities - soldier; citizen; Iranian. The
account and its conclusion also display some of the related
issues we discussed earlier regarding the oppositional use of
a category pair such as 'army/people'. One must remember
here that members do not routinely use category-concepts as
mere labels, but as methods for organizing their knowledge,
belief, perceptions, tasks, moral relationships, etc. Hence
their use of them as self-identifications is an essentially
*serious* use - and the problem of the simultaneous practical
relevance of two, contextually oppositional, categorial incumbencies for a particular situation is an intelligible problem in
those terms. Situations where such a problem arises are,
routinely, ones where the question 'What to do?' is askable.

Where the simultaneous relevance of two category incumbencies is co-produced in a setting by two persons, we might
have something like the following examples:

*A*
S1: I'm a doctor.
S2: But you're also my husband.

S1: You're my husband.
S2: (But) I'm also a doctor.

*B*
S1: I'm an Imperial Guardsman.
S2: (But) you're also an Iranian.

S1: You're an Iranian.
S2: (But) I'm also an Imperial Guardsman.

These kinds of exchanges are describable as 'conflict'-
generated and 'conflict'-displaying. Each sequence is also a
relevance-displaying sequence. The location of each part of
a sequence as a first or second displays an order of relevan-

ces at hand. *A* and *B* are different. The categories 'doctor' and 'husband' are neither contingent on nor inclusive of one another. The category 'Imperial Guardsman', how- ever, may accountably be treated, for some practical pur- poses, as contained within the category 'Iranian', for 'Iranian' may be treated as a collection inclusive of the category 'Imperial Guardsman'. In type *A*, therefore, a disagreement over the relevance of a particular categorization in a practical situation may only be resolved through the assignment of *categorial precedence* to one categorization over another *for some practical purpose*, issue or task at hand (although this *may* also result in the assignment of *general* precedence). Conversely, it may be done through *entirely deleting* the relevance of one of the categorizations for the practical con- cern at hand. When I say 'resolution' I do not by that intend to mean definite or final agreement by the two or more parties in that situation. Rather, this is intended to indi- cate the point at which argument may warrantably cease, at least for that occasion. It is the response of the person whose categorial incumbency is at issue that is of interest.

In type *B*, however, there is another alternative (which intimately ties back to our earlier discussion of category- feature disjunction or context-of-use disjunctions). If 'Imperial Guardsman' is treated as a separate category from 'Iranian', then one or the other category may be given prece- dence over the other or be assigned exclusive relevance (even though this may generate some moral judgments of the incum- bent). But the two categorizations may be treated as inter- twined or related, in which case one of them may be treated as *fulfilling* (or fulfilling more effectively) *the proper obli- gations of the other*; for example, fulfilling one's category- tasks as an 'Imperial Guardsman' may be seen as best fulfilling one's obligations as an 'Iranian'.

Such conflicts/disagreements, I said earlier, are related to the practical (and normative) problem of 'What to do?' or, indeed, of assessing 'what *X* did', 'what *X* will do' or 'why *X* did *Z*'. In other words, they are tied into normative *action contexts* - and the questions above are all questions about *actions*. But the actions under consideration in such instan- ces are actions that are category-relevant or category-genera- ted in that they are actions that are produced and treatable as expressive of, or fulfilling, or yet violating category-bound obligations, rights and tasks. They are morally assessable *in these terms*. Now, such considerations will, in certain situations, observably and expectably, lead to an impasse. Category use and relevance is occasioned by the setting within which, and the tasks for which, such use or invocation take place. Regularly, one will find that a conflict arises for the person contemplating action in terms of which particular set of

category-bound obligations to orient or attend to rather than
another, if both are made practically relevant but are also
practically irreconcilable.   Not only does this sort of problem
arise for a speaker/actor, but others may orient to just this
problem, or this sort of possibility, in attempting to understand, describe, report on or 'influence' a speaker/actor in
context.   An example of this comes from the reporting on the
Iranian situation - the attempt to explain or 'predict' the
behaviour of Iranian troops;   the projection of the possibility
of *a split in the army*, etc.   The description of these practical problems is ultimately in terms of categorizational relevances:   soldier or citizen?   The problem, in this case, rests
on and displays the oppositional understanding of the army/
people category set for the practical situation at hand - recall
our earlier discussion.   Both are features of the environment
of categorial relevance, but for any person, *one* alone may be
made relevant, or take precedence over the other, or be
treated as subsumed under the other category.   But there
will be occasions when resolution is very difficult or perceiv-
ably impossible.

Where such a problem *is* resolved, it seems to be so resolved
by the setting up of a *hierarchy of relevance* or *consequence*.
Dilemmas are resolved through generating hierarchies (orders
of precedence) for practical purposes.   But such hierarchies
as are set up cannot non-consequentially be of any kind or of
any order - there is cultural agreement on what would be
acceptable as an intelligible or appropriate order of precedence, just as there is over what could count as a good
reason, although there is a latitude for disagreement within
each.   Just as it is not a good enough reason to hurt someone just because you feel like it, it is not acceptable that a
man places his chess-club membership above his obligations as
a doctor, should they conflict, or that a woman gives precedence to her identity as a 'socialite' over her identity as a
'mother'.   We do not in *this* culture ordinarily accept that
such identities are generative of serious *moral* dilemmas.
Should a woman give precedence to her identity as a socialite
*over* her categorial identity as a mother, for instance, we
treat this *as morally implicative* - in such a case the precedent-
assuming categorial identity 'socialite' (and the concerns bound
up with it) works *as the reason* for situatedly failing to fulfil
her category-bound obligations in respect of her other identity
as a mother.

Many of the old and recurring existential dilemmas operate
around the simultaneous relevance of two membership categories for a person in a practical situation, e.g. citizen/family
member.   One thinks here of the old problematic of a doctor
who, while treating war injuries, finds that his son is among
the critically wounded and faces the question of whether to

leave him till his turn comes or treat him first.   Here it is
not only obligation conflicting with obligation alone, but also
a category-bound right/concern conflicting with another category identity's obligations.   Numerous novels and dramas on
social issues turn on just such problems.

## DESCRIPTIONS, CATEGORY-ORGANIZED KNOWLEDGE AND BIOGRAPHICAL KNOWLEDGE

In order to introduce some further complexities into the analysis of categorizational work, let us return to our Hell's
Angel data set.   Consider the following (H.A. Data):

65   A:   No - what you're saying these Hell's Angels people
          have actually been breaking into the Planet work-
          shops...

66   R:   That's what I mm consider myself - my own personal
          opinion.

67   A:   Yeah.

68   R:   I mean to say, I went in one night when there was
          erm half a dozen of them there or ... the place was
          open, the lock was broken on the door, there were
          tools lying all over the place, on the floor, round
          about er screwdrivers, er, saws, pincers, hammers
          ... everything.

69   A:   Mm.

70   R:   It's just asking for, er, trouble.

What we have in *R*'s second utterance is a simple description
of a scene:   a group of people, a broken lock, tools lying
around.   This description is being provided as the *grounds*
for *R*'s belief that the Hell's Angels had been breaking into
the Planet workshops - the scene is thus implicitly presupposed and treated as being self-evident and self-contained,
and a particular tie between the people present and the
features of the scene is being proposed, namely, that of
*agency*.   However, it is clearly the case that the presence of
anyone at the scene may be accidental or contingent:   these
people might have arrived by coincidence right after the
break-in;   they might have gone there in order to apprehend
whoever it was who *was* responsible for the break-in (see
Appendix 3, *A*'s earlier utterance 'they act as sort of night
watchman');   they might have taken refuge from the cold
weather and *had* to break the lock, the tools having been left
lying around by others earlier in the day;   or yet *some* of

them might have been guilty and others not.  $R$ , however, does not see the presence of these people at the scene as either accidental or contingent - for him the scene provides for their presence there *as the agents of its production*.   A feature of $R$'s description that is important here is his identification of the group of people in question.   He does not say 'a dozen persons there', but rather 'a dozen of them there'. The 'them' clearly ties back to the 'Hell's Angels' who are the subject of the conversation at this juncture, and it is within the context of talk about an identifiable and particular group of people that $R$'s reading of the scene becomes analysable. If $R$ did not know these persons, if he had been a total stranger to them, he would lay himself open to the charge of taking the scene 'at face value', 'jumping to conclusions', etc. were he unqualifiedly to insist that these people had broken into the place without first acquainting himself with who they were and what they might have been doing there.

On the other hand, he would be equally laying himself open to blame were he to ignore completely the 'face value' of that scene, i.e. the unexplained presence of the individuals at the scene of the supposed crime.   What he would conventionally be expected to do, as a competent member, and as a policeman in particular, is to turn any noticed and noticeable feature of that scene into an investigable matter.   However, $R$'s description displays an identification of the persons there;   they are no longer thus treatable as an 'unknown quantity'.   But the identification retains some equivocality - is it simply of Hell's Angels members in general, or of *particular* members?   Identifying a group of people as Hell's Angels may be done through accepting their self-identification, or through identifying/ recognizing some criterial mark (emblem, costume, etc.), or through recognizing the particular persons B, C, D, etc., who are known to the speaker and known to be Hell's Angels. This identification is then usable as a resource.   $R$ can claim his account/perception of the scene to be correct given what is known of these people as a *group*, or by virtue of what he has come to know of these *particular* persons during the course of his work.   But the two knowledge-claims are different here;   they are not of the same order.   The first is category-organized:   it trades on the conventional knowledge of category-bound features for the category 'Hell's Angels', as well as on category-constitutive/generative/relevant features. The second is biographical knowledge of particular persons, e.g. previous convictions, character, membership in the Hell's Angels, etc.   These cannot be treated as two entirely distinct domains of knowledge, for much of biographical knowledge is given in terms of category knowledge, but neither is the relationship between them entirely unproblematic, in particular when the category involved is one like the Hell's Angels - a morally self-organized group.   In such instances, a *systematic equivocality* is encountered as between talk of persons simply as members of the group (biographical strangers) and talk of them as *specific* persons who happen also to be members of the group (biographically known persons). Let us unpack some of the issues.

It is clear that giving descriptions of scenes, indeed one's very perception of scenes, is organized by one's knowledge. This, so far, is a commonplace. But the relationship of knowledge to perception and description, as well as to inference from observed scenes and actions, or reports of them, is complex. Now, although in going out into the market-place, for example, we may spend hours among 'strangers', they are nevertheless only *strangers biographically*. *Culturally*, the persons we thus encounter *are not strangers* – we know them well, we know what to expect from them, what they will expect from us, we know some of the features of their lives, we can provide stories about them and the scenes we encounter them within are self-evident through *this* knowledge. But this knowledge is category-organized: child, woman, married man, bus-driver, saleslady, policeman, butcher, shoe-repair man, old woman, mother, businessman, husband, etc. It is in moving from this level of knowledge (and the consequent ascriptions, inferences and perceptions) to ascriptions, inferences and perceptions on a personal or individual level that one *may*, and routinely does, encounter problems of 'fit' between (a) the two levels of knowledge claimed or accessible and (b) the knowledge claimed by or attributable to a speaker and the contingent description/perception of or inference from a witnessed or reported scene or action. Such 'fits' are investigable and routinely become issues for members – how such 'fits' are achieved, investigated, accommodated or found wanting is of course of great interest here. (Note that the move from personal knowledge to talk about category collectivities and to knowledge-claims at the categorial level may also be problematic – something that is known, in certain contexts, as generalization. We will not deal with this here.) Let us take the first issue first.

The following is another extract from Elizabeth Gaskell's novel 'North and South', which quite elegantly captures the issue as it is encountered by members in the course of their interaction. The reference is to the novel's main male protagonist, Mr Thornton, who is in love with Margaret Hale (see earlier extract in Chapter 4):

He was haunted by the remembrance of the handsome young man, with whom she stood in an attitude of such familiar confidence and the remembrance shot through him like an agony, till it made him clench his hands tight in order to subdue the pain. At that late hour, so far from home!

It took a great moral effort to galvanize his trust - erewhile
so perfect - in Margaret's pure and exquisite maidenliness
into life;   as soon as the effort ceased, his trust dropped
down dead and powerless:   and all sorts of wild fancies
chased each other like dreams, through his mind.    Here
was a little bit of miserable gnawing confirmation.    'She
bore up better than likely' under this grief.    She had then
some hope to look to, so bright that even in her affectionate
nature it could come in to lighten the dark hours of a
daughter newly made motherless. (11)

Not knowing that Margaret had a brother (let alone that he
had been visiting his family at the time Thornton had spotted
Margaret with a young man), Thornton's reading of the scene
hinges accountably on the available membership categorizations
for the scene he witnessed:   simply, young woman/young man.
In the context of 'an attitude of such familiar confidence' this
becomes implicative of the categorizations lover/lover;   for
such an attitude between members of the opposite sex, given
the time period the novel is set in, would have been seen to
be bound to the categorization 'lover' or some category from
the device 'family'.    Had Thornton *known* of the brother then,
that scene of intimacy might have been perceived by him as
*just another family scene*.    We touched on an aspect of this
earlier when we discussed category-transformable features.
Here Thornton's struggle is between his perception of the
scene in terms of his knowledge of available membership categorizations and their features and his *personal knowledge* of
Margaret as a 'pure' and 'maidenly' young woman, whom he
would not have expected to be in such a relationship of intimacy with a young man.    There is no 'fit' between the two -
a resolution to this problem would have to emerge either
through a reconstitution of his personal knowledge of Margaret
(a reassessment), or through finding it deficient by the discovery of other *biographically relevant* membership categorizations that could transform the sense of that witnessed scene
(the solution proffered in the later stages of the novel -
Thornton later discovers that the 'young man' is her 'brother'),
or through *finding an excuse for it*, thus maintaining both
readings (an intermediary solution that Thornton looks for).
What *deepens* or transforms his reading of the scene in any of
the three cases is further *biographical* knowledge (including
that of relevant membership categorizations).

One can take it, then, that a first reading of any scene
rests on members' categorially organized knowledge with respect to the membership categorizations immediately available
for the persons within that scene.    And any scene makes
itself and is self-evident in terms of such membership categorizations and the knowledge organized by them;   it is as self-
evident as these categorizations make it.    That such readings

may get reconstituted through the discovery, invocation or
other use of further relevant detail does not necessarily reconstitute such scenes as having been 'ambiguous', 'unclear'
or 'problematic' (except in cases of disjunction, as in the
example above) but rather as scenes for which the dichotomy
of appearance/reality (or face-value/reality) is relevant.
Note that it is not illusion/reality that is the dichotomy oriented to in such instances - 'appearance' is quite a different
concept from 'illusion'; it represents a version that does not
capture the entire truth or reality of a setting/scene/action,
but one that is nevertheless grounded in real-world detail.
The possibility of a 'further layer' of knowledge or additional
contextual detail throwing light on present circumstances and
witnessed scenes (and interpretations of them) and transforming what is for the present a version of reality into a version
of its appearance, or what is (seems to be) reality into part-
reality only, is routinely present. Here we may see the significance of the court-room oath 'I swear to tell the truth, the
whole truth and nothing but the truth'. There is *in principle* always the possibility of more detail to transform some
perception, interpretation or description of a witnessed or reported scene; *in fact*, not all detail can be *account-trans-
forming*, nor is all detail perceivable as reality-structuring.
What is and what is not, and how that is achieved or provided
for, is itself a vast area of interest, bounded by the informal
logic of concepts, our forms of life and conventionally available members' devices. We will not, however, be concerned
with detailing this issue here in an abstract way. Scenes,
actions and utterances are oriented to as seeable/hearable/
understandable for what they are by competent others whose
looking and hearing is informed, unproblematically, effortlessly
and immediately by their knowledge - cultural (including category-organized knowledge), biographical (including relevant
membership categorizations and character), contextual and
even technical. Indeed, where scene and actions are made
out not to have been self-evident and really self-explicating
for a hearer/looker, that is done precisely through the *attribution of ignorance* to that hearer/looker. Thus, for
example, to charge that a description or reading of a scene or
utterance is a 'face value' one or only captures its 'appearance' is one way of articulating the availability of alternative
rational accounts - it is a device by which disagreement is
articulated, equivocality established, competence or knowledge
questioned, or motive called into account.

This brings us to the second issue of 'fit' indicated earlier:
that is, between the knowledge claimed by or attributable to a
speaker and that speaker's contingent perception/description
of or inference from a witnessed or reported scene or action.
(Inferences are grounded in described or describable events
and actions, providing on that basis what is not *empirically*

available in the *details* of that scene or event.)    Let us take
the following example, an extract from a court-room transcript:

> The Witness:    I would classify him as a person who has a
> vicious temper.    I don't think on the basis
> of those two episodes only, and assuming – I
> am assuming that I had investigated those
> things, and I say this because whenever I
> receive a report like that, one of the things
> I am concerned about was: Was there alcohol
> involved;  was he febrile, a person under a
> fever perhaps could behave somewhat
> irrationally;  was there any other condition
> surrounding this event that might have
> caused him to behave that way.    I don't
> think I could take it at face value and draw
> conclusions from that, but – (12)

The witness here is a psychiatric doctor and the court-room
investigation pertains to whether the subject can be judged
criminally insane or not.    Now there are a lot of issues involved in this which we will not deal with now but reserve for
later discussion.    However, it is clear at least that the witness is reluctant to 'draw conclusions' simply on the basis of
a description of the events provided him (that the defendant
tried once to throw his baby into the fire and another time to
throw the baby out of the window).    The witness is providing for the possibility of other things making different sense
of the nature of the events and displays his ignorance of possibly relevant contextual information, displays himself as a
stranger to the subject and the event.    His unwillingness to
'take it at face value' is articulated, not simply through an
avowed ignorance of possibly relevant detail, but through his
*displayed knowledge of available alternative accounts* or of
possible circumstances that could render any reading indifferent to them a faulty and 'face-value' reading.    The witness
is observably taking what might conventionally be called an
'objective' or 'detached' (even a 'scientific') stance.    Now
note that, as the policeman *R* did in our earlier data, to provide a description of a scene or make a conclusion from it
purely on its 'face value' or on the basis of category-organized knowledge only, *without* the investigation of its biographical relevance, is to lay oneself open to blame.    If
ignorance is attributable to the speaker (*R* earlier, the witness here), then such a description may provide for a categorization (or self-categorization) of him as a stranger or outsider.    If ignorance is attributable, then, a faulted descrip-
tion/perception/conclusion may constitute the speaker as a
stranger or outsider.    At the same time, his being a
stranger can then be used to account for that description/
perception/conclusion and disqualify it, rationally and account-

ably. Moreover, his being a stranger can then be used as
an *excusing condition* for his having arrived at such a perception or conclusion in the first place. However, that does
*not* apply for incumbents of certain membership categories.
A policeman's *not knowing* is no excuse for 'jumping to conclusions' - it is a routine part of his work (as we indicated
earlier) to set up an investigation procedure and it is expected, or at least preferred, that until then *final* judgment or
a 'final conclusion' is withheld. It is the same for a doctor;
to 'jump to conclusions', 'to infer' or to make 'categorial'
assessments *prior to* such investigations opens such category
incumbents, *if* their perception/conclusion is found faultable
through ignorance, to the charge of *prejudice* or *incompetence.*

Let us take another example: suppose *M* and her husband *O*
are shopping in a big downtown store and they stop to look
at a jewellery stall. Suppose that *M*, after looking at a
number of necklaces, walks away with one of them. Her
husband, on seeing that, points it out, returns the necklace
to the stall and afterwards reprimands her strongly for
attempting to shoplift. Now *M* may reject such an accusation
on her husband's part as illegitimate, pointing out to him that
he knows her well enough to know that she would not do a
thing like that. In the context of their relationship as
husband-wife (an S-R pair) he is expected to have, or is
credited with, enough knowledge to make his wife's action
transparent. If *M*'s husband persists in his declaration of
his perception of her actions as having amounted to an
attempt to shoplift, then that perception may be seen by *M* as
being 'strange' or 'motivated'. Suppose, however, that after
a very brief courtship *M* and *O* got married and are now still
newlyweds, then there is no way to attribute to *O* decisive
enough characterological knowledge of *M* to have rendered that
scene obvious to him for what it was, from *M*'s point of view
(i.e. a case of innocent absent-mindedness, for example). *O*,
of course, may be expected to orient to that scene's appearance to others who are perfect strangers biographically.
Still, given the category relationship husband-wife, and the
relationally bound set of duties and entitlements, *O* would be
expected to 'think better' of his wife, display 'good faith' and
'trust', i.e. to employ a charitable interpretation.

To recap briefly, then: the description and perception of,
or inference from, a witnessed or reported scene by someone
is not only implicative for the attribution to that person of
some membership category (as in stranger/outsider). It is
assessable in the context of some category incumbency that
he/she is presumed or known to fill and which is perceived to
be of practical relevance for the case at hand (in terms of its
known-in-common set of obligations, entitlements, opportunities

or knowledge). Indeed, that very incumbency is assessed in
terms of such a perception, as when a doctor gets judged to
be *incompetent* (or indifferent, which is morally implicative for
a doctor) by taking some report or scene or description at
face value, i.e. making do with little knowledge of a situation
that not only requires *more knowledge*, but *requires him to
seek* such knowledge in fulfilment of his category obligations.

## ATTRIBUTIONS OF PREJUDICE AND BIAS

What we have looked at so far are some issues tied up with
the relationship between category-organized knowledge and
biographical knowledge. However, taking this a step further,
another point of interest is the relationship between category-
organized belief (*or* knowledge) and personal description and
inference. The distinction here between category-organized
belief and knowledge is that the former can be identified as
that set of substantive features that are (loosely) perceivable
as category-bound, but whose use thus in talk by a speaker
is treatable as a display (or implication) of *belief* as opposed
to knowledge (even if claimed to be knowledge by the speaker).
In other words, they have, strictly, the status of a *belief*:
so that, for example, we may *believe* that women cry easily,
that politicians are devious, that young boys are unruly. We
cannot, however, be said to *know* such things in general.
Although some persons may claim for them the status of knowledge, they remain the sort of things which *are treatable as
beliefs* by other members, so that, routinely, knowledge-claim/
belief-claim disjunctions may arise for them. (13) Compare
them with other sorts of substantive category-bound features.
We may be said to *know* that babies cry; that soldiers fight
(although some soldiers may never have seen a single battle);
that children grow; that women have babies; that Italians
eat Italian food, etc. We cannot easily or properly be said
(in the context of our common culture) to *believe* those
things. And it is these latter types of features that may be
transformed into or made to work as normatively category-
constitutive in various contexts and for various tasks. So,
for example, a woman who does not have a baby, or doesn't
want one, or cannot have one, *may*, routinely and accountably,
be perceived and talked of as a deficient woman or 'lacking in
womanhood' (or, alternatively, as a 'liberated woman'). This,
of course, does not mean that there does or should exist total
collective agreement to such a formulation. Indeed not.
But it is a formulation that has *perceivedly orderly grounds*
for its production.

The distinction between the two different sorts of category-
bound features on the basis of the knowledge/belief dichotomy
of their apprehended character may be further clarified and

ramified by examining the different way *attribution of preju-dice* may be made in each case.   Attributions of prejudice
are routinely made where the conventional rules of inference
about persons and collectivities are perceived as having been
violated, or where perceivedly groundless attributions are
made to them of actions, beliefs, traits, etc. (this is a case
where 'logic' fights with 'belief').   The inferential or attributive moves thus implicated may be in either direction (from
collectivity or category to individual or vice versa).

Now, in the case of category-bound features that are formulatable as beliefs (category-bound features B), the problem of
'prejudice' is located *in their very character as category-
organized beliefs*: it is at the very level of the beliefs about
categories, their incumbents and category-bound features, and
situated inferences from them, that the possible attribution of
prejudice is *systematically available*.   Take, for example,
these two possible utterances after a mugging:

A:  He's a mugger - why try him?   He did it.

B:  He's a $\emptyset$ - why try him?   He did it.

(where $\emptyset$ can stand, say, for any collectivity such as Black,
Arab, Gypsy, Jew, Irishman, etc.).   In A the applicability
of the categorization 'mugger' is grounded in whether the
person did in fact do the mugging.   The ascription of this
category to a person depends on successful and appropriate
action ascription, and the action itself generates the relevance
of the categorization.   Whether the person committed the
action or not will settle the usability (but not necessarily the
use) of that categorization.   Regardless of what other problems one may have with such a formulation or utterance, we
can see an important difference between it and the second
statement.   In B the use of the category is in no way contingent on the act, whether in fact that particular individual
has indeed committed it or not.   And whether that person has
committed the act in question or not, the applicability of the
category cannot logically be tied to the possible action ascription and is not generated by it.   The formal structure involved in such an utterance would be something like the following:

$\emptyset$s are/do *X* (mugging).

This guy is a $\emptyset$.

Therefore this guy is/does *X* (is a mugger/mugs people).

Therefore this guy has done *this X*.

The problem is essentially located in the first clause.   Now

observe that, even if the formulation of belief takes the form
of '⌀s are/do X', rather than '*All* ⌀s are/do X', it is *in the
very inference to* 'therefore *this* guy does/is X' that the concept 'all' is enthymematically embedded (thus implicatively produced, displayed and traded on) and accomplishes that inference as a mechanistic move from categorial applicability.
Another level of the problem is 'therefore this guy has done
*this* X' (where a specific action is in question).   For this
inference to hold, one has also to hold, and indeed presume,
that *only* ⌀s do   (as well as that no other ⌀ could have done
this X).   In other words, the *class of* ⌀s and the class of
persons who do X *are identical* for all practical purposes.
At any rate, the systematic possibility of prejudice attribution
here is category-based – it rests on a belief regarding a certain membership category.   (Note that the same reasoning can
be made with a *positive* or solicitable attribute or categorization;   in such a case, prejudice or bias is attributable still.)

Now if we look at the set of features that are available to
members in the form of 'knowledge' of the social world, in
particular of membership categorizations, their features and
incumbents, the case is far more complex.   Firstly, comparing them with the above instances, we find that they are,
expectably, not assessments and judgments in the proper
sense, whereas the above examples all are (although some conceivably might not be).   Secondly, it is not important for the
formulation of such features to take the format:   All X are/
have Y.   Sacks, in his discussion of category-bound actions
(we have expanded the notion to talk of category-bound
features), delineates a very important property:   when a
member performs an action, and that member is not an incumbent of the membership category to which that action is perceivedly bound, then that person may nevertheless be described in terms of that membership categorization. (14)   So, a
man crying may be described as acting like a baby or 'being
a baby'.   This provides the conventional strength of the
category-boundedness.   Equally, then, a child fighting may
be described as 'fighting like a soldier', a person told to
'grow up' is being implicitly attributed with childishness (or
child qualities such as immaturity), a person who loves eating
Italian food may be described as an Italianized person (cf.
Anglicized, Arabized, Americanized, etc.).   We know, of
course, that only women have babies, hence the point of the
ad in an English birth control clinic showing a pregnant man
and of the many film comedy situations trading on this where
men are placed ambiguously – for some of the film's characters
– in maternity contexts, etc.

The point, then, is that in our very conception and knowledge of what it is to be a baby, a soldier, a child, a woman
and an Italian, etc. these other features have their place.

It is not the case that our use of these category-bound features in interaction then depends on and displays the literal implicit form: All $X$ are/do $Y$. Rather, where we encounter an $X$, the being or doing of $Y$ is *programmatically relevant*, so that where it is not found, *an explanation or redescription is required*. Often, judgment follows hard on the heels of explanation or redescription. However many exceptions there are, they are still subsumed under the rubric of category-boundedness and do not *challenge* its basic validity. But the rubric of category-boundedness of this kind emerges clearly thus as a *normative* one. Indeed, we see once again how deeply normative is the organization of our knowledge of the social world. In the case of category-organized *belief*, however, exceptions may indeed be used or allowed to challenge the validity of the status of substantive features as being category-bound.

When, then, may prejudice be routinely located in this sort of case? It is precisely in the formulation of *normative expectations* or obligations, or the formulation of judgments, either of individual cases or more generally. For, although our knowledge of membership categorizations provides for such specific features as being programmatically relevant for certain categorizations, their absence does not impose or entail a *negative* or *positive* judgment. An explanation may suffice; a redescription may do. For example, a woman who has been married for five years and has had no children may simply explain that she does not *want* any children. This may suffice - it is when having or wanting a baby is treated as normatively constitutive of being a woman that a charge of, say, 'sexism' (unfair discrimination by gender) may arise, for in this context it is displayed in a negative judgment of the particular woman.

Thus, it is in the reformulation of the category-bound feature as a category-constitutive feature that 'prejudice' may be attributed or warrantably located by members. If the feature is seeable as one that is positive, then 'bias' may be read.

Contrastively, if a woman's not wanting children is viewed positively, for example, if she is seen as a woman of character and independence, then the category-bound feature of women giving birth to babies is not being treated as category-constitutive. The issue with 'knowledge' is not always that it is *correct* for all time but how it functions in our language games and our reasoning - its status.

However, we indicated earlier that in this area the issue of 'prejudice' is more complex. It is not with all categories that if their category-bound features (K) (category-organized knowledge ) are treated as category-constitutive that 'prejudice' may warrantably be ascribed.   For here again, whether and how this is the case depends on the logic-in-use of that particular category-concept, since these features are an integral part of our knowledge and understanding of these categories. For example, if a baby doesn't cry at all - and the inference is that there is something wrong with the baby or that the baby may not be a normal one ('crying' thus being treated as category-constitutive) - then 'prejudice' (or 'discrimination') is not warrantably or reasonably attributable, for the language game in which attributions of prejudice may be made is not congruent with the language games within which one may talk of real babies;  prejudice has to do with the sort of normative and moral inferences that in the logic of our language are not applicable to babies.

In the case of both category-bound features (B) and category-bound features (K), such features are not *only* treatable by members as displays of belief and knowledge.   Rather, in situ formulations and displays of category-bound features are used in the accomplishment of various practical tasks, e.g. making inferences, judging, contrasting and assessing, displays of understanding of prior talk, disagreeing, disqualifying, exhorting, persuading, commending, etc.   My interest here was simply to outline some analytically available properties of some category-bound features, which may in various and methodic ways surface as 'troubles' for members or be used by them as devices to accomplish various tasks.

# Chapter 6
# Ways of describing

In his 'How to Do Things With Words', J.L. Austin wrote:

the perlocutionary act may include what in a way are consequences, as when we say 'By doing $x$ I was doing $y$': we
do bring in a greater or less stretch of 'consequences'
always, some of which may be 'unintentional'. There is no
restriction to the minimum physical act at all. That we can
import an indefinitely long stretch of what might also be
called the 'consequences' of our act into the act itself is,
or should be, a fundamental commonplace of the theory of
our language about all 'action' in general. Thus if asked
'What did he do?', we may reply either 'He shot the donkey'
or 'He fired a gun' or 'He pulled the trigger' or 'He moved
his trigger finger', and all may be correct. (1)

Let us look closer at this issue of 'unintentional' consequences which Austin indicates. Although it may be correct to
attribute to someone the action (with a gun) that resulted in
the donkey's being killed (and, thus, in describing the action
in any of the versions that Austin provides), there are,
routinely, contexts in which attributing to someone an action
that *causes* the donkey's death cannot be transformed into
attributing to him the action of 'shooting the donkey' *without*
some problems arising. This is because the ascription of an
action conventionally involves the ascription of knowledge and/
or intention. Even if, therefore, one did not intend to
actually shoot the donkey when playing with the trigger, a
person may be described as having shot the donkey, since a
person may be expected to know that guns are dangerous;
indeed, one may say, 'He shot the donkey; it's a good thing
he didn't hit any of us instead!' We see, thus, that one of
the essential issues in action ascription is the ascription of
*responsibility*. And where knowledge (or the obligation of
acquiring such knowledge) is attributable, responsibility is
also attributable. Therefore, an action for whose consequences a person may be held responsible is attributable to that
person. In such cases, also, an expectedly relevant action
that is not undertaken may be seen as having been *withheld*,
and the withholding is itself seeable as an action. Take,
however, the following case. A man is given a gun and told
that it was unloaded by someone in a position to know (say
someone who owns it and had just finished cleaning it); more-

over, the man is invited to practise aiming at a target hung
up on a barn door.   In practising his aim, the man pulls the
trigger just to give himself the sense of 'the real thing' and
finds that he has fired a bullet which kills a donkey kept
inside the barn.   Can one describe this, with no further
accounting work and no problem, as 'He shot the donkey'?
Perhaps on the very spot and in the heat of the moment,
someone may describe what happened as 'He shot the donkey!',
but would we be likely to accept this description as an adequate report, later, on what happened?   Would we not be
moved, *if we knew the story*, to append to the description,
indeed reprovingly, 'by *accident*', since the description has
interactional consequences?

Another example, to sharpen the issue, would be the following:   suppose that in saying of someone 'She poisoned the
whole family' one simply means that the woman in question, by
pumping contaminated water to the house tank, had been the
agent of the family's drinking this contaminated water and
their being poisoned.   Clearly, however, if she did not *know*
or have reason to suspect that the water was poisoned, she
cannot be said to have 'poisoned' the family without further
clarification and qualification;   in that event, such a description would be routinely considered misleading, and deliberately
so, even if the family had died by poisoning, and no one else
had had anything to do with it.   In fact, irony is fashioned
out of such material:   while she thought she was doing them a
good turn by pumping the water up to their tank, she was in
fact setting a death-trap for them.   To say of this woman
simply that 'She poisoned them' is to *suppress crucially relevant detail for the description of the action* - qualifying
detail that would transform the very *nature*, but not the
*machinery*, of the action in question.   In including the consequences of the action in the description of the action, without
qualification, such that the consequences are constitutive of
the action category ascribed, the describer may then be engaged in implicatively over-attributing to the actor such
matters as knowledge, intention, responsibility, etc.   What
we would have is a problem of *over-attribution*.   And such
over-attribution is routinely a serious and delicate interactional problem, and a possibility which various legal procedures are partly designed to ensure against.

Now suppose that a man (let us call him Ken) shot another
man (John);   as above, if there is no way that Ken can be
said to have known, or suspected, that in pulling the trigger
of the gun he was holding a bullet would be caused to shoot
out and hit John, then to say simply that 'Ken shot John'
would be treatable as an over-attribution to Ken.   Nevertheless, this circumstance could be the basis for the development
of a problem in court.   In the witness-box, Ken can be put

into a bind when faced with a question such as 'Did you shoot John?'. He cannot properly answer '*no*', and he cannot genuinely answer '*yes*'. To predicate 'shoot John' of someone is to be involved in attributing some *specific* description to a *specific* person - it is *both* attributive and referential. Which dimension is to be attended to as a preference? If a simple yes/no answer is required from the witness (a device routinely used by court-room counsel), someone in Ken's position may be faced with a logic/convention disjunction: although there may be some dispute as to the manner and specifics of the description, there can be no doubt that these specifics, whatever they may turn out to be, can be predicated of no one else. To answer 'Yes' alone would be for Ken to be answering to more than the referential query and would involve him in permitting an over-attribution to himself of the action's consequences and intentions. To answer '*no*' is equally a problem - seeable as an attempt to delete the referential appropriateness of the description.

Suppose, however, that when Ken had pulled the trigger, he *had* intended to shoot John. To report what happened then simply as 'Ken shot John' would not (if Ken's intention was established) have any negative interactional fall-out for the speaker. (Indeed, what might remain an issue is whether Ken 'murdered' John - if that were the description provided, then it might still engender debate in some circumstances.) Suppose, moreover, that it is also true that John is 'the President'. Then the description 'Ken shot the President' is ambiguous with respect to whether Ken simply shot John and the speaker knows that John is 'the President' and describes him as such or whether Ken knowingly shot the President. To say 'Ken shot John (who happens to be the President)' is quite different from saying 'Ken shot the President', if the formulations were taken to indicate the *object* of Ken's action as he constituted it for himself. Moreover, the action, abstractly, of shooting a president is different from the action of shooting any man, just as the action of killing one's mother is different, morally and practically, from the action of shooting just any woman. This kind of ambiguity rests precisely in the availability of different forms of reference that can be made of persons (different ways of categorizing them and referring to them), all of which may strictly be accurate. (This ambiguity is, of course, also available for other classes of referent than persons.)

The above kind of ambiguity in reference is formulatable in terms of *transparent and opaque contexts*. Fodor writes:

Opaque ascriptions are true in virtue of the way that the agent represents the objects of his wants (intentions, beliefs, etc.) *to himself*. And, by assumption, such representa-

tions function in the causation of the behaviors that the
agent produces.... So, for example, to say that it's true
*opaquely* that Oedipus did such-and-such because he wanted
to marry Jocasta, is to say something like (though not, perhaps, *very* like:  see Fodor (1978)):  'Oedipus said to himself, "I want to marry Jocasta" and his so saying was among
the causes of his behavior.'   Whereas, to say (only) that
it's true transparently that O. wanted to marry J. is to say
that among the causes of his behavior was O's saying to himself 'I want to marry ...', where the blank was filled by
*some* description that J. (and J. alone) satisfies. (2)

Using Fodor's example, it would not have been true *opaquely*
to say of Oedipus at an early part of the play that he 'wanted
to marry his mother', although it would have been true transparently.   However, it would have been true opaquely to say
'Oedipus wanted to marry Jocasta'.   At a later stage of the
play, however, it would have been opaquely true to say
'Oedipus plucked his eyes out because he killed his father
and married his mother.'

If we apply these concepts to our earlier example, we can
say that, if 'Ken shot the President' is said in an opaque
context, it would presuppose that the speaker knew that Ken
knew that John = the President before he embarked on his
course of action.   If this presupposition were untrue, it
would then only be true transparently to say 'Ken shot the
President'.   And much may hang interactionally on this.
The contexts of ascription are not always clear and available
to third parties, of course;  hence, if the ascription were
done in a transparent context without that being made available to hearers, the speaker would be involved in *over-attribution* and masks the fact that the identities that are relevant
to the speaker and informed his categorial selections were not
those relevant to the actor, on the performance of his action.

The notions of opacity and transparency can be applied to
reports of sayings and avowals as well as to doings and
actions.   Here another distinction serves:

... an interesting class of ambiguities ... discussed by
philosophers since the middle ages as the distinction between
*de dicto* and *de re* interpretation.   The sentence
    19  Willy said that he has seen the woman who lives at
        219 Main St.
is appropriate either to report Willy's having said something
such as 'I saw the woman who lives at 219 Main St.' (the
*de dicto* interpretation) or to report his having said something such as 'I saw Harriet Rabinowitz', where the speaker
identifies Harriet Rabinowitz as 'the woman who lives at 219
Main St.' (the *de re* interpretation).   This ambiguity is

brought out by the fact that the sentence can be continued
in two ways, each of which allows only one of the two interpretations:

20a   ... but the woman he had in mind really lives in
      Pine St. (*de dicto*)
20b   ... but he doesn't know that she lives there
      (*de re*). (3)

It is clear from this that the 'de dicto' is the opaque reading and the 'de re' interpretation is routinely the transparent
reading of reports on what persons have avowed.

Ryszard Zuber casts the issue in terms of an interesting
paradox:

First a short remark concerning the intentionality paradox.
As is well-known, in some contexts (opaque or intentional)
the substitutability of identicals or truth functionally equivalent statements fails, giving rise to a change in truth
values.   This result is sometimes considered as paradoxical
because of the general principle that the same predicates
should yield the same truth value when applied to identicals
(identical objects).   Verbs of propositional attitude are
examples of opaque contexts and (28) and (29) is a classical
illustration of the phenomenon:

28   *Caesar thought that Rome was on the Tiber*
29   *Caesar thought that the Holy City was on the Tiber*

These two sentences do not necessarily have the same truth
value despite the identity of the object denoted by the sing-
ular terms 'Rome' and the 'Holy City'.   But, following the
discussion above, (29) being a contingent sentence, presupposes (30) which is evidently false:

30   *It was possible for Caesar to think that the Holy City
     is on the Tiber*

This example makes the following point: any substitution
changes some presupposition and thus substitution in an
opaque context may give rise to false presuppositions. (4)

It is also clear that such a substitution may change the context from an opaque one into a *transparent one* and transform
what would be a de dicto rendition into a de re one, although
the actual status of the statement may not be available to
hearers.   Note, too, that while both the opaque and de dicto
accounts of a person's sayings and doings tell us something
about that person's beliefs, objects, etc., the transparent and
de re ones do not do so to the same extent.   The latter tell
us something about the speaker's beliefs, state of knowledge,
etc., *were we to hear them in their appropriate modality*; and
we *may* take them as telling us something about the world.
Fodor writes in this connection:

Ontologically, transparent readings are stronger than opaque ones: for example, the former license existential inferences which the latter do not.   But *psychologically* opaque readings are stronger than transparent ones; they tell us more about the character of the mental causes of behaviour. (5)

In giving descriptions, such ambiguities are systematically possible; if one were to take a description proffered in a transparent context for one meant in an opaque context (the manner in which the ambiguity more routinely arises), then *over-attribution* may become an interactional problem.

In both the sorts of cases we have discussed there is an embedded ambiguity of description.   This ambiguity is locatable either in the proposed relation between the actor and the action-as-described attributed to him or in that between the actor and his action's object-as-described.   This relationship may be systematically masked in the description and is a *cognitive* one.   The problem in interactional terms may be whether one is involved in, or heard as, attributing more to the actor than can be justified on the grounds of correctly attributable knowledge/intention or belief.   Such a hearing could be generative of a disjunction between the parties.

Such ambiguities may be routinely encountered in newspaper descriptions of events and actions.   And as encountered in these contexts (as opposed to the exemplifying contexts of theoretic discussions) they mask another equivocality.   Two examples will suffice.   In the media reporting on the Iranian Revolution of 1979 many of the descriptions were couched in terms of the Iranian people's opposition to 'modernization'. Now, if the reader or hearer does not know what context such descriptions are operating within, she may remain unsure whether the Iranians indeed saw themselves as opposing modernization, or whether they saw themselves opposing some *other* development or set of practices which the reporter identifies as 'modernization'.   However, unlike in many other examples of possible transparent substitution (such as those given in the philosophical literature), what remains ambiguous is also whether indeed these practices can be taken to be what *we* (or the reporter) would mean by 'modernization', and whether indeed the reporter really believes that these practices being opposed are what most people would mean by 'modernization' or simply wishes the reader to believe that. This is quite different from substituting 'Morning Star' for 'Evening Star', or 'Oedipus's mother' for 'Jocasta' in an opaque context.   The latter examples are of substitutions we generally know to be correct.   The assignable status of the speaker's belief is therefore not muddy.   In contexts such as the Iran description, the reporter may make a substitution which he alone believes and/or which he wishes his hearers to

come to believe as correct.    In contexts where the reader
understands the description transparently, i.e. understands
that a substitution in an opaque context has been made and
what the opaque referent would have been (e.g. that the
Iranians are opposed to 'Westernization' or to 'foreign influence'), it still will not necessarily be clear to the reader, if
she does not concede the practical identity of the referents,
whether the reporter is lying or believes falsely that x = y
(i.e. that 'foreign influence', 'imperialism' or 'Westernization'
= 'modernization').    These issues have been at the core of
much of the discussion, reporting and counter-reporting on
the Iranian Revolution.    Another example is drawn from the
descriptions given of the conflict in the Lebanese civil war:
'To drive the Christians out of their strongholds, the Moslems
last week also imposed a tight *cordon sanitaire* around Christian areas' ('Time', April 12, 1976).    The implication is that
the persons categorized (perhaps correctly) as 'Moslems'
wanted to drive out persons whose relevant identity for the
purposes at hand is 'Christian'.    Strictly, it is not ever
clear-cut, in such cases, whether the description is being
offered in an opaque or transparent context - i.e. do the
people involved in the offensive constitute the objects of
their offensive as 'Christian' or is it the reporter who identifies them as being Christian and uses this categorization?
The implication of an opaque context is strong, however, precisely because of the co-selection of the categorization
'Moslem'.    However, if the reader had reason to understand
the description as operating within a transparent context -
perhaps because earlier in the same report there is talk of
*right-wing* Christians, or of *Phalangists*, or mention is made
that within the forces indicated as being on the offensive
there were a number of Christians;    perhaps through independently held belief about or knowledge of the nature of the
conflict - then it is still an issue whether the reporter really
believes that there is an identity of referents here, i.e. that
x = y, for practical purposes, or believes so wrongly, or is
intending to mislead, or does not think it much matters.


## ELISIONS AND ACTION ASCRIPTIONS

Suppose that Ken, while playing with a gun, and believing his
gun to be empty, pulled the trigger and by consequence John
was hit by a bullet and killed.    Can one, in such circumstances, describe the event as 'Ken fired his gun', or 'Ken played
with his gun', or 'Ken did some shooting practice'?    One
would here have to provide for the consequences of Ken's
handling the gun, for not to include them in a description of
what happened would be taken as *hiding them* ('If you've done
nothing wrong, what have you to hide?!').    One would have
to say, in order to give a proper description (and not just a

literally correct one), something like 'Ken shot John while
playing with his gun', or 'Ken fired his gun and shot John
as a result', or 'Ken shot John by accident', etc.   We can
neither simply say 'Ken shot John' nor can we say simply
'Ken fired his gun'.   Both would be inappropriate - but
notice that the descriptions that we can appropriately provide
are descriptions of what happened rather than simply of what
Ken did or of Ken's action.   The description of the *action* in
such a context would be either over-attributive or under-
attributive;   what we are constrained to give is a description
of an action *plus* its consequences, or a *mitigated* action description ('by accident').   The grammar employed in constructing an account has to be shifted from a grammar of 'doings' to
a grammar of 'happenings'.

On the other hand, if Ken had intended to shoot John, we
still cannot say 'Ken fired his gun' - we would have to say
'Ken shot John', which is a *description of Ken's action in
terms of its consequences*.   Since the description 'Ken fired
his gun and as a consequence shot John' can be non-problem-
atically attributed to Ken, the description of the action can be
*elided* with the description of its consequences, in Eric
D'Arcy's terms. (6)   Suppose, however, that Ken is a member
of a cult and shot John to satisfy some macabre notion of
entertainment that the cult members subscribed to.   Ken's
action cannot, in these circumstances, according to D'Arcy, be
described such that it is *elided* with its consequences:   'Ken
entertained his friends'.   Such an elision of action description with the consequence of the action is *morally* inadmissible.
Just as it is an under-attribution to say of Ken 'he fired his
gun' when he had intended to kill John and succeeded in doing
so, and thus to exclude the consequences of the action from
the description of that action, so it is also an under-attribution to elide the action with its consequence so that we have
'Ken entertained his friends';   this latter elision, as D'Arcy
correctly points out, obscures the nature of the action and/or
the means used to attain it:

> Certain kinds of act are of such significance that the terms
> which denote them may not, special contexts apart, be elided
> into terms which (a) denote their consequences, and (b)
> conceal, or even fail to reveal, the nature of the act
> itself. (7)

To illustrate this, D'Arcy uses an example from the Eichmann
trial where it was said that a Nazi research institute had
asked a concentration camp commander to supply it with
infant bodies for its experiments.   To comply, the camp commander had a number of Jewish babies gassed.   D'Arcy
points out that to describe the commander's action as 'assist-
ing medical research' (even if scientific knowledge *had* been

advanced by the research) would not be admissible. As
D'Arcy puts it, 'in certain cases there is one point at least at
which an "act"/"consequences" line *must* be drawn'. (8)   He
formalizes some of his points (and this may also serve as a
preliminary formalization for some of the points emerging in
this text):

As a rule, then, the line between 'act' and 'consequence'
may be drawn at different points when the elements of a
given episode are being analyzed.   If *a* is the number of
relevant elements comprised in the term which is used to
denote the act, *c* the number of relevant elements comprised
in the term used to denote the consequences, and *t* the
number of relevant elements comprised in the description of
the whole episode, so that

$$a = t - c$$

then while *t* is of course a constant for a given episode, *a*
and *c* are variables. (9)

Therefore, there are 'values *below which a* does not extend'
and 'values *within which a* may vary' and 'values *above which
a* does not extend'. (10)   Let us try to put the matter somewhat more precisely:

| Action Ascription 1 | Action (Consequences) Ascription 2 |
|---|---|
| A   Shot John intentionally | Entertained his friends |
| B   Fired the gun | Shot John intentionally |

In case A one cannot appropriately go beyond description 1,
by eliding the action with its consequence to produce description or action ascription 2.   In case B, on the other hand,
one cannot stop at action ascription 1 and avoid its elision
with its consequence to produce action ascription 2.   We can
formulate the issues we have ranged over in the following
rule:

The moral ascription rule

In intentional-action ascriptions, the ascriptive vector stops at
the point of highest value of moral implicativeness.

We indicated that with *un*intentional and *non*-expectable consequences there are basically two alternatives;   the description
provided must be of the episode, rather than of the action, or
it must be a mitigated action description where the action is
not elided with its consequences but where the consequences,
if serious or of relevance, nevertheless have to be provided -

the *distinction between action and consequence is maintained in the presentation of both.*

But what of cases where the consequences are unintended and unexpected *but might have been foreseen or avoided* if some care or generally available knowledge had been employed? We pointed out earlier that action ascriptions have something to do, after all, with the ascription of responsibility for the consequences or the state of affairs that results from the action. If I throw a brick out of the window, not intending to hit anybody and even supposing that there would be no one passing underneath at that time, but I do hit someone on the head, causing his death, then I am still responsible for that consequence. And if his wife were to scream at me that I killed her husband, it would only be in a weak tone that I would be able to say, 'But I did not intend to'. People could still say of me that I 'killed him'. And in that they would be blaming me for his death. D'Arcy seems to intend just this when he writes that 'A more general point seems to be that X is elidable into Y to the extent that Y is the *anticipatable* consequence of an act such as X'. (11) We can recast our modal ascription rule into a second version to fit this kind of case, then.

The moral ascription rule (version II)

In action descriptions, the ascriptive vector stops at the point of highest value of moral implicativeness compatible with assignable responsibility to the actor.

An illustration of the above can be taken from the example of the brick; if, while in a rage, I pick up a brick and throw it, causing it to hit the window, the window to break, the brick to hit a man on the head, and the blow to kill him, I can be assigned responsibility for all these consequences; they are the sorts of consequences a flying brick may be expected to result in on some occasion, even if they are unintended. And *if that* responsibility is assignable to me, so an action incorporating the consequences for which I am responsible may be ascribed to me. But it still cannot be said simply that I 'broke the window' or 'hit a man on the head', suppressing the most important and morally implicative consequence: that the man was killed.

If, on the other hand, I had thrown the brick into a street after seeing that it was empty, it made a loud noise as it crashed, the woman next door was startled by the sound as she was climbing to reach for something from a high shelf, lost her balance and fell to the floor, breaking her leg, I cannot easily be assigned responsibility for her breaking her leg. It would be extremely misleading for someone to describe my action as 'breaking Mrs Brown's leg' or, if Mrs Brown had died by her fall, as 'killing Mrs Brown'.

Note two points about the rule as we have formulated it:

1 Responsibility is not something assignable a priori in fixed ways; the very assignment of responsibility is itself a complex matter for assessment and investigation on the occasions of its relevance. Much of the legal process deals with just this issue, even where explicit intention is not ascribable.

2 Persons may disagree on the relative values of different consequences and on the relative moral implicativeness of certain acts in context. This itself is taken to be morally 'revealing'. That there is widespread agreement on certain issues, and that the boundaries of disagreement are fixed by certain consequences, is clear. This still does not prevent the possibility of radical disagreements arising. A matter of interest here is the organization of compelling and hierarchized relevances and values. But some of these issues must await the next chapter.

## TEMPORAL ELISIONS

Let us now turn our attention to a different sort of elision in the description of actions. Take the following data (S.T. Data A11-12):

Q: May we take it then, Doctor, you accepted the assurances of certain people living in the vicinity of I suppose the lower Falls, as a general term, that there was a necessity for this clearing station on the 13th?

A: It was not - well, any post that was set up - it was not a clearing station then, it was purely a first-aid post on the 13th.

Q: Whatever we call it, a first-aid post or a clearing station, somebody on the 13th assured you this was a necessary step to take?

A: Yes.

The discussion (see the full data transcript in Appendix 2) between *A* and *Q* centres throughout this sequence on the question of the need for the actions of *A*'s Order in setting up a medical centre external to the hospital services during the troubles in Londonderry on August 13 to 15. As I read it, *Q* is attempting to *question* the authenticity of that need, or the claim that it could have been grounded in and occasioned by the observable details of the situation.  Through this $Q$ seems to be trying to constitute the setting up of that centre as something motivated by expectation or knowledge of some *forthcoming* state of affairs rather than as an answer to a *previously* perceived actual need.  $A$ is trying to deny or fend off that reading by providing for the authenticity of the perceived need (S.T. Data A5):

Q:  Did you ask from anybody why they thought this was necessary?

A:  If the personnel on the spot thought it was necessary, I would be quite happy to go along with it.

Q:  It appears, Doctor, rather than dealing with an imme-diate problem they were trying to anticipate a future problem;  is that not the position?

A:  Not really, no.    There were injuries.

In the former exchange (S.T. Data A11-12) one can locate one kind of machinery for accomplishing these tasks.    In that a first-aid post may be viewed as answering to lesser or milder forms of injury and medical needs than a casualty clearance station (commonsensically), $A$'s correction of $Q$ - that it was not initially a clearing station but a first-aid post - provides for a grounded and ordered transition or upgrading in response to needs as they developed.    $Q$ had all along used the setting categorization 'casualty clearance station'. But it is only at this point that $A$ corrects it thus.    I sug-gest (again commonsensically) that this is in part grounded in the manner that $A$ justifies the need for the centre   (S.T. Data A7):

Q:  What I am trying to get from you, Doctor, is whether this problem on the Wednesday, that is on the 13th, could not have been dealt with by the ordinary hospital services;  why it was necessary to set up this quite exceptional, as it were, clearing centre?

A:  I think if there is a problem people are not going to go from the Falls to the Royal because you get a scratch with a stone or something like that, and this chap who belonged to the area - he did not live there actually but his mother lives there and he was visiting and saw that there was the necessity, that these things were neces-sary, that treatment on the spot could be given instead of going to the hospital.

Given the *nature* of the injuries used to justify the need for the centre, its categorization as a casualty clearance station becomes a problem for its continued characterization as a centre answering to observable, rather than foreshadowed, needs. (Note in Appendix 2 *Q*'s insistence on the matter that the *hospital* services were not used.) Thus, the setting categorization which *A* substitutes is one tied into displayed need.

In the description of what the Order did then, in the description of the set-up (embodying an initial action taken, as well as a set of organizational practices), *A* is attempting to separate the final outcome/transformation ('casualty clearance station') from the initial intention and outcome ('first-aid centre'). In doing that he constitutes *Q*'s description as a temporal elision between a state of affairs $S_2$ at some time $T_2$ with time $T_1$. Let us put it this way:

| Action A $(T_1)$ | Action B $(T_2)$ |
|---|---|
| Description D(A) | Description D(B) |

If description D(B) is substituted for D(A) at time $T_1$ (to cover action A), then the latitude for providing for the reasonable or natural transformation of course of action A at $T_1$ (or setting $S_1$) to B at $T_2$ (or setting $S_2$) is delimited. If a person P is described as having simply done D(A) and D(B), without any analysis into the separate temporal locations of each action (temporal parsing), a method often used in court-room settings, it is possible to 'delegitimize' the action D(B) by denying it its genuinely occasioned grounds. The natural and practical sequencing of the two actions is obscured, and so, therefore, is their methodic grounding in their natural and real context. The question is not simply of sequences in the abstract; not of A coming before B or after. Rather the temporal spread between the two actions, which accountably provides for their practical discreteness one from the other, is eliminated – it is this temporal spread that routinely directs us to look for separate grounds or reasons for each of the two actions (although some kind of relationship may nevertheless be maintained in the formulation of the two actions and their grounds). 'Time' is treatable by members as a *location*: specifically, as a location of intentions, motives and courses of action and events. A temporal location is a matrix of possibilities, of organizational and practical features that are resources both in the actual accomplishment of practical tasks and in the design of prospective or retrospective accounts of such actions, events and tasks. It is thus a locus for a variety of practical and moral trajectories. *To contract the temporal spread between two actions is to dislocate an action from its own grounds and constitutes an elision of the grounds for action A with the performance of action B,* **or** a *packaging of two separate actions under the* *same description, culminating in an upgrading or escalation in the character of the attributable reasons or grounds for acting* (since action B is thus cumulatively appended to action A). An illustration of the latter point may be provided by the following examples:

1 A: So you gave him the sleeping pills and you struck him.

   B: Well, it was after/

   A: Yes or no?

   B: I gave him the pills, but he did not fall asleep – he was full of energy ... he wouldn't fall asleep ... it was getting towards midnight, so I thought if I could knock him out some other way;  so I waited behind the door;  I didn't mean to kill him.

The suppression of the temporal spread between giving him the sleeping pills and striking him on the head provides for both these actions as displaying one determined and conjoined attempt to get him under, even perhaps to kill him.

2 A: So she gave him the sleeping pills and struck him on the head.

   B: No, not straight after ... *that* was three hours later.

   A: Oh?  So what happened?

The temporal unpacking of a sequence of actions, temporal parsing, is more than simply an academic matter.  Let us look at the following example (S.T. Data A27-29):

Q: The fact remains, Doctor, in the heart of the lower Falls, before the trouble had in fact escalated, there were preparations being made to receive very heavy casualties?

A: Well, they were not made by us or by anybody we know of, and as far as I know there were no preparations because the bandages and things that we got were from people having to tear up sheets initially before we could get to the hospital to get some.  People brought in sheets and pillowcases that they tore up, of their own.

Q: Perhaps it is a matter of emphasis;  some people might think that bringing in 12 or 14 beds and ringing up for doctors and nurses and so on is making fairly substantial preparation for casualties?

A: I do not think I should be a director if I did not anticipate problems. There is not much point looking for
beds at one or two o'clock in the morning if the trouble
escalated, as I felt it might, from the night before's
reaction.

The compression and temporal elision of the action of bringing
in the beds (performed during the day - see Appendix 2)
with the action of asking for the doctors (performed during
the night *after* the casualties started to arrive in serious
numbers) enables Q to describe both actions as 'substantial
preparation', whereas each alone might not be so describable.
That is to say, this elision allows him not only to select the
kind of description he needs to accomplish the task at hand
(i.e. to imply that the centre's activities were not simply the
response to situated need) but also to bring *both actions*
under the rubric of *one* description, a description that obscures the temporally located contextual variability of the
separate actions rather than a description that might preserve
their distinct features such as, for example, 'doing medical
work', 'helping the injured', etc. Indeed, the description
thus selected by Q provides that both actions are *in fact* one
action, performed on the basis of some presumed purpose or
desired consequence, and not separate actions sensitive to
emergent needs that have some specific character in common,
or some family resemblance between them. Thus Q is also
hearable as involved in an instance of over-attribution. Just
bringing in twelve or fourteen beds might be seen as a simple
precaution (after all, it was individual initiative on the doctor's part - see the data - and could be tied into his category-
tied obligations as a director); but doing that and ringing up
for doctors and nurses may well be seen as a more serious
undertaking, a more determined attempt at being prepared,
and prepared for something more serious. Such methods of
temporal elision are, of course, usable in building up a case;
the more items that can be attributed or collected under a certain description, the less easily defeasible becomes that description, provided there is some perceivable 'fit' between the items.

In this chapter I have been concerned with elucidating the
nature of practical descriptions of agents and their activities,
concentrating upon the intertwining of practical and moral
interests in the construction of accounts. We shall return to
take up some related matters in Chapter 8.

# Chapter 7

# The inferential environment of hierarchies and contrasts

Hierarchies are members' ways of ordering their relevances, their concerns and their values, in the course of the situated accomplishment of their daily tasks and the resolution of their practical problems. Where a hierarchy is procedurally constructed thus by members, it is done by reference to some standard and to some practical concern which sets that standard for the occasion. In other words, hierarchies both display and depend on a standard for their construction and use. Wherever there are standards, one finds that, generically and programmatically, there are also actual or available assessments. Such assessments, moreover, will sometimes be comparative and/or contrastive in nature. Therefore, we can assume that contrasts and comparisons are routinely occurring phenomena since the very fabric of speech and interaction is interwoven with standards and assessments, both moral and normative.

Clearly, I shall be neither concerned nor able to elucidate exhaustively the varieties of contrastive work and structures, nor all the relevant features of hierarchical work. That would be not only unrealistic, but misconceived. Rather, I shall attempt to show *that*, and *some of the ways that*, contrastive work is embedded in the normative and moral infrastructure of speech, reasoning and activity and that, indeed, contrastive devices are not only embedded in, but are essentially complementary to, categorizational work and the work of hierarchical ordering in the course of accomplishing interactional tasks, and thereby in the production and reproduction of social order. In other words, they provide complementary resources in the accomplishment of solutions to problems and puzzles in the praxis of daily life. To put it crudely: categorizations 'collect' features, hierarchies 'order' them, contrasts 'differentiate' them, and this ordering and differentiation of features takes place against an ordering and differentiation of tasks, relevances and values. Let us begin by considering a transcribed extract of data from a group therapy session in which the therapist himself was absent: (1)

F: Ye ... don't seem right to call him William outside here though does it?

C: Well, if you call him William in here you may as well bloody call him William outside.

For $F$, one may call the therapist (William) by his first name in the therapy session, but not outside.   For $C$, given that one calls him by his first name in the therapy session, one may equally call him by his first name outside that setting. Now, we may hear those two different formulations of permissible action in the following way:

1   For $F$, calling the therapist 'William' in that setting does not provide for that form of address elsewhere.   For $C$, it does.   $F$ is setting up a distinction between setting $S_1$ and other possible settings $S_n$ where he might meet the therapist. $C$ does not, on the face of it, appear to be doing that.   One possible hearing is that, whereas $C$ may be seeing a precedent, $F$ is not.

2   For $F$, then, it may be that the type of relationship operative between himself and the therapist in $S_1$ that provides for that form of address is not operative elsewhere.   $F$ may be orienting to a possible feature of mental health therapy sessions, where informality (first-name address) and the ability to talk about oneself (facilitated by first-name address) may be just such a feature of the therapy itself, and indeed the orientation to this feature may be treated as an index of one's understanding of, and willingness to enter into, therapy.   So $F$ would then be providing that, in some sense, $S_1$ is a *special setting*;   one where calling the therapist by his first name is especially provided for, and given the absence of such provision elsewhere, that form of address is not extendable to any other setting (presumably by the patients).   Conversely, we may say that, for $F$, $S_1$ is the type of setting where he may have most reason or permission to call the therapist by his first name.   Or that $S_1$ is the type of setting where it is particularly expectable that he might call the therapist by his first name.   Compare $F$'s utterance with the following example.   Suppose that a couple are seen arguing in public; it is routinely the case that in such instances other members deem such behaviour inappropriate, regardless of what they do in private.   Indeed, members may be heard to wish or recommend that such behaviour on the part of the couple be reserved for the privacy of their own home.   Such examples occur widely – some actions are 'all right', 'passable', 'adequate', 'expectable', even 'appropriate' in some settings *but not in others*.

3   For $C$, on the other hand, 'outside' may not be different from 'here' in any criterial way.   The informal mode of address is thus, according to this hearing, extendable to other settings.   What would admit the use of a first name for the therapist in $S_1$ is *not* absent in $S_n$.   $C$ may be seeing a precedent.   But a precedent has on each and every occasion for following it to be seen and made applicable to that

setting and that occasion.   In doing that one judges and
provides that the features of this setting $S_2$ are in a criterial
way 'the same' as those of setting $S_1$, where the precedent is
thus seen and provided for as having been established.   *C*
may be doing just that in her utterance.   Heard that way, a
*licence* to act is also heard as being formulated in her utterance, arising from the established precedent.

4   There is another, and perhaps stronger, way in which we
may understand *C*'s utterance, which is that she may in fact
be providing, like *F*, for a distinction between $S_1$ and possible $S_n$'s.   But, whereas *F* may be heard to have been
making $S_1$ out to be in some special way accommodating to an
informal mode of address, and therefore criterially different
from possible other $S_n$'s, *C* may, according to this hearing,
be making it out as in a special way accommodating to
forms of address such as 'Dr Lawrence', ones which orient to
the 'official' identities by which that setting was organized in
the first place.   Instead, it would be that *C* may be setting
up a *contrast* between $S_1$ and possible $S_n$'s.   Here, addressing the therapist by his first name in $S_1$ is in some way
'more of an issue' than doing so in any setting $S_n$.   If in
*that* setting, $S_1$, the informal mode of address is used, then
it may equally be used in other settings.   Since that setting
is particularly appropriate for forms of address *other than*
informal ones, then if the informal address is used *here* it may
certainly be used outside.

I want now to take up some implications of these observations.

Given *F*'s proscription in our data to the effect that calling
the therapist 'William' in the session does not entitle one to
call him 'William' outside, one might then take it that for *F* to
hear someone call the therapist 'William' *in* the therapy session would not provide him with grounds for inferring, assuming, taking for granted or expecting that this person, at any
time and anywhere that she meets the therapist, calls him by
his first name.   Moreover, it could be taken that, should *F*
hear that person call the therapist 'William' in some other setting, this would furnish grounds for him to assume the existence of special provisions or entitlements for that (for
example, that the two are actually friends), or to see the
person as cheeky, presumptuous, impertinent, a social climber
or some equivalent of these characterizations, depending, in
part, on the appropriate membership categorization that one
may relevantly find in the first place.   This possibility
derives, of course, from his use of culturally available conventions of category-bound and other entitlements circum-
scribing the first-name usage.

This brings us to a focus on the following point (which we

have already encountered both in our previous data and in
our analysis of it), namely, the relationship that obtains
between conventionally available entitlements and possible
inferences. Some notion of entitlements may be seen as
often *presupposed* in inferential work. Now, in this case it
is the *absence* of an entitlement that one can say is being
presupposed in the inferential work. To be more precise,
it is a normative constraint or proscription that is implicit in
the inference. An example of an entitlement's being presupposed would be where $F$ might know $X$ to be a friend of
the therapist, and therefore entitled to call him by his first
name, and he observes that $X$ does not do so. From this he
may infer that $X$ is trying to be formal, has had a quarrel
with the therapist or that they don't call each other by their
first names in front of patients, etc. Thus, what we have
here is an example of how 'moral notions' (to use a vague and
general term for the moment) get presupposed in some inferential work. Some aspects of this inferential work will be
examined later in much greater detail. For now, $C$'s utterance brings us to look a little closer at how this can operate.

If $C$ is providing that there are no critical differences between $S_1$ and possible $S_n$'s, then one can take it that, for her,
hearing a member of the therapy session call the therapist
'William' *outside* such a setting may provide for her that he
would do the same *in* the context of the session. And hearing a member of the therapy group call him 'William' in the
session may provide for her that he does so wherever and
whenever he may meet the therapist. On such a hearing,
one can take it that the real issue for $C$ might be getting
onto first-name terms at all. Once a patient has got onto
first-name terms with the therapist, then it may be a noticeable matter, indeed a surprise, for $C$ that the patient is heard
elsewhere calling the therapist by his surname. The specific
provisions for first-name address that $F$ may be heard orienting to as being operative within the session (and thereby their
character as *exceptions*) may not be oriented to by $C$ at all,
or at least not treated by her as exceptions that mark this
setting out from others.

If, on the other hand, $C$ is hearable as setting up a contrast
between $S_1$ and possible $S_n$'s 'outside', as I indicated earlier,
then it would seem that where one calls another by his first
name in a setting where it is particularly problematic, then to
do so in other settings is 'no issue', the 'no issue' character
of those settings being provided for hearers by virtue of the
implicit contrast. Thus, one can take it that, for $C$, to hear
a patient calling the therapist 'William' *outside* may not make
available the inference that he would do so during the therapy
sessions, where after all there is special business to attend to
and other patients to deal with, for which, perhaps, operating

a standard and formal therapist-patient relationship may be
most appropriate or preferred.   Hearing a patient calling the
therapist 'William' in the session, however, may provide for $C$
grounds for a host of inferences, such as 'He's trying to make
out he's friends with the therapist', or that he is emphasizing
his friendship with him, or that he's very relaxed and at ease
in therapy situations, or that he's being cheeky, or aggres-
sive, etc.   Moreover, it might be taken to provide $C$ with
grounds for inferring that he would no doubt call him 'William'
outside.   What we might then be entitled to take as being the
real issue for $C$, according to this hearing, is the matter of
getting to call the therapist 'William' *in the therapy session*.
It is clear here that a notion of 'appropriate' or 'permissible'
forms of address may be presupposed in inference as to how
someone might address another in various settings, based on
observation of that person's behaviour and/or (attributions of)
knowledge of that person's categorial incumbencies.   This
inference about another's action trades on the known-in-
common cultural conventions, *as well as the attribution to
the other of a reciprocity or mutuality of perspectives regarding actions*, especially those for which a latitude of
assessment may hold.   But let us note here that one may, of
course, observably make such an inference about another's
action, trading on knowledge of the other's notions of appropriateness without necessarily *sharing* in them;   however, it
may be that unless this is especially provided for, a hearer
might be able to invoke a conventional warrant for attributing
such notions to the speaker herself.

I wish here to emphasize a number of points:

1   The 'exact' hearing of $C$'s utterance is *not* the issue under
discussion;   whichever way one may hear it in terms of its
implied assessment of the features of setting $S_1$ ('in here'),
the point is that both hearings have this in common:   that $C$,
or those sharing her orientations, can move inferentially from
setting $S_1$ to settings $S_n$.   That is to say, whether $C$ considers $S_1$ and $S_n$ as essentially, and for the purposes of
address, of the same order or not, $C$ can expect that, if
someone uses the informal mode of address in $S_1$, then that
person will use it also in $S_n$.

2   What we would seem to have, then, is *the possibility of
inferences from actions that are seeable as disjunctive or
inappropriate to the settings within which they are performed
to a projectable performance of that type of action in other
settings*.   They work, if you like, as a lens, refracting and
thus 'fixing' the character, concerns, practices, actions and
relationships of the actor for others.   Such setting-disjunc-
tive or setting-inappropriate actions serve as a reference
point and conventionally provide for inferences to other such

actions. To take our earlier example, members overhearing
a couple having an argument in their own home would not be
surprised to see them treat each other amicably and with love
in front of others. But if they have heard them having a
big argument in public, they would not be at all surprised if
they also argued in private; indeed, it would be routinely
presumed that this happens. We can say that this would not
be a *discoverable* matter for members, but a routinely presum-
able one. It is still a *discoverable* matter, however, that
the couple overheard quarrelling in private would also do this
in public.

3 We have already noted the difference in $F$ and $C$'s implicit
formulations of the therapy session as a setting or occasion.
Both seem to be implicitly employing the standardized relational pair 'therapist/patient' in organizing their formulations and
their notion of appropriate behaviour. But they do it *dif-*
*ferently*, and differently, I suggest, in a very interesting
sort of way. The S-R pair, 'therapist/patient', is a locus of
a set of asymmetrical rights and responsibilities, knowledge
and need. We called it (in Chapter 5) an asymmetric category set. In treating the setting $S_1$ ('here') as being different from possible $S_n$'s ('outside here') such that it is appropriate to call the therapist by his first name here only, $F$ is
focusing attention on those aspects of the S-R relation which
*enable the patient* to call the therapist by his first name
here, but which are not present for him or her outside the
boundaries of that relation, where presumably first-name
address is returned to its usual framework requiring called-
person's permission. In other words, $F$'s focus seems to be
on the *patient's* needs and rights, etc. as organizing the
therapy session. $C$'s employment of the S-R pair, however,
seems to focus on the *therapist's* rights, status, etc., within
the therapy session, since the issue is that of the patient's
getting onto first-name terms at all with the therapist. It is
this asymmetry of focus between $C$ and $F$ that provides for
their different inferential horizons and their clearly different
displayed notions of appropriateness. This is an asymmetry
that, I suggest, is systematically available and grounded in
the very organization of standardized relational pairs; it is
an asymmetry that can develop into a full-blown disjunction in
the case of asymmetric S-R pairs particularly and be locally
generative of divergent moral positions on specific practical
matters. It represents a difference or contrast in the *pair-*
*relational focus*.

4 It is clear that both $C$ and $F$ are providing for a categorization of settings in terms of some action's inappropriateness
in inferentially generative ways. Hence, it is clear that settings, like persons, can be given various contexted, ad hoc
categorizations constructed by reference to the practical tasks
at hand and organized by their relevances.

5   Where $F$ makes a distinction between $S_1$ and $S_n$, he is
providing that distinction in terms of the *difference* of the
settings in relation to the issue of calling the therapist by
his first name.     There is an implied *contrast of difference*.
On the other hand, inasmuch as a contrast is heard projected
in $C$'s utterance, it is a *hierarchical contrast* between the
two kinds of setting in terms of the appropriateness of first-
name address.     (We will take up points 3 to 5 later.)

6   Suppose, for example, that someone is heard shouting at
his wife in a restaurant.     The following inference by members who are witness to this is both routinely accountable and
regularly occurring:   that if he shouts at her in public,
'imagine what he's like with her at home'.     That is to say,
the projection from an observed action in public to a possible
action in private is not restricted to the kind of action observed in the public setting.     Now, shouting at one's spouse in
public may be characterized as a setting-inappropriate action.
Members conventionally orient to moral constraints as operative in certain settings vis-à-vis various types of action, and
their contravention can provide an issue for members.     In
this example, we are trying to indicate that there can routinely occur an inference from such a contravention to the possibility that, where these constraints are conventionally weaker
(or non-operative), the nature of the contravention is exacer-
bated - for example, that the man would do more than shout,
perhaps even use very insulting language and may, on occasion, hit his wife, should he get drunk.     (Think here of the
saying 'I'd hate to meet him on a dark night!')     There are
fewer constraints on family members shouting at each other 'at
home' or in private than there are if they shout at each
other in the presence of other people or 'in public'.     Members then orient to the 'on-record' character of their own and
each other's public sayings and doings.     Moreover, given the
S-R pair 'husband/wife', the public display of such contravention comes off as a double failure of obligations and intensi-
fies the very character of that contravention;   one does not
shout at one's spouse in public since, amongst other things,
that may undermine one's position as a pair vis-à-vis others.
That members can be observed sometimes acting inappropriate-
ly, rudely and the like, *in public*, can be provided for as
strongly inferentially generative.     The use of setting-inappropriate actions as a device by members enables them *to extend
their inferential horizon not only along a descending order of
settings categorized and ordered thus by reference to that
action*, but also along an *ascending or escalating order of
possible actions in those settings*, thus *maintaining a consistency of evaluation of a person's in situ actions*.     Such a
consistency of evaluation, of course, often and routinely,
displays itself in character ascriptions.

7   Let us take another example of what may situatedly be
seen as a setting-inappropriate action.   If $X$ makes passes at
a secretary in the middle of an important business meeting,
one might conclude that $X$ is so attracted to her that he is
oblivious to the priorities or proprieties of a situation.
Alternatively, one might infer that he is in the habit of
making passes at women, or that he will almost certainly try
to do that at the firm's party that night, or that the rumour
one heard, that $X$ made a pass at $Y$ the other day in the
corridor, was probably true after all.   Such inferences may
thus provide, by implication, for the setting-inappropriateness
of an action and be treated as presupposing it.   And the
action projections involved in this may be accomplished *prospectively or retrospectively*, or the inference may be to
character or personality.   Such character ascriptions can
then serve as umbrellas for the ascription or projection of
other character-tied actions to a person.   And the character
ascriptions serve to underpin and provide a standard for
evaluational consistency, as we indicated above.

Before returning to our data, let us look a little more
closely at what we have so far, namely, the device of setting-
inappropriateness.   The question one might ask here is
whether this device is derivable from another positively formulatable one:  that is, do we need to look at setting-
*appropriate* actions?   Could we derive the former from the
latter?   What setting could be characterized as one where,
for example, flirting is appropriate?   A party, a picnic on
the river, a dinner for two, a chance meeting on a corridor
or lift?   It does not seem likely that one can locate and
specify a setting for which flirting is available as an appropriate activity – the party, picnic and so on are settings
wherein it is *permissible* that flirting be done, but they
cannot be said to be settings wherein it is expectable that
flirting will or should occur.   Again, are there settings
where, say, dressing is appropriate?   There are ways of
dressing that are appropriate for certain settings;   there are
some settings where it is inappropriate to dress, such as in
public places, but as long as there is no chance of being
seen it is 'all right' to dress anywhere.   Yet again, whereas
it makes sense to say that it is inappropriate to smoke in a
non-smoking carriage (indeed it is not allowed), it sounds
clumsy to say that it is 'appropriate' to smoke in an open
field.   One may say to people joking during a council meeting, 'This isn't a public house'.   But one would not conventionally say that to people joking at a party, over dinner,
travelling to work or in a myriad of other settings.   The
issue involved in the use of 'setting-inappropriate actions' as
a device *is not that an action typically appropriate to
another setting was performed in this setting and by virtue of
that is seen as inappropriate to this setting*, or provides

thus for categorizing this setting in terms of another's features, but rather that an action inappropriate to *this* setting was performed.   By virtue of that, of course, members may be seen as treating this setting as though it were another kind of setting (one in which typically or routinely that activity does get conducted). (2)

Which brings us to the distinction between setting-*inappropriate* actions and setting-*tied* actions.   Consider the following question:  'Did you go  to bed?'   This question can situatedly provide for an activity that is conventionally tied to bed;  the provision of the action in terms of some setting can enable one to hear the relevant activity being implied or presupposed, namely, sexual intercourse.   Another example might be 'What's she doing?', to which a proper answer might be 'She's in the kitchen', from which one could take it she is cooking or washing up, although one is not necessarily correct in this conclusion;  there remains here a latitude for possible activities that are typically done or doable in the kitchen.

The actions we have been looking at above are the kind that are evaluatively characterizable and circumscribable by *exceptions*.   The formulation of a setting-inappropriate action can be heard to be the formulation of a normative or moral breach. (There will be more on such issues in our last chapter.) Let us now return to a consideration of the issues arising from the data.

Presumably, a hearer of *C*'s utterance might warrantably take it, or come to expect, that should *C* herself begin to call the therapist by his first name in the therapy session then she would do the same 'outside'.   We located this kind of possible inference earlier as trading upon a hearing of a *hierarchical contrast* between one setting and another as being formulated in the utterance.   *F*'s utterance, on the other hand, provides for a different kind of contrastive understanding of the two settings.   Now let us consider an analogous kind of utterance as an example and see if we can further elucidate the issues:  'If he can repair the TV, he can certainly fix the fuse.'

It would seem to me that one conventionally possible contextualization of such an utterance (in other words, one routinely occurring usage) is that a hierarchy is being set up (an ordering) as between the capacity to repair a mechanism as complex as a TV set and the capacity to repair a fuse (or perhaps between the time it takes to repair one or the other, or the importance for the needs of the household, etc.).   Let us suppose that the notion of *skill* is the relevant one on some occasion;  then the former skill is being used to generate

the expressed inference to the latter skill – to project it.
A state of skill or practical knowledge is being attributed on
the basis of the observed capacity to repair a TV that would
*include* the capacity to repair a fuse.   Notions of hierarchy
and displays of hierarchical ordering can be employed as resources for generating contrasts – hence the sense of 'complex' and 'simple' in my own text above.   Such hierarchical
contrasts, as accomplishments, can be defeated by the invocation of a *contrast of difference*;   a hearer might choose to
point out that learning to repair a TV set's special mechanisms
may not include learning to fix a fuse at all.   Think of an
utterance such as:   'Well, if he can learn to do X, he can
learn to do Y'.   And the retort 'They're quite different
things!'   Often inferential work is accomplished and displayed
by members in the course of an interactional sequence in a
manner that trades on the observability of a hierarchy, as
seen in the following examples:

A:  Al repaired our TV set the other day.

B:  Oh, great!   I'll ask him to fix the kitchen fuse, then.

or

A:  He couldn't fix the fuse.

B:  Pity, ...  I was going to ask him to look at our TV.

or

He's not going to help a stranger if he doesn't help his
own brother.

In the latter sort of example one can hear a grading being invoked and displayed as between helping a brother and helping
a stranger, so that the inference to the possibility of the
latter is observably generated from the former.   Where X
doesn't help a brother, one may see it as likely that he will
not help a stranger in some similar predicament.   One way,
then, of hearing this is that a hierarchy of entitlements and
obligations is being invoked, where a brother is entitled to
and can expect help from a brother more than a stranger can.
It may be said that the notion of a hierarchy or ordering is
superfluous here, since a brother is treatable as a pair part
of an S-R pair whereby he has a set of rights and obligations
that are not present for a stranger;   in other words, that the
issue can be treated in terms of the absence or the presence
of rights and duties, and that such contrasts as are projected
in those terms (cf. in our example) are projected on that
basis.   This sounds reasonable, but absence/presence of
some feature or relevance may be treated practically by members as a kind of in situ *ordering grid* for which other items

may be found or fitted (on) at other relevantly provided positions on that ordering grid. For example, if someone were to say to the speaker of an utterance such as the one in our example, 'His brother doesn't really need his help', this would be hearable as a re-ordering of relevances in terms of some notion of 'need' to provide that the 'stranger/non-brother' may in those terms be placed in a higher order. This, however, trades on and displays that some person categorizable as 'stranger' may indeed have some rights and expectations (where the implicit categorization in use here is one such as 'person requiring help') vis-à-vis another, so that if his need is greater than a brother's, someone may attend to him rather than to a brother.

Hierarchies, then, can be traded upon and used, constructed and displayed in the production of priorities and agendas - 'I'll help you pack your books, but you'll have to wait till I've done mine' - where what comes first is not a contingent matter. The agenda can be said to be normatively organized, but in this it displays, as does our just prior example, *an interlocked pair of orderings – the normative and the procedural: the hierarchy of relevances and the order of consequences, where the second turns on the first.*

I want to emphasize some points here. Let us construct the following example (suppose we were engaged in writing a radio scenario):

1  A:  Where's John going to sleep, then?

2  B:  He'll have to go on the floor...

3  A:  He won't like that.

4  B:  Why?

5  A:  I put him on that old couch the other night, and he was grumbling the whole morning after.

6  B:  Well, that's bug-infested, the floor isn't.

Turns 1 to 5 can be treated as providing for a hierarchy with couch and floor graded in terms of sleeping comfort, where that hierarchy is locatable by virtue of the *inference* provided. Turn 3 is constituted as an accountable inference by turn 5 by trading on the observability, in this sequence, of the hierarchical contrast of 'couch' to 'floor'. If John found sleeping on the couch a complainable, he would also find sleeping on the floor a problem. Commonsensically, 'couch' and 'floor' are provided for as being contrastable in the *degree* of sleeping comfort afforded by them, where the couch is being produced as 'uncomfortable', yet still a 'higher-comfort' item, i.e. higher up in the order. Thus, any member of a formulated hierarchical contrast set can be demonstrably and accountably used to display beliefs or to generate expectations and inferences of one kind or another about possible actions, responses or behaviour vis-à-vis the other member of the set. The following kind of inference, for example, can be made: that X won't mind sleeping on the couch because he is normally happy sleeping on the floor, where the floor is being constituted as uncomfortable and the couch less so.

Action located at one point of a hierarchy, *by virtue of the inference observably being drawn*, can be made to provide accountably for the possibility of action thus located at another point on the hierarchy. If X (for example) can sleep on the floor, he can sleep anywhere. But where the relevant feature is formulated or assessed in 'negative' terms (as in the case of setting-inappropriate actions), *the inferential vector moves conventionally only along one direction; from a point located by the speaker higher up on that hierarchy to a point located lower down.* (3) The hierarchical contrast in these cases is accomplished by virtue of inferential work, but is itself the machinery by which that work is made observable and accountable, the two are reflexively tied to each other.

In response, a second speaker might, as B does in turn 6 of our example, make sense of the first speaker's usage of a hierarchical contrast device although displaying what is hearably a disagreement as to its applicability in this particular case. This is done by invoking a *contrast of difference*, in our example between floor and couch, where the latter is made out to be bug-infested. This difference can be heard as defeating the inference A provided for by the use of the hierarchical contrast. *Contrasts of difference are conventionally usable to defeat the use of hierarchical ordering devices* and are not usable for the same kind of inferential work as the latter. B in our example might wish to undercut the relevance of the hierarchy set up by A and provide for a different one using an alternative feature of the items used in setting up the hierarchy. Or alternatively he may wish to reverse the hierarchy: to provide for a 'proper' reversal of the positions of couch and floor in the hierarchy, by reversing the relevance or consequence of the feature or attribute used to set up the original hierarchy. An example of the former procedure might be were B to answer in turn 6, 'Well, the floor's much cleaner, and I know he's fussy about that.' An example of the latter might be where the attribute of hardness (or sleeping comfort) hearable as organizing the hierarchical ordering in our original example is informed by the

relevances of someone who, for instance, has a 'bad back';
so that, instead of the couch being placed as higher in order
to the floor in terms of comfort, because it is softer, it is
placed lower in the order for precisely that reason. Thus,
we see two things from this example:

1 In focusing on a different feature from the one originally
used to establish a hierarchy for some items, and in order to
defeat the relevance, force or propriety of that hierarchy,
one may use this new feature either to formulate a contrast of
difference (the couch is bug-infested; the floor isn't) or to
set up an alternatively relevant hierarchy (the floor's cleaner
than the couch).

2 Relevance organizes the ordering of a hierarchy by feature:
indeed, one may map an order of relevance onto an ordering
of items by feature to reverse the *upshot* or significance of
that feature in context (hardness, sleeping comfort).

Let us now look at our data again, and briefly make some
last remarks on it:

F: Ye ... don't seem right to call him William outside here,
though does it?

C: Well, if you call him William in here you may as well
bloody call him William outside.

F: Ehahaha ... yehehe.

1 Although $F$'s utterance seems to be proposing that there is
some distinction between setting $S_1$ and setting $S_n$ it is not
available to hearers whether indeed this is because $F$ orients
to the two sorts of settings as simply different or whether he
orients to a hierarchy of settings but one ordered such that
$S_1$ is lower on that hierarchy (constraint on calling the therapist William, since he requires it in the session), and thus
activities performed there or rights acquired there cannot be
projected onto $S_n$: the inferential vector does not conventionally move in that direction. But in the latter case, the hierarchy, if one is being oriented to, *is systematically masked
from hearers, by virtue of the unavailability of inference or
action-projection.* It does not, therefore, make any practical difference for the purposes of this analysis.

2 We remarked earlier that according to one hearing there is
an implicit difference in the pair-relational focus between $C$
and $F$. One may say, as an initial observation at this point,
that it is this focus shift that provides for the ability to
generate a hierarchy in response to $F$'s distinction and provides for the character of the exchange as an '*assertoric*

*sequence'* where disagreement is articulated. This notion is
taken from Jeff Coulter; (4) he identifies assertoric sequences
as a basic sequential structure. The assertions he is involved in analysing are declarative assertions, and the base
structure he outlines is: assertion-agreement/counter-asser-
tion/disagreement token (adjacency pair alternates), with re-
assertion or backdown as major options following counter-
assertion. If we look at the data we can see that it can be
treated as an example of an assertion/counter-assertion
sequence; in producing a counter-assertion to *F*'s assertion,
*C* has made a *topic-relevant focus shift*. I wish here only
to indicate that such topic-relevant focus shifts are routinely
a feature of disagreement and argument sequences as well as
of discussion sequences. In our data, the focus shift we
have identified is a pair-relational shift which can routinely be
transformed into a full-blown disjunction. There are other
kinds of focus shifts that may be operated in conversation.
We said earlier that membership categorizations carry a cluster
of conventional features with them; we also indicated a form
of categorizational disjunction which we called category-feature
or context-of-use disjunction, by which a disjunction over a
category feature may arise in terms of whether it is bound to
or constitutive of that category or not. However, even in
the absence of disagreement over which features are bound to
or constitutive of a membership category in question, a different set of relevances may inform which features of those
bound to or constitutive of the category should be the focus
of topic-related talk, e.g. the rights *or* duties of a spouse
vis-à-vis a certain issue. One may have a discussion or
argument arising contingent on this. Focus shifts of these
kinds provide for the orderliness and accountability of disagreements, transformations on the sense of the talk, reorder-
ing of items and relevances, etc.

A rather complex example of topic-relevant focus shifts is
available in Jeff Coulter's data (although he attends to different analytic issues). In the following sequence John is repri-
manding Mary (both residents of a half-way house) for getting
up late every day and wasting her time.

27 John: N'd you'd just got up at eleven o'clock and you
were back in bed at one and I asked you why
you were in bed ... at two an' you said you
were depressed an' I said O.K. you can be
depressed standing up now ouda bed 'n' I had to
come back up - up an hour later to do the same
thing.

28 Mary: Is this a house or a hospital anyway?

29 Paul: Both.

30   Mary :   Both?

31   Paul :   Mm hm.

32   John :   W-wrong it's a house ... I'd do the same thing
for my brother if he were in bed since I don't
have any sisters I have to put it on that level.
(2.0)

33   Mary :   So *I* would do the same thing if I were in a
hospital.
(1.0)

34   John :   Well, O.K. -

35   Mary :   - (as if I'm sick)   (    ) I'm *depressed*.

Mary's question raises the relevance of the settinged-tied
S-R pairs:  family member/family member and doctor (nurse,
etc.)/patient.    The former is a symmetrical pair, the latter
an asymmetrical one (in which the patient's needs are routinely
defined by the incumbent of the professional category, and
her freedom circumscribed by him).    In John's answer ('a
house', utterance 32) he provides for the relevance of the
symmetric S-R pair, but instead of focusing on the *rights* of
incumbents of such a pair, he focuses on the *obligations*,
enabling him to say, 'I'd do the same thing for my brother'.
Mary, in response, shifts focus explicitly to the setting categorization 'hospital' (made available in Paul's answer, 'Both',
utterance 29) and implicitly not only to her *right* to rest, but
also to her *need* for it;  thus strongly reasserting the warrant
for her previous position 'I - I *do* need my rest' (which occurs
earlier on in the data sequence).    It is clear how such focus
shifts are methodically available due to the organization of
category features.

Throughout our discussion of these topics, we have encountered the pervasively normative and moral character of members' practices.    It is now time to address ourselves to some
philosophical considerations in the light of our analytical
observations so far.

Chapter 8

# Rationality, practice
# and morality

In this final chapter I shall be concerned with marking out
some issues that are of relevance to, and emerge from, the
problems and questions we have been addressing so far.
The treatment that I shall give these issues will be much less
than exhaustive, for they are deserving of a detailed and
independent study themselves.    I shall be content to indicate
some directions for further analysis and study that I believe
to be necessary in this field, and some of the points that
seem to me to arise from the logic and substance of our
earlier discussion.

Throughout the previous pages we have seen how moral
matters - standards, criteria, judgments, implications, etc. -
are bound up with various other practical matters - categorizations, descriptions, inferences, etc.    It is not the case
that this relationship is between something called a description
or a fact on the one hand and a moral notion, or a value, on
the other hand.    Rather, as we have seen, description (and
'fact') rests for its character and specifics on moral and other
normative standards;   for members it is routinely and unproblematically constituted that way.    Action ascriptions,
action projections, inferences, competences, expectations,
judgments, descriptions of 'what happened', etc. are organized through and through in a moral way, and with respect to
moral or other normative standards.    Some of these other
normative standards have to do with issues of rationality that
are not strictly moral as well as normative standards operative
for certain language games and domains - science, aesthetics,
logic.    Whichever way one may delineate other kinds of normative standards for rationality, however, *in practical life*
(as distinct from the theoretic pursuit of domain-specific
tasks) it is difficult to draw hard and fast lines between the
operations of moral and other normative standards.    As we
indicated above, and elucidated earlier in the text, *competence* for some categories of person is routinely bound up with
moral assessments of performance, for the very description of
a person as a doctor or a mother provides for certain obligations that are treatable as constitutive features of that description.    Here I would like to look briefly at a phenomenon
of members' practices that displays the interrelationship, *in
practice*, between rationality and morality in a particularly
interesting way.

Take the following extract of court-room data:

The Defense: Suppose after that interview you had been told and believed that on two occasions in two different homes Stewart tried, actually tried, to put his little baby in a burning fire and was prevented only by physical intervention by at least one person, maybe two or three, and that on another occasion he gave every indication of wanting to throw his baby out the window and was again prevented only by physical force from doing so; suppose you believed he did those things, would you classify him as normal? (1)

The defence's question about the subject's 'normality' or rationality is tied into the description of supposed actions - a serious attempt on two occasions fatally to harm his own baby. (2) In part, it is the special ties expected to exist between the standardized relational pair parent/child that make accountable the strength of the moral breach provided for in this talk. To throw babies into furnaces at all is not ordinarily justifiable or excusable. But it is done recurrently in some circumstances - by soldiers in wartime, by guards in concentration camps, etc. The descriptions provided routinely for such actions are that they are savage and that the persons committing them are vicious, brutal, depraved, etc. We refer to such persons as 'inhuman'. What we do in such circumstances is condemn them *morally* (if we hold, that is, to a certain morality); or at least by condemning them we exhibit our shared moral auspices. But in this case, apart from the fact that there is no wartime context to provide, if not the grounds, then at least an environment of possibility for such actions (and a *collective* framework for them (3) that makes it difficult to judge each person's actions on *their own grounds completely*), there is an added dimension. To throw one's own baby into a burning furnace, when one is expected to love that child in the first place or at least to discharge one's responsibility of caring and providing for him, may be seen to be a very great moral breach indeed. Here we have *not only a proscriptive breach but also a prescriptive breach*; it becomes treatable as a breach that is not understandable at all. The person committing it becomes a candidate for insanity ascription, for being seen as 'irrational'.

Let us unpack some of the issues involved. Rationality is bound up with the grounds for action (necessarily but not exclusively). Any person found killing any baby may become a candidate for the ascription of irrationality; babies are not treated as actors, nor therefore as providing rational grounds

for such behaviour towards them.   Given the category-tied
features of 'baby', the sorts of actions that may be taken
towards them are not routinely ones where killing is an
understandable, if condemnable, action.   Killing one's own
baby undercuts even more the availability of rational grounds
as an account for the action.   The behaviour of soldiers in
wartime may be on occasion somewhat differently treatable
since, as noted above, where a group of persons engage in
such activity, it is difficult to attempt to ascribe insanity
*collectively*. (4)   Therefore they are judged to be barbar-
ians.   We also judge the concentration camp commandant who
sends scores of babies and children to the gas chamber daily
to be criminally depraved and brutal.   But don't we, in
some contexts, also call him insane?   Has Hitler, for example,
not been described as insane?

Let us approach the subject from a different direction.
Who are the 'criminally insane'?   Routinely we will find that
they are persons who have killed for what are considered to
be reasons that are not good enough or for no reason at all,
except the wish to kill.   It is not that such persons are
automatically seen to be 'insane' by all and sundry;   rather
they become candidates for such ascription, for their actions
are deemed to be 'irrational'.   But compare these to other
persons categorized as 'insane';   we will find that in this
case the issue is not one of logical intelligibility but of *moral
acceptability*.   Or, in other words, the intelligibility of an
action is bound up, ultimately, with standards and criteria
and here, in *this* case, we are talking of *moral* standards.
But unlike logical criteria, moral standards, although shared
to a large extent, are also standards on which we can *take a
position*.   Therefore, they are changeable, and are standards we can disagree on.

What we are doing when we label some killer 'insane' is
saying that he has no acceptable (and *in this sense* understandable) reason for killing.   But we are not logically
obliged to treat such a person this way, and routinely, whilst
treating such persons as criminals responsible for their
actions (the Nazi leadership, for instance), we will still call
them 'mad' in the contexts of *other* language games we may
play with respect to these actions of theirs.   When we do so
we are drawing our boundaries of *membership*.   It is not
simply drawing the boundaries of moral membership as when
we call someone 'inhuman' or treat him as 'deviant';   we are
going further – we are almost calling that person non-human;
*we are drawing the boundaries of rational membership through
the use of a standard of moral membership*.   In other words,
we are denying that person the status of membership at all.
But this need not be the case;   for although his actions are
treated as morally unacceptable, and we may say that they are

'incomprehensible' or 'unintelligible', we can, and routinely do, on other occasions, treat such actions as intelligible - they are moral actions after all and not mistakes in calculation, or colour-blindness, or a belief that one's head is in the basket on the table. They have a different logic. An example of a court-room sequence dealing with this issue is the following:

The Witness: And much of his hostility was - practically all of his hostility was directed outward against other people.
At this time, this last test, there was no evidence on any tests that showed this boy had any feeling of conscience or regret; he was completely swallowed up with thoughts of hostility, of vengeance, of being captured, and escape, and electrocution, and all etcetera, associated with his present life.

The Defense: Mrs. Kirby, doesn't this make him as identifiable as easily as a bad boy as a sick boy?

The Witness: No, because of the difference in the strength of the ego from the two dates shows that this boy has lost control, voluntary control of his behaviour. Also that his intellect has been so warped by his fantasy that he no longer sees things as real, as they actually are; he no longer interprets reality as it actually is.... (5)

The above data clearly indicates that certain actions are treatable by members equivocally as evidence of either being 'sick' or being 'bad'. That is to say, the very same action that is treatable as being evidence of 'irrationality' can be treated intelligibly as simply a morally 'bad' action. The witness in the above interchange provides 'psychiatric' evidence of irrationality in other domains in order to defeat the interpretation of 'badness' and provide instead for that of 'sickness'. The point is that where an action is deemed morally so groundless, so unacceptable, that membership is denied the actor, through the ascription of irrationality, then paradoxically this ascription serves to excuse that actor from full responsibility for his action, from moral responsibility. The choice for members then becomes whether he is to be made to carry this responsibility or not, and the language games tied up with such cases are regularly tied up with the issue of responsibility.

The question is, just because we find some actions or set of actions horrendous, terrible, actions that we would not or *could* dream of doing, or for which we can find no practical mitigating or qualifying conditions, does that mean that others who do them are to be treated as morally not responsible for them? As excused from their consequences? When we say yes, we are saying that such actions fall entirely outside our collective standards, that their agents cannot be seen to be genuinely acting as moral agents (nor, therefore, as rational agents). But some will, and do, say no. Look, for example, at the following extract of data from an article by John White called 'Guilty is Guilty, Insane or Not':

We can agree that Jim Jones was insane, but does that mean that if he had lived he should have been found not guilty by reason of insanity? Or Adolf Eichmann?

The Nuremberg trials declared loud and clear that people must be responsible for their acts, even in time of war. Trials in America today, however, declare that people are *not* responsible for their acts because their state of mind excluded reason. Consequently, criminals have been handed legal means to get away with murder....

Legislators should correct this most gross miscarriage of justice - a miscarriage based on the foolish idea that your state of mind has a bearing on your innocence or guilt in criminal proceedings. If you did it, you're guilty - period. Whether you remember doing it or whether you could make a rational decision at the time doesn't matter at that point in the proceedings. Your state of mind and other possible mitigating circumstances should be taken into account only in passing sentence. Irresponsible behavior can never be condoned to the point of murder. ('New York Times', February 25, 1979)

I am not trying here to take one position rather than another - I am merely showing that either position is logically intelligible, that the same action-in-context may be treatable as either simply 'immoral' or 'irrational' as well and that, routinely, the judgment as to which way to treat some criminally constituted action and its agent is often dependent on other matters (evidence and criteria ultimately *external* to the action and its immediate context, e.g. tests and psychiatric examinations, etc.). The disagreement on *how* to treat such a case (6) is not ultimately resolvable through the ascription of irrationality to one of the disagreeing parties. If one party (prosecution, a witness, a juror, a layperson) insists on seeing, and demanding, that that action be treated as one for which the agent was morally responsible (possibly thus denying the status of 'irrationality' to the actor), and if another party insists on seeing that actor as 'irrational' as evidenced by that action, the disagreement is itself a *moral one*.

If one were to disagree with the writer of the above text, for example, the outcome of that disagreement would not sensibly be that the position is itself, say, 'irrational' in a *logical* sense, but would simply be a *moral formulation* of the position.   And vice versa.   If, on the other hand, someone were to claim that he was Napoleon, and a disagreement arose between two parties as to whether this person was rational or sane, then the disagreement would be seeable by one party at least as *itself* being illogical.   Anyone who believes that a person who seriously claims to be Napoleon is sane is himself open to the ascription of the same irrationality or insanity and on the same grounds.   In the above text, the writer is clearly using the notion of insanity as a *moral judgment*, for he uses it side by side with the ascription of responsibility to the actors.

What I am trying to elucidate are some of the moral grounds and criteria for the ascription of rationality and irrationality to an agent.   And to point out that there remain, therefore, some moral grounds for challenging such ascriptions.   Jim Jones is an interesting example. (7)   Although some people may call him *mad*, he would claim for himself and his beliefs the status of an *alternative moral system*.   Another very striking example is the case of the Moors Murderer, Ian Brady, in Britain.   In this case, despite Brady's arguments during the trials that he was an ideological sadist, there was an argument made for his insanity on the grounds of his terrible crimes - indeed, his insistence that his actions were taken on the basis of an explicit (if unacceptable) 'moral' view could be taken as further evidence of his insanity. Yet he argued for what he constituted as a different moral-philosophical viewpoint.

So it is clear that certain sorts of action can be seen as irrational on the basis of *moral grounds*, by which very same procedure that view could be challenged.   Moreover, in the very descriptions that provide for the *outright* and *complete* moral rejection of some actions (the ascription of insanity to the agent) such actions can be *excused*.   But this *is* part of our criteria of rationality, paradoxical as it may seem; such inconsistency is rooted in our very 'forms of life'. (8) There are no *ultimate external criteria* for the decision between such available judgments (even if we could acknowledge that in certain instances some person is working with an alternative moral system, we may still view *that* as insane), even though we may practically look for and find such criteria in particular contexts.   Which of two such judgments is made in any case is ultimately a *practical* matter, and various grounds can provide for its accountability for practical purposes.   This is not an attempt to simplify the procedures and standards whose use on practical occasions provides for the accountability of the outcome, but simply to indicate a basic feature of the logic of such available procedures - we are here at the point where rationality and morality *just are* intertwined.

Before moving on, I wish to indicate another interesting point about our reasoning with regard to 'deviant' or morally condemnable actions. We noted earlier how for homosexual activity, a person is characterizable by members as a *homosexual* if he engages in such activities for themselves and not for reasons outside that kind of activity, e.g. for money. Indeed, it seems as though the distinction between doing an activity for no specific reason outside that activity and doing it for a reason (purpose, motive, interest) *beyond* the activity itself is one that is regularly important for members in their categorization of persons. Now we find a further dimension to this. Certain reasons for action and certain actions by their very nature make relevant for members the ascription of insanity (Nazi concentration camp planners). Crucially and routinely, however, the person who, say, *murders for the sake of murder*, or for no reason other than that he wished to do it, or for some pleasure that the act of murder gives him, is a candidate for insanity ascription, whereas a man who murders for *profit or gain* is judged in explicitly moral terms alone. We will find, if we think of a list of *morally proscribed* actions, that this is a routine feature of our logic of reasoning about them; where they are done for no specific reason external to them a person (the agent) is judgeable as somehow irrational or abnormal. Homosexuality, in the past, has been treated as 'unnatural'; a person who steals for pleasure or for the sake of stealing may be categorized as kleptomaniac; a person who enjoys beating others is categorizable as a sadist; a person who just kills for no specific reason is categorizable as a psychopath. (9) In the past, in this culture, such actions may all have been treated as evidence of 'possession'. (10) Today, these categorizations are made to operate as various descriptions usable under the rubric of 'sickness', and some, like homosexuality, have in certain places been freed from this treatment. (This is essentially a denial of the status of moral choice to the agent's actions by defining not only what *counts* as membership, but indeed what can *be* such membership.)

We have seen how standards of rationality and standards of morality are intermeshed. They are intermeshed thus in practical ways, and the various language games we can play with the concepts of 'irrationality' and 'insanity' are tied up with practical purposes which provide the clue to what might seem to be, from our above discussion, an inconsistency in usage. Let us look more closely at the practical character of the interrelation between rationality and morality, using some other kinds of example.

In his book 'Moral Notions' Julius Kovesi discusses the
importance of moral principles in organizing our life - our
attitudes, problems, considerations and decisions about
actions. (11)   He gives an example of a sort of situation
that members may view as 'a predicament', to show how even
circumstances we consider extraordinary are thus for us by
virtue of our moral principles and notions, rather than
because we have none to fit the situation.

It is only by the help of moral principles or other moral
judgments, or at least by the help of complete or incomplete
moral notions, that an existentialist can produce his
examples of extraordinary situations where no principle can
help the moral agent to make his decision. (12)

But the example Kovesi gives can serve to make another
point.   He proposes the following scenario:  George is condemned to death by due process of law and Philippe is to be
the executioner;  but he is the only one who knows that
George is innocent of the crime for which he has been condemned.   He also knows, however, that George works for
the Gestapo and is about to discover who the leaders of the
local Resistance are.   Kovesi suggests that Philippe's predicament and his need to make a decision is intelligible in terms of
the principle that murder is wrong and asks if, knowing
George's innocence, Philippe would not be murdering despite
his *legal* right to execute George.   What I would like to
suggest is that, though Kovesi is right in principle, such a
situation as he instantiates would not in fact necessarily be a
predicament at all (if, that is, we sustain Kovesi's own
assumptions about the case).   Why not?   Because, although
morality is not reducible to *interest*, it cannot be totally
abstracted from it either.   Morality organizes our prudential
affairs and interests, but it is informed by them as by *our
forms of life*.   I suggest that in the above example, given a
context of war and occupation, given the implications of what
capture by the 'Gestapo' would mean, given that the total context would be perceivable as a struggle for, and about, life
and deeply conflicting basic interests, Philippe would not
necessarily (nor would anyone in his place) find himself in a
moral predicament regarding George, if he was sure he was a
Gestapo agent.   This is only possible as a moral predicament
for people *outside* such a *practical* situation of interest, and
indeed only if we were to think of Philippe *as a specific sort
of character*.   If George were a Gestapo agent, his execution
by the Resistance would probably be on the agenda *anyway*,
and the *practical interest* involved here is both constituted
by and a constituent of the moral stance.   It is *a moral
interest*.

What I am trying to say is that, by virtue of one *considera-*

*tion* (the issue of the Resistance and the Gestapo), the *other* consideration (whether to execute George for another crime despite his innocence) is *practically* overshadowed, so that there is no necessarily real predicament at all.   And indeed, if Philippe were to return without having executed George, he would be considered by others who share with him, at the very least, an interest in protecting the Resistance and fighting the Nazi occupation, as someone who doesn't really place that much value on it after all and/or as someone who *does not understand the situation*.   Genuine moral predicaments are not abstract issues of principle - they are practical matters.   Let me give another example.

Take a man who undergoes torture but will not tell the torturer what he wants to know - the names of his comrades, for example.   He maintains his silence in the face of absolute pain and the risk of death.   We *recognize* the reason for his fortitude; we recognize its 'virtue'.   He wishes to save others the same fate, perhaps even to protect the entire process of a cause he believes in.   We can admire him.   We call him courageous and we can recognize his courage even if we did not share his cause.   But take a man who will not speak - to save a puppy.   We would find him 'crazy', 'irrational'.   We even find it difficult to imagine such a situation. We can imagine a situation where a man might jump into the water to bring out an injured dog, but what would we think of him if he decided to jump into the sea to save this dog when he could not swim at all?   We would not think of him as 'right' or 'wrong' morally - we might say that he 'lost his head', or we would think him irrational even as we might marvel at his loyalty;   we might even think that he was imbalanced or at least did not possess enough intelligence.   Or take the man who will not tell a lie at the risk of being put to death.   Well, how we judge that depends on the lie - if a little unimportant lie would do the trick, and he refuses to tell one 'on principle', then for us he may be 'irrational', even though he may be 'acting on principle', unless there are other serious considerations involved.   Of course, 'we' and 'for us' already here demarcate a specific set of shared moral auspices that tacitly define the parameters of rational membership.   In finding someone 'irrational' for such reasons we are displaying and relying on *our* criteria of membership. The general point remains, however.   It is clear that 'acting on principle' in abstraction from the practical assessments of relevances and consequences is not enough;   it is not a standard which members routinely use.   'Acting on principle', the use of principles and values, is itself a matter of evaluation, and evaluation in terms of other values and ends.   And *not* in an arbitrary but in a deeply embedded and integral way.   The *relevance* of a specific principle in a situation is a matter of practical moral judgment *itself* and such a moral judgment is not separable for members from a consideration of *what is at stake*. (It is in the light of *such* considerations that, paradoxically, risking death rather than tell a small lie, for example, may turn out to be rational.) I am *not* saying that, for members, the 'end justifies the means' - simply that some ends justify some means. And some do not. And whether they do or do not depends on a contextual judgment of consequences and responsibilities that is far more complex than Kovesi's scenario. Further, I am saying that such ends (and the *ends* themselves are evaluatable) and consequences are also practical matters of interest and self-interest, in morally relevant ways. Not that such interest is sovereign in moral reasoning. But there is a limit beyond which it can be flouted and a member·deemed still rational, or moral, from within any given morality. Of course, in Kovesi's example, a person in Philippe's position may indeed feel himself to be faced with a moral predicament. But we would not necessarily *recognize* this predicament. Indeed, were we to have been his comrades we might have found that very sense of predicament morally telling and implicative, possibly irrational. The relevance of a moral notion or principle cannot be formulated in a mechanistic and a priori manner. As Wittgenstein says, 'Not only rules, but also examples are needed for establishing a practice. Our rules leave loop-holes open, and the practice has to speak for itself.' (13) Wittgenstein makes a further point of great importance for understanding the *complexity* of practical reasoning. His remarks are about empirical judgments, but they apply just as much to moral judgments: 'We do not learn the practice of making empirical judgments by learning rules; we are taught *judgments* and their connexion with other judgments. A *totality* of judgments is made plausible to us.' (14)

We cannot agree with this without seeing that it has consequences for our life and our language games. Any situated judgment made or position taken may be relevant to a multiplicity of interconnected standards, practices and outcomes.

Julius Kovesi glosses much of the complexity of moral practical reasoning and members' judgmental work. He makes a distinction between what he calls '"open terms" (where further specifications are needed to enable us to make a judgment on the act) and "complete terms" (where these further specifications have been included in the term already)'. (15) He says further on in his discussion:

When a notion is not formed completely from the moral point of view (e.g., 'killing') then it includes both morally right and wrong acts and in these cases the words 'right', 'wrong' are used for selecting from a mixed class the types of acts that are different from the moral point of view.

When a type of act selected completely from the moral point
of view receives its own term (e.g., 'murder') then the
words 'right', 'wrong' are used only as reminders, they
remind us what was the point of forming such notions.    I
would like to call such notions complete notions. (16)

Still talking of the distinction between 'complete' and 'incomplete' moral notions, Kovesi makes the following point:

So when an act is specified by a description which is incomplete from the moral point of view then we cannot say that
it is good in itself.    On the other hand, as I indicated
earlier when I referred to the intuitionists, an act specified
by a complete term can be said to be good in itself.    It is
good in itself because all that we need to know in order to
judge it good is incorporated in the term that specifies that
act in question.... We have to give further qualifications to
an incomplete description or specify certain conditions in
order to be able to judge these acts always good.    *Once
these qualifications and/or conditions are incorporated in
a term then an act referred to by that term can be said to
be good without qualification or unconditionally good.* (17)
(My italics)

Kovesi is here formulating the notion of complete and incomplete moral notions with regard to 'acts', although he uses
some examples later on (e.g. prejudice) which are not about
classes of act at all.    I take it that his points hold for those
acts judged 'always bad/wrong' as well.

In fact, we have few, if any, single terms that specify
actions generally deemed good such as we have for negatively
implicative actions such as 'murder'.    In the former case, we
have constructions such as 'act of courage', 'act of honesty',
'act of loyalty', etc.    The 'act' description here may deliver
a judgment, but it remains essentially polymorphous and in-
determinate in terms of possible and actual referents.    Therefore, it is difficult to see how Kovesi's notion of a 'complete
moral term' could begin to apply here.    This exhibits the
kind of problem systematically encountered when a philosopher
produces *generic* formulations and claims without detailed
empirical analysis of, or sensitivity to, members' actual practices.

D'Arcy makes the same point about actions that are positively implicative in terms of a distinction between what he calls
'moral-species-terms' (instances of which constitute recognizable kinds of act) and 'moral-genus-terms'.    He makes the
following further observations:

Genus-terms frequently have opposites in a way that species-terms have not: we have 'honesty' and 'dishonesty', 'chastity' and 'unchastity', 'justice' and 'injustice' and so on; but there are no corresponding opposites for 'theft', or 'rape', or 'calumny'. Furthermore, both these types of term commonly have a noun-form and an adjective-from; but, when expressing an opinion about an act, we more commonly use the noun-form of a species-term, and the adjective-form of a genus-term; that is, we are more likely to say, 'That was a lie', or 'That was murder', than to say, 'That was mendacious', or 'That was murderous': but we more naturally say, 'That was dishonest', or 'That was unjust', than 'That was dishonesty', or 'That was injustice' (or even 'an act, or a case, of dishonesty or injustice'). It would be interesting to pursue this, if we were engaged in a wider study of the language and logic of moral evaluation; genus-terms seem to be much less 'descriptive' and much more 'evaluative', and they lend themselves much more readily to the function of predicate than do species-terms; and an investigation of the reasons why this is so might be illuminating. (18)

To return to Kovesi's discussion: there is a difference, is there not, between saying that an act of murder may be said to be always wrong (or unconditionally wrong) and saying that we can all agree on what an act of murder is on each and every occasion of a 'killing'. There is also a difference between saying that we use the concept 'murder' to describe an act of killing we are condemning and saying that the acts (of murder = killing we condemn) are acts that *everyone* will or does deem to be wrong. For then we might ask the question, why does anyone do such acts? Are we to think that everyone who has committed what we call 'murder' is haunted by 'guilt' all his/her life? The most we can say is that they will probably seek *another* description for their acts (one that is not bound up with the conventional judgment of 'wrong' or 'bad') if they wish to claim our same moral auspices or to make a moral claim on us. But between the two descriptions there is sometimes no *empirical* court of appeal.

There is a difference here between the *linguistic accounting* and the *human (or moral) practice*. Our moral concepts are closely bound up with judgments which we learn *together* with the use of those concepts. Such judgments embody *standards*. And as Wittgenstein says, 'We use judgments as principles of judgment.' (19)

Thus we know in common what are the standards conventionally bound up with our concepts and their use - and we know what the standards for *our actions* are. And the possibility of *this* distinction is what makes moral concepts differ-

ent.   Such standards as we learn with our concepts, that
we know in common, are standards we can orient to, seek to
change, deny, secretly reject, understand, etc.   *We do not
have to share them all, although we may recognize their force
in and for our life and their interconnection in various ways
with a complex network of other judgments.*

We can imagine someone calling another's action 'cheating'.
We can also imagine the rejoinder to be 'You can call it what
you want, but I am not going to risk X for the sake of ...'.
It is not an uncommon utterance type.   What such an utterance expresses is the recognition that some action can *formally fall under some description*, together with the denial
that that is *morally relevant* for the issue from the point of
view of the speaker.   What is important here is that such an
utterance remains *logically intelligible* (even if for another
party that displays a morally objectionable attitude).

If '"murder" is wrong' is to be treated as an unqualifiable
absolute, how do we understand *mitigation*?   British law
recognizes *provocation*, which mitigates a judgment from
murder to manslaughter (a legal, not a commonsense, category).   Note that what is mitigated *here* is not *the literal
description of an act*; rather what is being provided for is
that, whilst the act is not being condoned, it is *not being
absolutely condemned either*.   (One can of course take a
moral position on such laws. (20))   This is not only true of
the law, but is, I suggest, routine for members' judgments.
How many of us would *wholeheartedly* condemn the killing by
a person of his torturer?   Or of a particularly pernicious
blackmailer?   We might not condone the latter instance, but
would we be insistent in absolutely condemning it?   Might we
even, in some cases, not condemn it at all?   And some people
who would not themselves ever think of killing someone might
even say, 'Serves him right'.   Yet it would still be, technically, murder.   We would often, in such cases, simply feel
thankful that we were not in *that* position.   Or we might
say, 'I don't know what *I* would have done in his place.'
And this sort of position is *endemic* to the nature and procedures of *moral practice*.

Take now, as an example, the case of a mercy killing.
Persons have various moral positions on this, and that is a
fact of our contemporary moral scene.   Some persons may
say this is evidence of 'the breakdown of contemporary morality', or 'the dissolution of value', but all that they would be
saying is that their morality is *their* morality.   Now, legally,
mercy killings, or euthanasia, are 'murder'.   In his example
of Philippe and George the Gestapo agent, Kovesi asks whether
George's execution would cease to be 'murder' just because
Philippe is legally entitled to execute him.   Kovesi seems to

be recognizing that 'legality' and 'morality' are not identical.
However, his formulation of the issue still rests more on a
legal framework than anything else: the *moral relevance* of
the notion of 'murder' for him is precisely because Philippe
knows that George has not done what has been ascribed to
him by legal procedure and that the law and its intentions
and 'spirit' have been *misapplied*, through a jury's ignorance
of legally relevant facts.   The action of executing George
would then only cease to be murder, according to this treatment, if he were guilty of the crime he was condemned for.
But can one not simply say in some such case that this is
*legalized murder*?   Suppose the crime the law condemns a
man to death for (according to the statutes) is something we
do not consider a crime, or do not consider as the kind of
crime that merits this sort of sentence?   Can we not call
this 'murder'?   Are we unintelligible here?   I think not.
And where the law says that an action is 'murder', we might
not want to condemn it, although we might recognize that it
fits that *legal description*, as in some kinds of mercy killing.
What I am trying to say here is that there is no necessary
identity, indeed there is routinely a divergence, between the
legal use of the notion of 'murder' and the lay member's use.
The law, of course, enters our life and *provides further
instances of our use*;   in some areas it may eventually not
only introduce new language games or new steps into our
existing language games but it may change some of those
games over the years.   But *in the first instance*, the law
provides a formalization of some lay uses and procedures and
is not simply identical with them.   Routinely, what is legally
relevant is not taken to be identical with what is morally
relevant.   Even if we agree on the description of an act as
legally 'murder', we might not then agree on the moral relevance of that act or that description.   And if we do not
agree on its moral relevance we may seek to give another
description, although it may not be a description encapsulated
within some specific category-term.   And if we coin a category-term such as 'euthanasia' or 'mercy killing', for example
(comparable to Kovesi's example of 'saving-deceit'), it would
still technically or legally be an instance of 'murder' just as
saving-deceit remains an instance of lying, as Keith Graham
correctly points out. (21)   And if we coin the term 'euthanasia' can we decide and provide in advance that the acts
covered by that term will be necessarily right or wrong?
For everyone?   And what of the killing of a 'murderer'?
Technically and legally that may still be 'murder' (although it
may be mitigated, depending on the circumstances), unless
the killing is done by the state: an *execution*.   We come
back full circle now, and are compelled to ask whether an act
of killing is condemnable (or merits the full force of the description 'murder') only if it is not legally sanctioned?   Clearly, the answer has to be no, if it is to deliver the character

of members' ongoing orderly practices. Where the answer is
yes, it is partisan to only one kind of context of use and
*one* moral viewpoint that may be systematically adopted by
members. That more or fewer members may practically adopt
one viewpoint is another matter. What is pertinent, however,
is that as members we know what the conventional implications
are of any description in context and what the conventional
implications of particular disagreements and defeasances are,
and we can design our talk and action accordingly. Does
this mean, then, that 'murder' is not a complete moral notion
after all? Or that simply no moral notion can be treated as
a wholly complete one if by that we mean close-textured
(regardless of the manner in which open texture is ruled
out), despite the embeddedness in it of certain kinds of judgment? I suggest that the latter is the case.

Let me recapitulate briefly. I made a distinction earlier
between a linguistic accounting practice and a broader human
or moral practice. I shall make a distinction here between
the technical or correct literal applicability of a description to
some action and the moral relevance of that description.
Note that this is cognate with the methodological and analytic
issues of membership categorizations. In our discussion of
the latter, we indicated some of the parameters of open-
texture for certain categories, for example, their use in context as domain-of-practice descriptions, as moral performance
descriptions, as competence descriptions, etc., and the use of
certain category features as category-bound or category-constitutive. We can think of and handle action categories in
ways similar to the ways we thought of and handled membership categorizations. This remains a pressing analytic task.

Kovesi argues that in a disagreement regarding a moral
notion, e.g. murder, the disagreement is not about the evaluation of particulars under some description, but about
whether they are relevant to one description at all rather
than another, i.e. is it murder or self-defence? For him, if
the description 'murder' is applicable to a set of particulars,
then those particulars are already and necessarily being described from a specific moral point of view and the act is
thereby being condemned. It is what he calls the 'formal
element' that determines the relevance of some particulars to
a description. Our examples earlier of legal uses were meant
to show that even where a particular description such as
'murder' is found technically or legally applicable (since we
might have no other description for *that* case, or even for
that class of cases), its moral relevance may be situatedly
denied or rejected (a rejection of the action-bound value or
category-implicated judgment) without any loss in intelligibility. As Graham correctly points out, (22) not one but many
descriptions may be applicable to some action or set of partic-

ulars.   And the many descriptions available may all be *moral*
descriptions.   Kovesi's own example of the Gestapo agent is
enough to show this - instead of treating the two moral considerations as two co-existing or simply alternative ones, they
may be treated by members as two *competing* ones.   Here we
can again see the relevance of Wittgenstein's point about the
*totality* of judgments made available to us and their learned
interconnection.   Graham criticizes Kovesi for not making a
distinction between wrong $_G$ and wrong $_D$, (23) where the
first is applicable to action types that may generally be said
to be wrong and the second to actions that situatedly may be
said to have been the wrong thing to do.   Both, Graham
says, are important in the understanding of moral decision-
making.   His point is appropriate.   The issue of moral relevance is not automatically decided by appeal to correct applicability.   There are, then, instances in which the *same
action* may be described as 'murder' by some party (where
this description is used to condemn that act) and differently
described (and condoned or mitigated) by another party.
And there may be no *empirical* court of appeal to decide
between these two *disjunctively* used descriptions, e.g.
soldiers' behaviour in wartime; abortion.   Further, there
may be instances when the legal or technical applicability of
a description may be recognized, but its moral relevance or
implications denied or disagreed on (a *practical* fact-value
disjunction or action-relevance disjunction, indicating - if
indication is still needed - how and that a programmatic fact/
value dichotomy is a spurious one).

Kovesi's problem is that he makes what he calls 'the formal
element' do too much work. (24)   It is used alternatively
(and interchangeably) to cover the common property between
various instances of the same action (or term);   the relevances that organize a description;   the practical purposes
behind some description;   the features bound up with a concept;   the definitional sense of a term, etc.   Graham points
to the confusion in Kovesi's discussion between what he terms
the C-type accounts as to why we call something by a certain
name (given by that feature which is in common between it
and other instances falling under the same description) and
a P-type account (given by the purpose or point of the concept, e.g. to excuse, to condemn, etc.). (25)   It is such
confusions that prevent Kovesi from drawing the requisite
other distinctions, which make available the variety of language games we can play with moral (and other) concepts and
the multiple, methodically usable, standards bound up with
them.   He therefore ends up conflating their different
features.

Morality, then, is a *conventional* matter;   and moral concepts are, like other concepts, *open-textured* and not amen-

able to a logical formalization that would render them, or
render some of them, into a strict calculus and enable us to
use some idea of *logical entailment* in understanding the
interrelationship between description and judgment, or between
value and description. Kovesi is right in maintaining that
moral concepts describe and do not simply evaluate what is
otherwise described. But he is still falling prey to the
dichotomization which he is trying to argue against when he
maintains that they describe the world of evaluation while
descriptive concepts evaluate the world of description; (26)
he still seems to be maintaining here a division of domain
between description and evaluation which I find somewhat incoherent. Of course, given the way he sets up this division, it is not too difficult thence to move to a conception of,
at least some, moral concepts which are formed completely
from the moral point of view (e.g. murder) as opposed to
others which are not (leaving the curious question as to what
other points of view are involved in forming such concepts,
e.g. lying). These complete moral concepts are supposed to
describe the corresponding acts with no need of situated
qualifications in their implied moral judgment. Neither this
position nor the classical one which maintains a strict dichotomy between the task of describing and the task of evaluating
(a position I presume Kovesi was trying to get away from) is
analytically adequate. In other words, neither the idea that
judgments may be logically entailed in descriptions (even in a
limited domain) nor the idea of a strict and encompassing fact/
value dichotomy will do to understand the complex world of
members' moral praxis.

Kovesi entirely misses the issue of defeasibility conditions,
as well as the occasioned practical nature of moral judgment.
And those wedded to a working conception of a fact/value
dichotomy to describe the social world deeply misunderstand
the conventional character of this world. The moral conventions bound up intimately with the use of moral concepts, the
judgments embedded in the use of these concepts, and the
conventionally implicated values bound to them as features of
action categories, the multiplicity of criteria for the use of
action categories, and the multiplicity and interconnection of
diverse judgments all provide for our shared standards, the
possibility of contravention without unintelligibility, the
orderly defeasibility of moral ascriptions, etc. Where a concept like 'murder' is used it strongly implicates a negative
moral judgment of act and actor, *an implication that cannot
be ignored*. An action like 'killing' is a morally implicative
action. But the conventionally available implication is neither
a logical entailment nor an expression of an arbitrary individual interest. It is, to apply a notion used in connection with
membership categorizations, *a programmatically relevant implicativeness*. The procedures by which such implicativeness

is defeated, transformed or mitigated are also conventionally
available to members within the culture.   The *values* that fix
the objects of such procedural work (and are constituent of
our situated judgments) and that are presupposed, displayed,
implied by and avowed in the course of such work are often
matters that we share widely, but neither necessarily nor
fully.   Our values and *what* we especially value are themselves matters rooted in our life interests and our forms of
life, as are those matters over which we expect agreement. (27)   But these values are not abstract matters that
are automatically applied or which automatically provide for
their own application.   'We express (or try to express) judgments of value, not just any time, but in circumstances in
which it makes sense to do so.' (28)

There are matters, of course, which, from *within* a given
morality, we like to, and can in practical circumstances, treat
as absolutes, whilst others, from within that *same* morality,
are allowed qualifications, etc.   From *within* some morality,
given the interconnected totality of judgments (empirical and
moral) available to us, certain actions and courses of action
can be treated as being clearly, for practical purposes, irrational, and at any rate as unqualifiedly unacceptable.   Genocide is, for *me*, just such a matter.   It does *not* mean that
the commitment of genocide is *logically* unintelligible - just
morally so, *for me*.   It means that here I have reached bed-
rock and, *as a member*, I will treat this issue, and regard the
negative moral implications of the concept of 'genocide', not
as conventionally available, but *as givens*, *as moral facts*:

> If I have exhausted the justifications I have reached bed-
> rock, and my spade is turned.   Then I am inclined to say:
> 'This is simply what I do'. (29)

And in 'On Certainty', Wittgenstein says:

> Where two principles really do meet which cannot be recon-
> ciled with one another, then each man declares the other a
> fool and heretic.

> I said I would 'combat' the other man - but wouldn't I give
> him *reasons*?   Certainly; but how far do they go?   At the
> end of reasons comes *persuasion*... (30)

Both from the foregoing and from the substance of the previous chapters it becomes clear, not only that moral reasoning
is practical, but that practical reasoning is morally organized;
that is to say, whilst we do have moral concepts and procedures of reasoning that are explicitly moral in character, the
entirety of our interactional reasoning is morally and normatively constituted.   Moreover, at this point I wish to propose

that 'morality' has, *essentially*, *a modal logic*.   I shall enlarge on this presently.   First let me here say some words
on what I believe to be a central feature of the traditional
approach to moral matters that has characterized much of
moral philosophy to date, and thus place the perspective of
this work in relation to that field.   The feature I refer to
here is the conception of a relatively well-defined domain of
moral discourse;   a conception which, I believe, serves ultimately to obscure rather than enlighten the character of the
everyday moral world.   'Moral discourse' is a theoretic
abstraction from various moral displays and accomplishments
within the practical world of members' activities and concerns.
For a member, an utterance which a philosopher has tradi-
tionally treated (or would have so treated by virtue of his
methods of analysis) as outside the realm of moral discourse
can still be said to have 'moral undertones' and 'moral over-
tones'.   This latter character that members may and do
assign to utterances, stories and stances is of great interest
and importance.   What is observable in the everyday world is
a variety of judgments, verdicts, notions, inferences, presuppositions, descriptions and actions, etc. that have a moral
character.   Moreover, that moral character is itself displayed,
detected, made sense of, relied on, pointed to, evaluated and
defeated in orderly methodic (conventional) ways. (31)
'Morality' is a *cluster* of real-world phenomena.   The actual
occasions of use of the term 'moral', for instance, are not exhaustive of morally relevant talk;   rather, the use of the term
*topicalizes* moral matters and morally implicative features of
the practical world.   Such topicalization further involves a
situated display of relevances and moral auspices that is a
fundamental oriented-to feature of talk.

The treatment of moral matters by many philosophers has
systematically exhibited a confusion (and at best a neglect of
the distinction) between topic and resource on two levels,
analytically and methodologically.   They have failed to distinguish clearly between the topicalization of moral matters in
practical contexts, members' moral *theorizing*, their talk
within *moral contexts* and their use of *morally organized procedures and moral standards* in the conduct of their everyday
affairs.   They have also thus glossed over in their own work
the distinction between substantive moral theorizing and the
analysis of moral methods - the differences between a theory
of morals, a moral theory and the enquiry into moral reasoning.

Different moral philosophers exhibit this confusion or glossing of the distinction in different ways and to different
degrees.   Classical moral philosophy has, of course, been
particularly guilty of this.

A good contemporary example comes from R.M. Hare's 'Freedom and Reason'. Despite Hare's insistence that ethics as a form of enquiry is morally neutral he allows himself to fall into the trap of one-sided stipulation. He writes:

> Ethical theory, which determines the meanings and functions of the moral words, and thus the 'rules' of the moral 'game', provides only clarification of the conceptual framework within which moral reasoning takes place; it is therefore, in the required sense, neutral as between different moral opinions. But it is highly relevant to moral reasoning because, as with the rules of a game, there could be no such thing as moral reasoning without this framework, and the framework dictates the form of reasoning....

> The rules of moral reasoning are, basically, two, corresponding to the two features of moral judgments which I argued for in the first half of this book, prescriptivity and universalizability. When we are trying, in a concrete case, to decide what we ought to do, what we are looking for (as I have already said) is an action to which we can commit ourselves (prescriptivity) but which we are at the same time prepared to accept as exemplifying a principle of action to be prescribed for others in like circumstances (universalizability). (32)

But 'universalizability' is itself usable as a *device* of moral argument by members and as a practical criterion that constitutes and displays a *particular* moral position: *Do unto others what thou wilt have done unto thee*. It is used as a moral criterion and standard by which actions and judgments get specified and assessed from a particular viewpoint. It is not, by any means, one that is used or accepted by all members. This leads Hare to the curious position of deriving an evaluative conclusion from what he claims to be a non-evaluative premise (a violation of his own precept about moral reasoning). Given that he builds 'universalizability' into 'morality', as one of the 'rules of the game', he allows himself the claim that most people, if informed and made to use their imagination, and possibly with the help of the moral philosopher, would drop what 'extraordinary' (discreditable, intolerant, racist, etc.) moral positions they may have, through the exercise and process of moral reasoning. The remainder are a few 'fanatics' - as if 'fanatics' were not a construct of moral exclusion.

My own theory does not get the content into our moral judgments by verbal legislation; *we* have to put it in by exploring the logical possibilities. There are real alternatives between which we have to choose. But unless we are prepared to take the fanatical line, and opt for a certain principle regardless of even our own desires, we have to allow our choices to be circumscribed by the desires of other people. This is the logical consequence of universalizability, when coupled with prescriptivity. (33)

G.J. Warnock in 'The Object of Morality' writes:

... there have been white men who, loyal and considerate and so on towards other white men, have seemed to recognize no such claim to consideration of other persons who happen not to be white. Such codes, as I have said, are often spoken of as moral codes; it would be orthodox usage enough to remark that 'the morality' of, say, the head-hunting tribesman regulates his dealings only with fellow-members of the tribe, and does not apply to his relations with any other persons. Such talk can be readily understood, and so far is no doubt unobjectionable; but I believe that it can also be said, with point and truth, that such a code, while indeed it can be called *a* morality, is not morality - to see things so is not to see them from the moral point of view, and such notions, while wholly understandable, are not moral notions. But if to say this is not to be just arbitrary, what justifies one in saying it? Well, one can at least begin, in my view, by saying that it is *analytic* that principles of morality are not thus circumscribed in their application; it is part of the concept - the 'special' concept if you like - of morality that no person is simply excluded from moral consideration, and furthermore ... that if he is to be considered differently from some person, the difference made must be justified by some morally relevant ground of distinction. (What is morally 'relevant' follows, of course, from what morality is; it is not an arbitrary matter, or a matter of choice or opinion.) (34)

Warnock is similarly engaged in a stipulative and *morally judgmental* procedure here. He recognizes that persons may organize their moral positions and commitments round certain category identities, identities that are selective and demarcate for them the boundaries of practical membership. But then he goes on to say, like Hare (see Introduction), that a non-universal moral code articulated in this manner, while it can 'be called *a* morality is not morality' and that such notions as are embedded in it are not moral notions. He is thus incorporating his *own* moral position into a definition of what is 'moral'. Perhaps the problem lies in the analytic attempt to say what 'morality' and 'the moral point of view' are in general terms rather than simply looking at moral and practical reasoning itself, an attempt that seems to enmesh the analyst hopelessly in producing abstractions of the various language games we play with the notion of 'morality' and 'moral'. (35)

Another consequence of the glossing over, or neglect of, the distinction between topic and resource has been the conception indicated earlier of a defined domain of moral discourse. As an example of the way this domain formalization has been more problematic than revealing I wish to look briefly at Hanna Pitkin's discussion of moral discourse. (36)    This is not because I think she provides the best analysis within that kind of tradition, nor because I consider it the most significant, but rather because it provides a stark and simple example and because, although it is written ostensibly from a Wittgensteinian perspective, it yet fails to make the necessary and appropriate break with traditional approaches.

In her chapter, Language Regions, Moral Discourse, and Action, (37) Pitkin discusses the notion of different types of discourse, or language regions, as developed in the work of F. Waismann, G. Ryle, M. Oakshott and, of course, Wittgenstein.    Pitkin notes that:

Wittgenstein's discussion of language games and forms of `life suggests that we might think of language as being subdivided into clusters of similar and related concepts, used in similar and related language games. (38)

Later, she goes on to say:

Wittgenstein himself speaks at one point about 'regions of language', and again invokes the analogy between language and an ancient city:  'a maze of little streets and squares, of old and new houses, and of houses with additions from various periods;  and this surrounded by a multitude of new boroughs with straight regular streets and uniform houses'. (39)

Pitkin says of Waismann, Ryle and Oakshott that each of them agrees that there are 'significant subdivisions within language, differing in fundamental ways'.    They are called by Waismann 'language strata', by Ryle 'language categories' and by Oakshott 'voices in the conversation of mankind'.    The subdivisions are supposed to differ 'not merely in vocabulary or subject matter, but in the way that language is used:   in grammar, logic, structure'. (40)

However, Pitkin goes on to say that Ryle 'warns that the idea of language categories is merely an idiom, harmful if pressed too far'. (41)    She says:

The idea of regions or strata or categories in our language is likely to foster the illusion of systematic rules, of sharply distinct, fixed subdivisions whose boundaries may not be violated.    We are likely to want to list the regions, cata-

logue them, and thereby classify the world.... But any
subdivisions we distinguish within the main body of our
language will be only questionably distinct;   the categories
will be categories *we* set up because we happen to have
concepts available for them:   'science', 'morality', 'religion'.
... One may treat mathematics as a language region, but
one may also see it as a whole collection of different language regions with different rules. (42)

Having delivered the above warning, however, Pitkin goes on
to examine in greater detail 'the region of moral discourse',
emerging with too legislative and narrow a conception of it
(even if analysis were to be restricted to topicalized moral
discourse):

From the perspective of our ordinary employment of language in the region of morality, moral discourse particularly
centers on actions, and on action gone wrong.   It has to
do with the assessment and repair of human relationships
when these have been strained or damaged by the unfore-
seen results of some action. (43)

Are we to take it that, for Pitkin, the employment of language in the region of morality (whatever that may turn out to
be) is the same thing as moral discourse?   At one point she
talks of 'moral argument' and takes the position that the point
of such argument is not agreement on a conclusion but 'successful clarification of two people's position vis-à-vis each
other'. (44)   Is she not talking here of only specific (theoretical) kinds of moral argumentation?   At another point she
says that moral discourse is supposed to 'result in truthful
revelation of self;   it must be conducted in a certain manner
of style', that not 'just any conversation about action is a
moral one'. (45)   And at yet another point she talks of
'moral discussion'. (46)   In much of this her analysis follows
and draws on Cavell's work in his 'Claim to Rationality'. (47)

There are a number of confusions in Pitkin's positions.
Firstly, a moral argument could conceivably be one where
there is disagreement on the moral description of an action -
e.g. a lie or an act of consideration, murder or self-defence.
Such descriptions of actions are themselves morally implicative
for the description of persons - deceptive, kind or cowardly
(depending on whether a person is seen to have deliberately
lied or been tactful, or simply could not bring himself to tell
the truth).   Or the argument could be about *who* is to blame
in some occurrence (implicative for action descriptions, e.g.
the description of X's killing Y as having been an act of
murder or an act committed in self-defence).   Or it could be
an argument about what would have been the right or wrong
thing to do in certain circumstances.   Or about whether *A*

was the right thing for $X$ to have done. Or it may be about
*why* X did A (also tied up with some agreed-on moral description of action $A$ and implicative for the description of $X$'s
character). Or it may be an argument about *a moral principle*. Moreover, there remains that all-important distinction
between talk *about moral matters*, and talk whose immediate
character or point is the making of moral judgments, and talk
involving, invoking and using moral concepts and morally
organized procedures. For instance, Gerry may be telling
Ken that he believes John stole his fountain pen because he
had discovered him lying in the past and nobody else had had
an opportunity to steal it (the use of a morally implicative
past action as grounds for ascribing a morally implicative
presently relevant action). This cannot properly be con-
strued as a moral discussion, although it may give rise to one
were Ken to begin arguing with Gerry on the merits of his
case against John. Or it may simply give rise to an argument about John, with Ken defending him and insisting that
his lying does not mean that he would steal, possibly even
accusing Gerry of being prejudiced against John, etc.
Gerry's talk, then, invokes moral conventions, uses moral
concepts, involves moral judgments, displays a moral position
and could well raise a general moral issue. It is both embedded in a moral context and generative of moral matters and a
moral focus for the conversation. It cannot be excluded from
analytic concern.

Furthermore, 'talk about morals' could be: talk about his
morals; my talk about my morals; your morals; your talk
about my morals; talk about a particular situated display of
morals, i.e. as relevant to a particular action; or talk about
morals in general, specific moral principles or the morality of
certain institutions. Here again, even where 'morals' are
topicalized, we can find a diversity in what that talk could
*amount to*. Talk about *his* morals, for example, may be in
the context of discussing such principles, relevances, etc. as
might arise therein *in and for themselves*. Or it could be
designed around an interest in the person himself; that interest could be practical or 'idle', as in gossip. Gossip is not
an instance of 'moral discussion', yet it both generates moral
issues, relevances and characterizations and relies on them.
My talk about your morals could be abuse, commendation, complaint, query, clarification. My talk about my morals could
be a display of superiority, doing contrast work, display of
remorse, self-clarification, etc. Talk about moral issues that
does not involve reference to any *particular* persons at all
could be advocating a position, complaining, justifying a practice, etc.

So a 'moral discussion' is not the same as a morally relevant
argument and neither exhausts the 'use of language in a moral

context'.  Pitkin seems all too often to be taking 'moral discourse' as being simply one or the other, and even then in a
very limited mode (see quotation above).  Pitkin's problem is
that she cuts off the 'moral' from the 'practical', whereas the
moral is the foundation of the practical and indeed *is*
supremely practical.  The discussion of possible action consequences, of contemplated action, is as common as the discussion of actual consequences of past actions.  No doubt Pitkin
would agree with this, yet she keeps it out of her analytic
focus in discussing action and morality.  Evaluation of goals
that people have, beliefs they hold, character, interests,
attitudes, the *manner* in which they do things (sincerely, effi-
ciently, promptly, honestly, etc.), *what* people routinely do,
how they spend their time, etc., are all subject to the kind
of scrutiny we call moral.

In her talk of 'language regions' Pitkin moves from divisions
such as 'science, morality, religion' (48) to talk of the divisions that Cavell employs:  'It is by virtue of these recurrent
patterns of support that a remark will count as aesthetic, or
a mere matter of taste, moral, propagandistic, religious, magi-
cal, scientific, philosophical.' (49)  She talks further of the
regions of (truths of) 'mathematics, science, poetry, and even
political opinion'. (50)  She quotes Wittgenstein on the logic
of commands, Waismann on the logic of aphorisms and on the
'logic of half-faded memory pictures' (51) and talks of the
'truths of mathematics, ... science, poetry, everyday practical concerns, sensations, ethics'. (52)  She is involved in a
confusion of levels.  Are we to take it that these different
discourse/activity domains and language games (themselves
quite different sorts of thing) differ from each other in equivalent ways and are in some sense symmetrical?  Is the way we
would discuss commands independent and symmetrical to the
way we would discuss ethics?  Is morality different from
poetry in the same kind of way in which it differs from other
everyday practical concerns?  Is political opinion different
from science in the same way that mathematics is?  The implication of her treatment, throughout, is twofold:  that the different 'domains' she talks about are totally independent from
each other and, which is another side of the same coin, that
they differ from each other in identical measure.  To use an
analogy here, Pitkin seems to treat those 'domains' as one
might view non-identical twins (or quintuplets) and not as one
might view a *whole family* (father, mother, siblings, uncles,
grandparents) in terms of differences, asymmetrical relationships, dependencies, tasks, etc.  And that is precisely what
is wrong with her analysis.

Let us take poetic discourse as an example.  For this,
Pitkin draws on Oakshott's analysis.  According to Pitkin, he
says that the poet is 'always partly engaged in image-making,

not just in image-using;  he is always innovating on the store
of available concepts.   And secondly, poetic discourse is
"contemplative", which is to say that its concepts and images
are enjoyed for themselves'. (53)   Here Oakshott's model of
poetic discourse is 'poetry' itself and not talk about poetry.
Pitkin's model for 'moral discourse' is, however, at times talk
about moral issues, and not the performance *of* moral actions
(illocutionary acts):  accusing, excusing, condemning, prais-
ing, assessing character, finding guilt, allocating responsibility, establishing rights and duties, encouraging action, etc.
Clearly, there can be no strict equivalence of type, no sym-
metry between the two kinds of concern, or 'discourse
domains', as Pitkin sets them up.   If, however, as seems
reasonable, we are to include both the 'doing' and the 'talking
about X' into our conception of any specific domain for practical purposes, then one can consider the following:   No
amount of members' talk about poetic issues could be con-
strued as doing (writing, reciting, composing) poetry,
whereas their talk about moral matters is always still the
'doing of morality'.   It always involves the taking of a moral
position, the display of moral auspices and the use of moral
conventions, in much the same way as talk on logical issues
is also 'doing logic'.   Moreover, I think that it is quite mis-
taken to say that the concepts and images of poetic discourse
are enjoyed simply for themselves.   A poem is often and
importantly assessed in terms of what new light it might throw
on human experiences or on what is called the 'human condition';   it can be evaluated in terms of what moral stance it
reveals, or in terms of how true it is in depicting or evoking
some aspects or features of human experience.   The entire
debate on 'commitment' in art is intelligible in this context;
Oakshott's view, then, represents only a preferred standard
of aesthetics and, some members might add, of moral concern.
Although this type of evaluation is by no means one that all
find uniformly relevant or appealing, it is still a framework
which members can and routinely do use in their evaluation of
poems and other works of art (and consequently of the artist
herself).   We can say of a poem that it is insincere, honest,
committed, relevant, trivial, etc., in terms of *moral relevances*, and we can say these things of the artist merely by
scrutinizing his work.   We can also say of a poem that it is ·
moving, anguished, communicates a sense of suffering or
elation, etc., and these things have a curiously interesting
relationship to moral matters that is itself deserving of study.

On the other hand, it does not make sense to say, except
in a metaphorical mode, that some piece, say, of scientific
dialogue is poetic;  and we certainly do not judge or assess
moral positions with criteria derived from poetry or poetic
discourse.   And here, I believe, we get to the crux of the
matter.   Pitkin at one point says:

Wittgenstein suggests that we think of the specialized, technical subdivisions of language, such as the symbolism of chemistry or the notation of calculus, as 'so to speak, suburbs of our language', neat, clearly laid out, unmistakably separate. But in the old city, regions will be more difficult to distinguish or delineate precisely. (54)

If I may use and enlarge on the analogy, we find morality not only in the old city as overground locations (sidestreets, boulevards, squares, odd shops) but also and crucially as a maze, a foundation of underground connections that open up at different places of the old city - as the underground railway, if you like. Pitkin talks of the different *logical styles* of different language regions (a phrase she borrows from Waismann (55)), but she does not include 'logic' in her collection of different language regions or domains of discourse. This is probably because of her awareness that 'logic' could not stand in relation to other modes of discourse as some might to each other, e.g. science and religion. It is because we can assess all manner of findings and inferences in logical terms; our norms of rationality underpin our understanding of talk and action throughout. Similarly, I want to suggest, our moral conventions underpin our understanding of talk and action throughout; we can assess all manner of actions, relevances and concerns in *moral* terms. Logic and morality are the twin guardians of our discourse and activities; they provide our fundamental source of normative criteria for the conduct of our practical human life.

The different language regions, then, are not distinct or independent of each other in a clearly defined way, apart from the technical sub-divisions; they have various relationships to each other, such that contrasts and comparisons between them are done accordingly in different ways. These domains cannot be delineated from each other abstractly according to fixed criteria, but rather any distinction is made and used situatedly, in terms of practical relevances and tasks, and is embedded in the practical context of the talk. One does not talk always, or even often, exclusively in one domain. I could say of a poem that it is 'honest' and the sense of that remark derives not only from the various senses of the word 'honest', but also from the fact that the object of the remark is a poem, and not a person. Wittgenstein's idea of language games is far more sensitive to the actual practical contexts of talk and action than is the idea of language regions or domains (albeit the latter has some uses), because of its implicit reference to living human activity: 'Here the term "language-*game*" is meant to bring into prominence the fact that the *speaking* of language is part of an activity, or of a form of life'. (56)

CONCLUSION

We proposed earlier that 'morality' be treated as essentially having *a modal logic*.   The following few points will serve to provide for the sense and character of this claim:

1   Many basic sorts of moral judgment are, as Wittgenstein said, *learnt*:   their use as principles of judgment is an occasioned practical matter.   Wherever we treat moral principles as rules, then, they may be said to operate with the 'etcetera clause' in Garfinkel's terms:

> Apparently no matter how specific the terms of common understandings may be ... they attain the status of an agreement for persons only insofar as the stipulated conditions carry along an unspoken but understood *etcetera* clause.   Specific stipulations are formulated under the rule of an agreement by being brought under the jurisdiction of the *etcetera* clause.   This does not occur once and for all, but is essentially bound to both the inner and outer temporal course of activity and thereby to the progressive development of circumstances and their contingencies....
> Not only can contingencies arise, but persons know as of any Here and Now that contingencies can materialize or be invented at any time that it must be decided whether or not what the parties actually did satisfied the agreement....
> That the work of bringing present circumstances under the rule of previously agreed activity is sometimes contested should not be permitted to mask its pervasive and routine use as an ongoing and essential feature of 'actions in accord with common understanding'.

> This process, which I shall call a method of discovering agreements by eliciting or imposing a respect for the rule of practical circumstances, is a version of practical ethics. (57)

2   The boundaries of the practical applicability of moral concepts, descriptions and judgments are drawn by exceptions. Such exceptions are not trivial, nor are they extraordinary. They represent the cross-cutting relevances that persons expectably and routinely have in the conduct of their daily praxis.   Were it not for such a complex network of cross-cutting relevances, it would be hard to locate the dynamic of change from *within* the moral order.   Such exceptions are conventional and provide for the orderly defeasibility of moral ascriptions, descriptions and inferences and for the possibility of *orderly challenges* to moral judgments.

3   Our earlier work with membership categorizations showed how, quite apart from categories that are explicitly moral in their character (e.g. thief, murderer), membership categoriza-

tions have a moral organization and moral features and
routinely operate within a moral context.   More precisely,
membership categorizations such as doctor, mother, brother,
friend, etc. have category-tied rights and obligations that
inform their practical use and members' practical assessments.
Such category-tied rights and obligations are category-tied
moral features of the social world - although we can, as members, talk generally of rights and duties that other persons
may or should have, it is routinely that rights and duties
(and therefore blame, assessments, responsibilities, etc.) are
organized in essentially localized and modally specified ways.
Whilst we can talk of a good person, we can also talk of a
good friend, a good mother, a good nurse, etc. and these
latter uses are neither identical nor dependent on the former.
Think of the difference between expressions such as 'a good
person' and expressions such as 'a good German' or 'a good
American'.   It is not simply that we can, if we want, organize our moral interests with respect to certain membership
categories in the conduct of our practical life, but that
indeed, conventionally, our moral understandings and interests
are already thus organized in large part;   the practice of
emphasis and selection is that of moral position-taking by
members and is generative in situ of diversity and disjunction.
However, one of the available modalities here *is* the moral
organization of the categorizations 'human being', 'citizen',
'people', 'species-member', etc.   These categories may be
used by members to organize their practical morality in various situated ways and in precedence over other categories;
they may also be treated as *subsuming* other categories.   They
may be treated as programmatically relevant device-categories
in various contexts.   It is *here* that the logical possibility of
moral universalizability is locatable, not only as an available
moral option for members, but as one that can be made
actually relevant in *diverse* situations and is treatable by them
as having genuine *moral force*.   It does not, however, mean
that universalizability is a rule of all genuinely analysable
moral reasoning, as Hare would have it.   Our earlier discussion of the police/people category set, the possible logic/
convention disjunction locatable in this and category-generated
dilemmas speaks to this point.

4  Our work on setting-inappropriate actions provides also for
the understanding of setting-localized moral features and judgments.   There is, then, a large class of actions (and beliefs)
that are generally 'all right' except in certain settings (for
various reasons), where 'all right' provides for variations of
personal taste, inclination and preference, rather than a conventional function.   Moreover, many moral positions and judgments are only possible and relevant in contrastive or hierarchical forms.   Routinely it happens that to do some action $X$
is not judgeable as particularly good or bad, right or wrong,

commendable or condemnable, but to do X *rather* than Y, or to do X *before* doing Y, etc., might be judged unfair, unkind, considerate, helpful, loyal, irresponsible, etc.

5 If we think of moral rules/principles as prescriptions and proscriptions (and not all moral judgments can be treated either practically or analytically this way), we will find, then, not only that some of them are tied to specifics but that within their domain of relevance they may be defeated in methodic orderly ways and have conventionally formulatable exceptions or non-applicability contingencies.

6 Should someone say, 'But all these modalities *simply express* general principles', we would have to answer that such principles are only available *in and through* the *specific practice*, and so we look at that practice. Take a category-bound duty: for example, a doctor's category-bound duties towards his patients. What is the *general* principle involved here?

That a person should help the needy?

That a person should help *sick* people?

That a person should fulfil his obligations towards others?

That a person should carry out his job?

We can ramify such formulations. But all these formulations (and principles) are members' practical situated rules, decisions, judgments, principles, etc. *The category-tied feature is used as a tacit resource*, generating the above sorts of formulations as practical devices. Here we remember with force Wittgenstein's remark: 'We *use* judgments as principles of judgment' (58) (emphasis added).

One last point must be made before bringing the discussion to a close. 'Morality', 'moral values', 'moral positions', 'moral beliefs' are not invisibly locked into the minds and feelings of persons. Rather, they are routinely displayed and available publicly in the very same instance as intentions and beliefs. In the very display and public availability of action-intentions and beliefs, in the very performance of actions and in the very organization of talk, moral positions, values and stances are displayable and publicly available. Indeed, they may thus be ascribable to agents *despite* their own avowals.

If we look back at our discussion of the moral ascription rule, we can see how, regardless of *what* the values and moral stances of a speaker/actor are, *they may be locatable for what they are by competent members*. The rule can be reformulated as a *hearer's maxim*: In any action description, the point at which the ascriptive vector stops *displays* the point of highest moral implicativeness or value for the speaker. (Of course, if the speaker is the agent of the described action, the action may speak for itself.) Alternatively, or at the same time, it can be taken to be expressive of the speaker's *recognition* of a specific moral implicativeness to the action and a *concession* to a morality different from that which the described action itself may be taken to display.

This public locatability of moral position and value stance is very significant and involves complex and varying procedures. It displays some of our basic agreements and constitutes a basic resource in moral persuasion and demonstration.

Thus, the conventionality of the social world provides both for the methodicity of ascriptions, inferences, judgments and descriptions, as well as for the methodicity of their defeasances, and the procedural possibility of change in the particulars rather than the methods of moral practice. Although the logical entailment of moral judgment from actions is not a practical issue for members, neither is an 'is/ought' dichotomy a methodological problem for them. The dichotomy itself is usable as a member's device for defeasance, excuse, justification, etc. It is itself a moral method.

The thrust of the above has been the elucidation of the conventional and practical character of members' moral matters and the foundational character of morality in organizing the ongoing praxis of members in the social world. Morality presupposes community, as community presupposes morality.

# Harvey Sacks on categorization: an overview.

Sacks introduced his notions of 'membership category' and 'membership categorization devices' in the following way:

> My attention shall be exclusively limited to those categories in the language in terms of which *persons* may be classified. For example, the categories: 'male', 'teacher', 'first baseman', 'professional', 'Negro', etc., are the sort I shall be dealing with. Frequently, such 'membership categories' are organized, by persons of the society using them, into what I shall call 'collections of membership categories'. These collections constitute the *natural groupings of categories*, categories that members of society feel 'go together'. They are not constructed merely as aids to my analysis; whether or not a particular category is a member of a particular collection is, in each and every case, a matter to be decided empirically. (1)

Thus, categories such as 'father', 'mother', 'son', 'grandmother' and so on are found to 'belong' to the membership categorization *device* 'Family'. Similarly, categories such as 'teacher', 'doctor', 'lawyers' belong to the device 'Occupation'; 'English', 'French', 'Chinese' to the device 'Nationalities' and also the device 'Natural languages'.

Given that everyone is an incumbent of more than one category than is assumed in any given interaction, Sacks locates the basis for his analytic problem: the selection rules whereby membership categorization is actually achieved by members in the course of their practical activities in society. He presses this analytical problem further by raising a variety of related issues: What are the conventional implications bound up with accomplished selections? What are the inferential consequences of accomplished selections? How is 'category knowledge' used and relied on by members in the production by them of descriptions of social scenes? From here, Sacks noted that there are conventional preferences for linking up a range of activities with a range of membership categories which members of the culture actually orient to (and they display their orientation). His analysis of 'category-bound activities' (2) was an attempt to demonstrate this; indeed, Sacks went on to argue that the selection of a membership category by any member to refer to or characterize any other member

(or even herself) could not be understood simply in terms of
criteria of 'correctness'. Rather, it involves considerations
of much greater analytical complexity, such as 'appropriateness', 'recipient design/recognitionality', 'implicativeness',
'orientation to already-used categories in the discourse so
far', and so on. (3)

Sacks, in presenting his formulation of 'membership categorization devices', proposed some basic rules for the application
of any device's categories to a population. (4)   His initial
claim being that for any population of size $N$ there are always
*at least* two devices which may be used to categorize the
members of that population, he observed that some devices
have the property of population-member exhaustibility; i.e.
that there are some devices whose categories can be differentially applied to every member of a given population of persons without remainder.   These 'Pn-adequate devices', as he
called them, would include the devices 'Sex' and 'Age'.   If
someone were to categorize an entire population, categories
drawn from either of these devices would be found sufficient
to categorize every member.   There are, of course, more
devices which are *not* Pn-adequate than are Pn-adequate, but
in the case of those which are Pn-adequate, the following
rules apply, according to Sacks:

*Consistency Rule.*   If some population of persons is being
categorized, and if a category from some device's collection
has been used to categorize a first Member of the population, then that category or other categories of the same
collection *may* be used to categorize further Members of the
population.   As a correlate of the consistency rule, the
following may be proposed:   *Category Relevance Rule 1.*
If any Pn-adequate device is appropriate for categorizing
some population, then any category of such a device may be
used on each Member of the population to provide a count
of how many are and how many are not Members of that
category. (5)

Subsequent to this quite basic rule and its correlate, Sacks
introduces a further rule of application of membership categorization devices, this time without the constraint that it
covers only Pn-adequate devices.

*Economy Rule.*   For any population N, on any occasion of
categorizing Members, whether the consistency rule or some
combining rules are necessary, the task may be complete if
each Member of the population has had a single category
applied to them. (6)

Adequate reference or characterization for practical purposes is achievable in our culture by the use of a single cate-

gorization, although there are clearly occasions on which referring to some Member as 'that man', or 'the professor' or
'the woman' will be found inappropriate.  Such occasions are
investigable for their features, and Sacks and Schegloff elsewhere note that at least one major consideration which requires category proliferation beyond the use of a single category is the local distribution of knowledge. (7)    Specifically,
they note that categorization terms are selected with reference
to the presumed state of knowledge of the hearer/recipient,
and that where this 'preference for recognitionals' breaks
down in interaction, category terms may proliferate beyond
minimal reference forms *until* recognition is achieved.

Continuing with his discussion of the most elementary rules
for device application, Sacks proposes that

Given the consistency rule and the economy rule, we have
the: *Repeatable Use Rule*.  The application of a Pn-
adequate device to a population N involves determining for
each Member of the population, in any sequence, which
category is appropriate, where any category may be repeatedly used. (8)

However, Sacks notes that for *some* devices their proper use
does *not* involve the repeatable use of categories.   He adds,
'Suppose, for example, one is using the device *baseball team*
("first base", "second base" ... "catcher") to select players
from a larger population than nine (or eighteen) potential
players ...'. (9)

To his basic notions of *membership categories* and the
*devices* in which they may be collected, Sacks adds two other
important distinctions.   These are the 'collection R' and the
'collection K'. (10)    The collection *R* has as its members the
*Standardized Relational Pairs* of 'husband/wife', 'parent/child',
'neighbour/neighbour', 'boyfriend/girlfriend', 'friend/friend',
'cousin/cousin', ... 'stranger/stranger'.   The following rule
provides for whether a pair of classes is a member of the
collection *R*:

Any pair of categories is a member of collection R if that
pair is a 'standardized' relational pair that constitutes a
locus for a set of rights and obligations concerning the
activity of giving help. (11)

Categories drawn from any collection *R* may be, in Sacks's
terms, 'inferentially adequate' for some aspects of members'
knowledge.    He notes:

Members' knowledge of how Members behave is so organized
that items of that knowledge may, discriminatively, be taken

as expectably descriptive if no more than a single referentially adequate category has been asserted to hold for some Member in question. (12)

Moreover, as well as their use being inferentially adequate, Sacks notes that categories drawn from collection *R* have the property of 'programmatic relevance'.  That is, a Member categorized with a category drawn from *R* can be found to have certain rights and duties such that their non-observance would constitute a noticeable absence, a violation or deviance, and *not* in the first instance merely evidence that she may not be an incumbent of that category.  From here, Sacks goes on to formulate his second Category Relevance Rule.

*Category Relevance Rule 2.*  Given the relevance of some categorization device whose categories are programmatically relevant (whether or not the device is Pn-adequate), each category of the device is usable on the population being categorized such that the product of the device's application may consist of a set of observations (facts) that are formulable and usable not only vis-à-vis the product (category member + population Member) but also (category member + no population Member). (13)

In other words, the use of a programmatically relevant categorization can lead a hearer to topicalize or notice that some member is *missing*, in the event that a categorization term from the device is not applied to some Member when the device is being used.  Non-incumbency may here be treated as an *issue* by members, or, as Sacks himself puts it, an 'observable'. (14)

Now let us turn to collection *K*.

Collection K is composed of two classes (professionals, laymen).... Let us first note that K is Pn-adequate and provide, second, for how membership is distributed between its classes.

All those occupational categories for which it is correct to say that Members of the named occupations have special or exclusive rights for dealing with some trouble(s) are occasional occupants of K's class (professionals).

For any given trouble for which such an occupation exists ... that occupation (or occupations) constitutes the category exclusively occupying the (professional) class, where all who are not Members of it are undifferentiatedly occupants of the K class (laymen).  Thus, for any given trouble, incumbency in one of the classes excludes incumbency in the other. (15)

Now we must turn to some very important corollaries of these abstract formulations provided by Sacks in his earliest work on membership categorization.   He develops his analysis in a later paper entitled On the Analyzability of Stories by Children. (16)   He begins by noticing that a 'hearer's maxim' may be formulated from the production version of his Consistency Rule (given above).   Whether or not the devices in question are Pn-adequate, the hearer's maxim corollary of the Consistency Rule is as follows:   'If two or more categories are used to categorize two or more members of some population, and those categories can be heard as categories from the same collection, then:   hear them that way.' (17)   Thus, in treating the utterance 'The baby cried, the mommy picked it up', Sacks notes that the category 'baby' could derive from either the device 'Family' or the device 'Stage-of-Life'.   The Consistency Rule tells us that further persons can be categorized now with categories drawn either from the device 'Family' or from the device 'Stage-of-Life'.   However, given that a second category has been used, and is heard to have been used, *if* that second category can be heard as consistent with only *one locus* (or Device) of a first, then the corollary rule tells us that we should hear the first as *at least* consistent with the second, the two categories coming from the same Device (in this case, 'Family').

This Device ('Family') is one of a set of Devices having the property of *duplicative organization*. (18)   Sacks specifies this property in the following way:

When such a [duplicatively organized] device is used on a population, what is done is to take its categories, treat the set of categories as defining a unit, and place members of the population into cases of the unit.   If a population is so treated and is then counted, one counts not numbers of daddies, numbers of mommies, and numbers of babies, but numbers of families - numbers of 'whole families', numbers of 'families without fathers', etc. (19)

A hearer's maxim corresponding to duplicatively organized membership categorization devices is the following: 'If some population has been categorized by use of categories from some device whose collection has the "duplicative organization" property (e.g., "family", "baseball team", etc.) and a member is presented with a categorized population which *can be heard* as "coincumbents" of a case of that device's unit, then:   Hear it that way.' (20)   (Emphasis in original.)   Thus, in the utterance 'The baby cried.   The mommy picked it up', our capacity for (indeed, our first preference for) hearing that the mommy in question is the mommy of that baby, and not some other woman who contingently happened to have been also categorizable as a mommy, is derivable from Sacks's

observation that the collection of categories 'baby' and
'mommy' belong to the Device 'Family', and that its duplicative
organization and corollary hearing maxim provides for our
locating the two categories in this instance as deriving not
only from the device 'Family' but from the device unit 'Same
Family'.

Finally, for present purposes, Sacks introduces his notion
of 'category-bound activities'. (21)    Sacks argues that 'cry'
is bound to 'baby', i.e. to the category 'baby' which is, in
combination with just that activity descriptor, hearably drawn
from the device 'Stage-of-Life'.    He imposes specific constraints upon what activities are to be admitted, analytically,
into the class of 'category-bound activities', and they include
the following.    Firstly, the activity which is category-bound
to a given category must be such as to permit the given category to be possibly and permissibly 'read off from' or 'heard
as implicated by' the reference to the activity.    Further, a
failure on the part of a categorized member to perform the
category-bound activity in circumstances warranting its production can entitle an observer to notice its absence and to
make some inference about the categorized member's possibly
having become an incumbent of a *different* category (e.g.
'You see, he's not crying!    He's no longer a baby; he's a
big boy now!').    And, in addition, persons not otherwise
categorizable with a particular category may, when observed
performing a category-bound activity, have that category
bestowed upon them (e.g. 'Stop moaning about the accident!
You're just a big baby', said of an adult).    Finally, Sacks
notes that categories selected to categorize some member performing a category-bound activity and categories selected to
categorize that activity are *co-selected*.    Thus, although it
is possibly correct to say of a baby crying that it is a male
shedding tears, it is not possibly recognizable as a correct or
appropriate description of the scene.    The 'preference' for
category co-selection is a strong and generative one and helps
us to understand some of the organizational and selectional
features of such utterances as the one with which Sacks
began:    'The baby cried, the mommy picked it up.'    Such a
scene *could* be described as 'The young male shed tears and
the biological female parent lifted it up', but neither the categories employed to identify the members nor the categories
employed to identify their respective actions are co-selected
and they do not exhibit the necessary orientation to the
category-boundedness of the activities they are described as
performing.

# Scarman Tribunal data

## SECTION A: DR D. MCALISTER

1 *Cross-examined by Mr Russell*

Q: When you went down to Helen's Bay on the 13th August last year, had you any inkling you were going to be called back to Belfast that night?

A: None whatsoever.

Q: You, I think, are in charge of the Order in Belfast, is that right?

A: No, Ulster.

2

Q: Who was it that called you back to Belfast?

A: James Allison.

Q: What is his position in the Order?

A: He at that time was a Sergeant in the South Belfast unit.

Q: No doubt it occurred to you, Doctor, when you went home for a social evening that this was a very extraordinary thing to happen?

A: No, because they know I am always available and that it is my job to correlate any problem or issue that
3 arises in the Order and I would be first to be told.

Q: Yes, I appreciate that. What I was saying was extraordinary was that it was necessary to set up a form of casualty clearing station in a city like Belfast. Did that not strike you as very extraordinary?

A: No, we get calls for all sorts of purpose. We attend football matches, race meetings, everything, and it is not unusual to be called. If there is any problem where we hope to be useful, we go.
4

Q: Had you, for example, set up a casualty clearing station to receive civilian casualties ever before of this kind?

A: No.

Q: Therefore if it was not extraordinary it was certainly an exceptional thing to happen?

A: It was exceptional, yes.

Q: Did you ask from anybody why they thought this was
5    necessary?

A: If the personnel on the spot thought it was necessary, I would be quite happy to go along with it.

Q: It appears, Doctor, rather than dealing with an immediate problem they were trying to anticipate a future problem; is that not the position?

A: Not really, no.    There were injuries.

Q: How many injuries on the 13th?
6
A: I do not know how many they treated before I came up there.    There were not so very many when I arrived because it was after eleven and in fact it was our personnel - I noticed that someone mentioned in the paper the other day the firemen who were burned in the car, two firemen;  I think it was our personnel who took them out from the car.

Q: Where did they take them to?

A: They did take them to the Royal.

Q: What I am trying to get from you, Doctor, is whether
7    this problem on the Wednesday, that is on the 13th, could not have been dealt with by the ordinary hospital services;  why it was necessary to set up this quite exceptional, as it were, clearing centre?

A: I think if there is a problem people are not going to go from the Falls to the Royal because you get a scratch with a stone or something like that, and this chap who belonged to the area - he did not live there actually but his mother lives there and he was visiting and saw that there was the necessity, that these things were necessary, that treatment on the spot could be given instead of going to the hospital.

8

Q: Why was it necessary?    Did you enquire from any-
    body why it was necessary?    Did you ask anybody?

A: If they thought it was necessary I was quite happy to
9   accept their judgment and they were on the spot.

The Chairman:   Just a moment - who are 'they'?

A: Well, first of all Allison and his unit who belonged
    around there, who live there, my Lord.    He was
    visiting his mother who lives right in the centre of
    the problem when the problem arose.

Mr Russell:   There had not been, on the 13th, anything
10   like a breakdown in the hospital services, had there?

A: Not that I know of, no.

Q: Did you speak to the hospital authority about the
    necessity for this centre in Sultan Street?

A: No, there was no necessity to.

Q: Did you enquire from the hospital authorities, for
    instance, whether they were stretched to the limit or
    whether there had been an excessive amount of
11   casualties on the 13th?

A: We were not in communication with the hospital at all.

Q: May we take it then, Doctor, you accepted the assur-
    ances of certain people living in the vicinity of I
    suppose the lower Falls, as a general term, that there
    was a necessity for this clearing station on the 13th?

A: It was not - well, any post that was set up - it was
    not a clearing station then, it was purely a first-aid
    post on the 13th.
12
Q: Whatever we call it, a first-aid post or a clearing
    station, somebody, on the 13th assured you this was
    a necessary step to take?

A: Yes.

Q: And you were prepared to accept that assurance?

A: Yes.

Q: And because of your position in the Order you, as it
    were, took charge of it?

A: I went along as soon as I could.

13

Q: What time did you leave on the 13th-14th night?

A: I think about two o'clock.

Q: You were there then about $2\frac{1}{2}$ hours perhaps altogether?

A: Yes.

Q: Was there another doctor there?

A: I do not think so, there was no necessity. I mean, there was just purely odd cuts from stone throwing and things like that.

14

Q: Is it fair to say on the 13th there was not very much of a rush on your services in that centre?

A: There was the feeling that anything could have happened, you know, that sort of way, but you could get a very bad knock with a stone or a piece of metal or something like that very easily.

Q: How many people did you take through in that $2\frac{1}{2}$ hours, just in round terms?

A: I did not make any record. I just really do not know.

15

Q: Was it dozens rather than hundreds?

A: Oh, there were not hundreds, no.

Q: Not hundreds?

A: No.

Q: Anybody seriously injured among the people who came in?

A: Not really. Sprains. People, as I said, falling over things and injuries and sprains and cuts.

16 Q: Pretty trivial stuff on the whole, Doctor?

A: Well, I suppose if you are getting maybe a 2 or 3 lb. stone thrown at you it might not be so trivial.

17 The Chairman: If I am walking down the main street of

my city and I got a brick on my head I would not regard it as trivial?

A: I would not either.

Mr Russell:  It could have been dealt with by the hospital's doctor, that is the point?

A: It depended on whether or not the problem escalated. If the problem escalated the hospital could not have dealt with it.

18  Q: But it did not escalate on the 13th anyway, as we know?

A: Not to a great extent.

Q: Now on the 14th, the day, were you up at the clearing station at all during the day?

A: No.

Q: Was there another doctor on duty?

A: No.

19  Q: Was there another doctor on duty at any time?

A: No.

Q: You were the sole doctor there the whole time?

A: Yes.

Q: And you got there about 7.30 to 8 and it was fairly quiet for about 3 or 3½ hours.

A: Yes.

20

Q: What time did you finish that evening?

A: Oh, some time about 7 the following morning, or 8.

Q: So you were very busy then for about seven or eight hours all during the night?

A: Yes.

Q: During that time you said that about 70 gunshot injuries came through your hands?

21
    A: Yes.

    Q: I take it that as you were the only doctor there you –

    A: Sorry, you asked me during the afternoon or during the day was I the only doctor, and I said yes. But that night another doctor came along and I rang the Royal that evening, or that night, and they asked for volunteers and four senior students plus a medical student who happened to be on holiday came around about 1 o'clock from the Royal.

22
    Q: You had two doctors, about four students or helpers?

    A: Yes, and nurses of our own unit or local nurses.

    Q: They would be volunteer nurses?

    A: Yes, volunteer nurses.

    Q: Just to get the picture, Doctor, how many people were involved in servicing the wounded on that evening? You said two doctors, four assistants to the doctors, as it were?

23
    A: Yes.

    Q: And who else?

    A: There would probably be in the region of – many of the units were out on duty, outside, so I would say there would probably be at any one time, there would be the trained medical personnel, nursing and medical personnel plus maybe 20 odd members of the unit inside.

    Q: So that there were about 30 people or thereabouts treating the casualties?

    A: There were.

24
    Q: Just to give us the picture is the hall a large hall, bigger than this court for example?

    A: It is a two-floor hall.

25 The Chairman: This is the Edel Quinn Hall?

    A: Yes.

Mr Russell: What was it like, trestle tables, or how were you dealing with people who were injured?

A:  This was the idea of the beds, that we would be able to put them on them and use them for that purpose.

Q:  You actually had beds, had you?

A:  Yes.

26  Q:  How many beds did you have?

A:  About 12 or 13.

Q:  Had they to be brought in specially?

A:  Yes, I brought them in in the afternoon.

Q:  It is obvious, is it not, that somebody on the afternoon of the 14th August last was anticipating very heavy casualties or the possibility of heavy casualties in this area?

A:  Well, the tension in the area was very great and I
27  saw from the night before that if this thing escalated from the night of the 13th, if there was any escalation at all, that we were going to have a lot of work to do, and it was purely on my own initiative and not on anybody else's initiative that these things were prepared.

Q:  The fact remains, Doctor, in the heart of the lower Falls, before the trouble had in fact escalated, there were preparations being made to receive very heavy casualties?

A:  Well, they were not made by us or by anybody we
28  know of, and as far as I know there were no preparations because the bandages and things that we got were from people having to tear up sheets initially before we could get to the hospital to get some. People brought in sheets and pillowcases that they tore up, of their own.

Q:  Perhaps it is a matter of emphasis;  some people might think that bringing in 12 or 14 beds and ringing up for doctors and nurses and so on is making fairly substantial preparation for casualties?

A:  I do not think I should be a director if I did not
29  anticipate problems.  There is not much point looking for beds at one or two o'clock in the morning if the trouble escalated, as I felt it might, from the night before's reaction.

Q: This was all within half a mile of the Royal Victoria Hospital complex?

A: Half a mile plus barricades.

Q: You mentioned, Doctor, you thought about 70 gunshot wounds went through your hands that night?

A: Yes.

30

Q: That presumably is within about seven hours you mentioned when things got busy?

A: Yes.

Q: Can you say when the gunshot injuries ceased to come in, or was it right up until 7 o'clock.

A: This is something I could not tell you because one has not a very clear idea of time, my Lord.   It is very difficult ...

31  The Chairman:  When did you leave Sultan Street?

A: The following morning round about 7 o'clock.

Q: You were there the whole night?

A: Yes, my Lord.

Q: Well then, do you remember a time during the night when the stream of gunshot wounds fell off?

A: I would think that it would be around two or half past two or around that time of the morning.


SECTION B: DR D. MCALISTER

*Cross-examined by Mr Chambers*

1  Q: On the 14th was any enquiry made as to the identity of the people who were treated in the first-aid station.   I am not asking you to give names of casualties or anything.

A: Did anybody ask us did we treat anybody?

Q: Was any enquiry made by the people who were treating the casualties as to who they were and where they came from?

A:   No.

Q:   Not even their names?

A:   Not even their names.

Q:   Was there any reason for that?

A:   First of all, there was not time, the rush was so great.

The Chairman:   Let me put it to you directly:   is it a
2       policy of the Order not to take the names of casualties
        presenting themselves to your first-aid station?

A:   We do not normally do this.

Q:   It must have been evident to you and to others that
     there would be more chance of doing a good first-aid
     healing job if embarrassing enquiries were not made?

A:   Yes.

Mr Chambers:   Is that the reason then why names were
     not asked for?

A:   I think you are twisting my Lord's last remark.   The
     first remark my Lord made was that we do not normally
     do this.

3   The Chairman:   That is right.

A:   And that was the remark I answered.   We do not
     normally take names and addresses of casualties
     particularly.

Q:   You are out there to relieve suffering?

A:   Yes.

4   Q:   And you know perfectly well if a person goes to hos-
         pital they have to give particulars or particulars have
         to be obtained?

A:   Yes.

Q:   But yours is a different function and that function
     might be diminished in its value if you made embar-
     rassing enquiries?

A:   Yes, that is what it is.

5  Mr Chambers: But what I am getting at is this: sup-
    posing you were attending casualties at a football
    match would you not take the name of that casualty?

A:  No.

The Chairman: You surely discover which side he was
    supporting, was he Chelsea or Manchester City?

A:  No, we would write down 'A patient treated for such
    and such a thing' but not necessarily his name unless
    he had a very severe injury and you had plenty of
    personnel.  But on this occasion there was not the
    time to do these sort of things.

6  Mr Chambers: And it was felt your value would be
    greater if embarrassing questions were not asked?

A:  Yes.

Q:  The situation is that you have no idea who these
    people were or where they came from?

A:  I have not;  I would not know one person.

7  Q:  They could have been Roman Catholics, could have
    been Protestants, could have been any religion at all;
    is that what you are saying?

A:  That is true.

Q:  And they could have come from the Falls Road, could
    have come from outside Belfast, anywhere at all?

A:  Any place.

8  Q:  Roughly what were the ages of the people who were
    treated?

A:  Again there is not a fixed age group;  it was a
    general age group.

Q:  You do not have to ask embarrassing questions about
    this in order to see whether they are young people or
    old people or teenagers?

A:  I am trying to think.  Remember this is a year ago.

Q:  I understand.

A:  I suppose the bulk ...

9　The Chairman:　The old men came in with heart attacks,
　　　the young men with bloody noses, is that not right?

A:　It is.

Mr Chambers:　Is that the situation?

A:　It is, yes.

Q:　The people who had what one might describe as
　　　wounds caused by violence were young men, is that
　　　right?

A:　And young women and young children.

10　Q:　But by and large were those who had sustained
　　　injuries caused by violence young men?

A:　Not necessarily.

Q:　The estimate that you have given of the number of
　　　people who passed through the clearing station having
　　　suffered from gunshot wounds is purely an estimate?

A:　It is purely an estimate.

## SECTION C: DR D. MCALISTER

*Cross-examined by Mr Chambers*

1　Mr Chambers:　You would certainly remember, would you
　　　not, if you had had reports of ambulances being
　　　stopped by armed men;　that is something you would
　　　not lightly forget?

A:　Oh yes.

Q:　So we can take it there were no such reports?

A:　Yes.　You are referring to the 15th?

Q:　I am referring to any date at all during which or on
　　　which this centre was in operation or any of these
　　　other centres were in operation?

A:　Yes.

2　Q:　Does your answer still stand that you had no such
　　　reports?

A:   I know of one occasion when I understand, apart from
Army searches which were quite frequent, an effort
was made by armed people to stop one of our ambulances one evening on the Albert Bridge.

The Chairman:   This is the sort of information Mr
Chambers has been trying to elicit.   Tell us about
that?

A:   We were taking a patient from East Belfast through
Mountpottinger region to the Royal - to the City - I
think it was the Royal - I am not sure of the hospital
now.   An ambulance was coming out from that area
this particular morning and six men got out of a taxi
or a car and produced guns and the driver accelera-
ted and they hopped into the car and they followed on
over the bridge towards the Markets.   I know that
as a fact.

3   Q:   Do you know what day that was?

A:   It was this year.

Q:   1970?

A:   1970.

Mr Chambers:   Was it at a time when there was violence
occurring in Belfast?

A:   Yes.

4   Q:   Was it at the time of the rioting in the early summer
of this year?

A:   It was, yes.

Q:   When there was considerable violence in that Albert
Bridge area?

A:   Yes.

Q:   That is the only occasion that you can remember?

A:   That I can recollect, yes.

5   Q:   Just think carefully because we want to be clear about
this:   is this the only incident involving any of your
ambulances that you heard of?

A:   You mean by civilian armed people?

Q: By civilian armed men, yes.

A: It is, yes, that I can remember.

Q: And there was nothing in any way related to the period in August 1969?

A: Not that I recall at all.

*Cross-examined by Mr McSparran*

Q: First of all if I understand correctly the questions which have been put to you here there is a rather oblique suggestion that there was something sinister about the setting up of this post in Sultan Street. Have you anything to say about that?

6

A: There was absolutely nothing sinister about it.   It was one of those automatic things that a first-aider does.   It is his duty to help wherever possible in whatever way he possibly can.

Q: And so far as the 14th is concerned were you in fact the person who was primarily responsible for the post being manned on the night of the 14th?

A: No, it was one of the Sergeants at that time had the post manned.

7 Q: I am sorry, the night of the 15th?

A: I was, yes.

Q: You were the person who suggested that some beds should be provided?

A: Yes.

Q: And that was done as I think you have said yourself purely from your own initiative?

A: Yes.

8 The Chairman: Of course you have to plan for these contingencies, do you not?

A: We have.

Q: Sometimes there are occasions when casualties do not arrive when you are expecting them?

A: Yes.

Q: You cannot be left unprepared?

A: Yes, I feel that we should be.

9  Mr McSparran:  I am a little confused about dates and so that we get that out of the way the first night you were there was on the 13th?

A: Yes.

Q: Am I right then that it was the 14th you made the suggestion about beds?

A: Yes.

Q: And you were the one who suggested people should come back that night?

A: Yes.

10  Q: In fact at that stage were there any medical supplies of any substance in the station?

A: None.

Q: Had you to obtain medical supplies in an emergency from various hospitals?

A: Yes, from the Royal and from the City and some from the Mater and whatever we had ourselves.

11  Q: As well as that were you and members of the post phoning chemists?

A: Yes.

Q: As a matter of desperation?

A: Yes.

Q: At the last minute?

A: Indeed, yes.  They came down and opened shops at one and two in the morning to give us any supplies they had.

12  Q: And purely because no preparations of any kind had been made?

A: No, this was not anticipated at all.

Q: It was completely unexpected?

A: Unexpected, yes.

## SECTION D: FATHER V.A. MULVEY

*Cross-examined by Mr Chambers*

1 Q: Let us see if we can approach the matter in another way. Would you agree with me that during the past twelve months the people of the Bogside and the members of the police have been more frequently in conflict than during any year prior to that?

A: Yes.

2 Q: Would you agree with me that a great deal of the underlying cause of that conflict has been what has been described as civil rights disturbances?

A: I could not accept that as it is put, no.

Q: Would you agree, Father Mulvey, that there are people, be they calling themselves civil rights workers, or revolutionaries, or anarchists, who have been deliberately placing the people of the Bogside in conflict with the police for the past twelve months?

A: No, I am sure I would not accept that in the sense of the whole community of the Bogside.

Q: Let us amend it to portions of the community of the Bogside.

A: I cannot think of any particular incident where some people have said 'Let us attack the police'.

3 Q: I am not asking you that. I am not meaning physical conflict, I am meaning where the police have been obliged, on the one hand, to restrain or to take action against the people of the Bogside.

A: There have been situations that have arisen as a result of protests organized by civil rights members, or people saying they were members of the civil rights movement.

4 Q: Those conflicts, I suggest, have been, by and large, in the last twelve months?

A: Altogether I suppose in the last twelve months.

Q: Do you think it at all possible that that is the reason for the deterioration in the relationship between the Bogsiders and the police?

A: No, I do not think that that is the reason.  I think that the civil rights demonstrations were originally, and probably still are, meant to be peaceful, that no-one at any time set out to create conflict with the forces of law and order, and that I think they had many things about which they had the right to protest.

5 Q: Do you accept that so-called peaceful demonstrations can lead to action which is anything but peaceful?

A: There could be action that is anything but peaceful in demonstrations that began as peaceful demonstrations.

Q: Do you agree that in dealing with, say, a sit-down the police may have to use physical force to remove the people concerned?

A: I would accept that.

6 Q: Would you accept, therefore, that this kind of thing is likely to lead to a deterioration in the relationship between the Bogsiders and the RUC?

A: Nothing quite as light as that.  I think it would need to be something more serious than the removal of people sitting in the street if it is done by two or three policemen without excessive violence.

Q: Do you accept that repeated small incidents may have a large effect?

A: I would accept that that is possible, yes.

7 Q: Do you accept that there are people - I am not saying necessarily in Londonderry, but in Northern Ireland - who would be highly delighted to see the relationship between the Bogsiders and the police deteriorating?

A: I think there probably are such people.  I am not saying that I know any one of them, but there are such people, yes.

Q: You see, what I am suggesting to you is this:  you have spoken of this deterioration in relationship and I am suggesting to you that that is no accident.   Do you think it is an accident?

A: I do not think anyone deliberately set out to create tension between the police and the people.

8  Q: I suggest to you, Father Mulvey, that that is exactly what happened.

A: I am sorry, I do not agree with you.   I think the deterioration resulted because of misuse of authority and partisan behaviour on the part of some policemen.

9  Q: You have said that for years and years the police were accepted in the Bogside.

A: Yes.

Q: And that in these past twelve months things have undergone a radical change.

A: Yes.

Q: Is it right to say that it is in precisely that period that we have had this civil rights agitation?

A: Yes.

10 Q: Do you not accept that the two are related?

A: I do not accept that they are necessarily related.

Q: Do you accept that they may be related?

A: They may be related, but not intentionally.

Q: How can you know that?

A: Because I do not know of anyone who has set out deliberately to cause bad feeling between the people and the police.   I can say that the civil rights movement gained respect because of its essentially non-violent nature.   I think if that non-violent character had been acknowledged and reciprocated we would not have the tension between the people and the police we now have.

11 Q: Do you accept that at some stage of its activities the civil rights movement became infiltrated by people bent on disorder?

A: To say 'bent on disorder' is a phrase I could not sub-
stantiate. I would accept it was infiltrated by people
who have private axes to grind who are not at one
with the main leaders of the civil rights movement.

Q: And who would be only too delighted if disorder
resulted?

A: I could not answer that.

12 Q: You have described your actions on a number of occasions where it is apparent that you have been going
to considerable trouble - and do not for one moment
think I am being critical - trying to quieten down
young people, mostly young men, young boys, from
the Bogside who were causing trouble in Londonderry?

A: From the Bogside or outside it, people I did not
recognize necessarily.

Q: You did not recognize them. Let me say people from
your community, meaning by that the Roman Catholic
community - and I do not by that suggest there are
two separate communities. That has been an occupation that has taken much of your time?

A: Yes.

13 Q: Does that mean that there is a hooligan element in that
community?

A: I am not prepared to use the word 'hooligan', I think
it is a rather artistic term.

Q: What term would you prefer?

A: There are youths who can get so hot-headed that they
are careless of what trouble they cause.

Q: Can you think of no other description for them than
that?

A: I would say irresponsible.

14 Q: These are irresponsible youths. You would not put
it higher than that? Are they vandals?

A: I would not use the word 'vandals' either. I think
if we enquire they are quite law-abiding.

The Chairman:  Would you use the word reckless of other people's safety?

A:  Yes.

Q:  Would you use the word reckless of other people's property?

A:  Yes, I would.

15  Mr Chambers:  These are people whom you have had occasion to attempt to restrain in one way and another?

A:  Yes.

Q:  And with varying success.

A:  Yes.

Q:  Sometimes you have been unable to achieve what you set out to achieve?

A:  That is true, yes.

16  Q:  Would you accept that such people can readily be stirred up to violence against other members of the community and against the property of other members of the community?

A:  I would agree with that, yes.

Q:  Having heard the evidence that has so far been given, do you accept that it was those people rather than any strangers or people from outside who started the trouble in Londonderry on the 12th August?

A:  I would accept it was probably that kind of person.

Q:  That is, people in this irresponsible element of the Roman Catholic community?

A:  I do not know if it was the Roman Catholic ...

The Chairman:  I do not know that the words 'Roman Catholic' apply, Mr Chambers.

Mr Chambers:  You have spoken of this incident in July when you say stones were thrown by the police. This was late in the evening, was it not?

A:  It would be early morning, 12.30.

## SECTION E: FATHER V.A. MULVEY

*Cross-examined by Mr Chambers*

1   The Chairman:   Just before we adjourn there are one or
       two short questions I should like to put to Father
       Mulvey.

    Q:   You have told us more than once that you think that
         there was a real risk of strangers coming in to
         Londonderry from outside and taking advantage of
         perhaps a comparatively small incident to provoke
         violence?

    A:   Yes, that was the fear.

2   Q:   I want to get a good deal of this Londonderry Inquiry
         into, perhaps, proper porupective.   I take it from
         that answer that you, knowing the people of London-
         derry, would have believed them able to live in peace
         with each other if some sort of external irritation
         such as you were envisaging had not been applied?

    A:   I would think so, yes.

    Q:   And when you give that answer you include, do you
         not, the police within the term 'people of London-
         derry'?

    A:   Yes, I would.

3   Q:   Therefore – I think this important – and I am sure
         you as a priest will see its importance – you are pre-
         pared to ascribe to the police motives as peaceful and
         as good as you would ascribe to your own flock and,
         in particular, to the people of Bogside?

    A:   I would like to think I would do that.

    Q:   You would agree?

    A:   Yes.

4   Q:   We know also you would accept, would not you, that
         both in July and in August the police action, however
         much or however little you may criticize it, was their
         reaction to a developing situation of violence?

    A:   Yes, my Lord, if ...

    Q:   They did not begin it, did they?

A:  No, my Lord.

Q:  And you would accept, would you, that perhaps with errors of judgment, perhaps not, they, citizens of Londonderry, eager like all others to live in peace, were doing the best that they could to contain a situation which was putting them under great strain?

A:  I am sorry, my Lord, I could not accept that entirely.

5  Q:  How far would you go?

A:  The criticism I would make of the police may be just a criticism of their judgment.

Q:  Exactly.

A:  But the point at which it became impossible to stop the disturbance and at which I say something in the nature of a revolt started, was the point at which the police led a civilian faction or at least acted in collusion with a civilian faction coming into the Bogside area.

6  Q:  But again, you were good enough to indicate that this is a criticism of their judgment?

A:  I think it may be, yes.

Q:  Not a criticism of their motives?

A:  I would like to think it is not a criticism of their motives.    If I am in order in saying this, unfortunately, the history of relationships with the police over the past year would lead people in the Bogside area to feel that the police wanted to get in and punish them in some way, and this was the reaction, and it was the reaction to this action in collusion with civilians that I was afraid of when I at first complained.

7  Q:  We have heard an enormous amount, no doubt rightly, in criticism of the police.    It takes two sides, does not it, to create the sort of unhappy situation that we have been considering?

A:  Yes.

Q:  And you have made some criticisms, and we shall examine them, about police action.    You would not be prepared to say that others were blameless, would you?

A: No, I would not be prepared to say that others were blameless.

## SECTION F: MRS E. MCKNIGHT

*Cross-examined by Mr Rowland*

The Chairman: How old a man is your husband today?

A: Thirty-three; he was 20 when he was interned for four years.

Mr Murray: He had been interned in 1956 for four years?

A: Yes.

Q: That was in connection with the IRA campaign of the mid-fifties, was it?

A: Yes.

Q: He is a member of the IRA, is he?

The Chairman: Before you answer that question, she might think it was not because it was an IRA campaign but because it was a police campaign.

Mr Murray: Was it in connection with the IRA outrages of the mid fifties?

A: That he was interned, yes.

The Chairman: You are saying yes. You see, Counsel sometimes put questions that quite unintentionally appear to be vague. I do not know whether you accept that there were IRA outrages between 1956 and 1962. Do you?

A: I say that my husband was interned at that time because he was a Republican. I am not saying that he is a member of the IRA. I am saying he was interned because he was a Republican.

Q: And there were (let us use a neutral word) troubles between 1956 and 1962?

A: Yes.

Mr Murray: He was interned for four years, you say?

A: Yes.

# Hell's Angels data

1 A : I was wondering whether you could tell me who's
  handling the business that went on (at the New
  Planet) last week

2 R : erm.  Well, Inspector Sullivan's getting some information together

3 A : ah, erm ... my name's Anderson and I'm chairman of
  the Trust and I'm really just trying to find out
  what's happening

4 R : well, there's not much happening yet as far as I know
  ... the only thing we know is that the place is being
  used by er all these er dropouts and er Hell's Angels
  and they're prepared to have a battle royal complete
  with er weapons and goodness knows what with a load
  of skinheads

5 A : yeah

6 R : er to my mind that was not the kind of thing this er
  effort was supposed to be for

7 A : yeah er I see I mean you don't know erm you don't
  know what's going to happen?

8 R : I've no idea er I mean its up to the city council that
  isn't it?

9 A : er no I wasn't meaning that ... I was meaning from
  your end

10 R : well er, all we're doing is just getting some information together as much as we can about this er Planet
  er playground affair...

11 A : oh I see yeah ... you say you say there's been a lot
  of this fighting going on

12 R : er well I won't say there's a lot of it been going on
  but er if we don't put a stop to it it'll certainly go
  on the increase

13  A:  er.   Yes ... er the only thing is that I keep y'know
        as chairman of the outfit I keep getting conflicting
        stories of what you know what happened and er I
        thought you know I'd come to the place where presum-
        ably there would be you know the full story as it
        were...

14  R:  well, there was quite an article in the Guardian I
        think the other week about it wasn't there...

15  A:  yeah ... I read that but then some of the things
        other people have told me don't quite you know there
        seem to be its a bit vague as to you know how many
        battles there were and this sort of thing ... and what
        actually happened at this battle and how many were
        involved and ...

16  R:  well the battle didn't actually take place because we
        er went to it beforehand...

17  A:  oh, I see ... so there wasn't a battle at all...

18  R:  no, not on this particular night

19  A:  ooh, I see...

20  R:  but there could have been ... but there could have
        been ... and it could have been deadly serious...

21  A:  yeah.

22  R:  but we're just not going to put up with stuff like
        that

23  A:  yeah, yeah, do you know, is there is there going to
        be ... there were some arrests made I believe weren't
        there ... this was the other thing I was...

24  R:  yes

25  A:  of er of er of what ... who were the people who were
        arrested do you know I mean er...

26  R:  ooh, I couldn't say offhand, I think these were about
        seven in all...

27  A:  yeah, were there some skinheads or ...

28  R:  no, no, not skinheads, these are Hell's Angels types.

29  A:  I see, er, do you get a lot of bother from skinheads
        as well?

30   R:   not particularly

31   A:   yeah

32   R:   er the Hell's Angels types are the people who er *don't* stop at home ... they sleep out, they sleep rough, they're a dirty, scruffy idle shower, they live off social security er plus er thieving er things here and there

33   A:   yeah

34   R:   we've er arrested a number of people in the past who've been sleeping out there...

35   A:   have you?

36   R:   yes

37   A:   er mmm, yeah.

38   R:   breakers, housebreakers, shop breakers, thieves, goodness knows what...

39   A:   yeah

40   R:   its juster a place for them to go and sleep er .. they've got no responsibility, they don't want any responsibility

41   A:   yeah

42   R:   they just want other people to keep them.

43   A:   yeah .. I see .. OK....

44   R:   its just er developing into a problem is the place.

45   A:   yeah

46   R:   you see

47   A:   yes er well the thing is, its a bit unfortunate its come to a head at this point in time as far as we're concerned cos we're planning to get, we're hoping to get the the thing the building made secure, you know, I don't know if you know about this.

48   R:   well, you could never make that place secure.

49   A:   we-e-ell, I mean insofar as building a wall and er

putting windows, doors and roofs on and things of
this sort ... er....

50 R: I don't think your windows would last very long...

51 A: oh ... you sound very pessimistic...

52 R: well (coughs) knowing these types and dealing with
them er ... one can't look at it any other way...

53 A: yeah ... well the people who work down there claim
that there haven't been any break-ins since these
people have been around in fact and that they act as
sort of night watchmen, er but I don't know er...

54 R: what?   These Hell's Angels?

55 A: yeah

56 R: but they're the people who're doing the break-ins...

57 A: sorry at the New Planet there haven't been any break-
ins, you know, but I don't know whether they've
been ... you mean...

58 R: well, I mean there's nothing there now, is there?

59 A: well, there are some workshops, yes, which have quite
a lot of tools and equipment and things...

60 R: well, er that's been one of the troubles, you see, er,
they've er ... er ... a lot of the things have been
left there relatively insecure

61 A: yeah

62 R: er, screwdrivers, saws, goodness knows what -
wonderful breaking instruments

63 A: oh ... I see

64 R: I mean its no good just putting a padlock on a building and saying well its locked up its secure, that er
that doesn't stop these people...

65 A: no - what you're saying these Hell's Angels people
have actually been breaking into the Planet workshops...

66 R: that's what I mm consider myself - my own personal
opinion

67  A:  yeah

68  R:  I mean to say, I went in one night when there was
        erm half a dozen of them there er ... the place was
        open, the lock was broken on the door, there were
        tools lying all over the place, on the floor, round
        about er screwdrivers, er, saws, pincers, hammers,
        everything

69  A:  mmm

70  R:  its just asking for, er, trouble.

71  A:  yeah I see ... er well I think that yeah we're gonna
        have a meeting with er you and the town council and
        one or two others so maybe we'll be able to come to
        some er solution, but I mean the point is the thing
        I'm concerned about really is that er ... er ... over
        the summer we are hoping to complete the building
        programme and then eventually er hopefully ... um
        ... appoint some qualified person to take charge of
        the place er...

72  R:  yes but its no use someone taking charge of it if
        they're not there ... its no good leaving it overnight

73  A:  what ... er you...

74  R:  ... and leaving it unattended...

75  A:  oh ... I see ... so you're saying that there's n ...
        no no point in having a place like that at all...

76  R:  not if its left unattended...

77  A:  what ... unless there's someone actually lives in you
        mean.

78  R:  yes

79  A:  yeah, what, do you think there ought to be a flat
        there for the organizers or something like this...

80  R:  oh, well, something like that because i ... its too
        easy

81  A:  yeah

82  R:  I mean to say the approach to it is er um wide open

83  A:  well at the moment it is, yes.

84 R: Yes, well, I mean to say the er, m, anyone can get to it from er one or two or three directions...

85 A: oh, yes, I see what you mean yes yeah...

86 R: I mean to say that the object of it is a children's playground, isn't it, initially?

87 A: yeah

88 R: well all its becoming is just a doss house for people who are a drop-out variety

89 A: yeh, well, on the other hand, I mean er one of the original things was to involve people who were drop outs as well and try and do something about them erm...

90 R: ooh dear me, I'm afraid you've got much more faith in human nature than I have

91 A: yeh well maybe with a bit of luck we'll see some of them pushing wheelbarrows this summer ... that'll be a turn up for the books ... er...

92 R: well er you might get them to push a few wheel-barrows, but what they'll do when they're not push-ing wheelbarrows I don't know er...

93 A: yeah

94 R: not a bad idea might be to go and get some work somewhere

95 A: yeh, quite, yeh

96 R: that's the solution for them

97 A: yeh

98 R: they should go and live at their homes

99 A: yeh

100 R: n ... not sleep out in dirt and filth...

101 A: yeh ... er do you know how many have...

102 R: I know dirt and filth nowadays seems to be er a bit of a virtue but er still perhaps that's my er er obscure way of looking at it...

103  A:  on this sleeping out thing, I haven't been able to
          discover how many people have been sleeping there,
          have you any idea cos you know we are concerned
          about it er...

104  R:  *six*, seven, eight, nine, ten at a time.

105  A:  really

106  R:  yes

107  A:  as many as that?

108  R:  Yes, th ... they light a fire there, they go round
          to Hargreaves at the front when they're delivering
          vegetables, get carrots and potatoes, things like
          that, help themselves

109  A:  do they?

110  R:  They do indeed

111  A:  yeh ... I see ... O.K. well thanks for your help
          anyway erm ... we hope er we hope we you know
          the thing doesn't get out of hand, its obviously
          worrying you

112  R:  th ... the only thing to say about the Hell's Angels
          is that the Angels doesn't apply but the Hell part
          does

113  A:  hahahahaha, what about the skinheads?   Ha ha ha.

114  R:  no, you'll find the skinheads may be a l ... little
          troublesome, but at least they do live at home.

115  A:  oh, I see, yes, and do they work as well?

116  R:  a number of them do yes

117  A:  yes, yeh ... (pause) I haven't actually seen any of
          these people, I haven't seen any skinheads actually
          ...

118  R:  you don't see much of the skinheads

119  A:  yes, yeh, must go around with my eyes shut I
          think...

120  R:  I mean to say th ... these Hell's Angels that've been
          going down to the Planet there these are the ones we
          turned out of this flat in South Road

121 A: oh are they

122 R: they occupied that place as squatters

123 A: yeh, when was that?

124 R: oh, perhaps eight-nine-ten months ago

125 A: oh as long ago as that mmm and they'd been living in an empty house had they?

126 R: they hadn't lived in it, they just took over an empty house

127 A: yeh, oh, I see an ... and you got you cleared them out of there.

128 R: er ... you get young girls going missing from home

129 A: yeh

130 R: I mean to say we've got one of 'em er one of them charged with an offense against a young girl

131 A: have you?

132 R: mm

133 A: one of the Hell's Angels?

134 R: yeh

135 A: oh, mm

136 R: that's the kind.   They're certainly not angels

137 A: no, quite, no ... oh well this sounds as though it's more serious than I'd anticipated.

138 R: I, I mean to say the cult that they have I mean to say they arrange their own wedding ceremonies

139 A: yeh ... do they?

140 R: they have this weird and wonderful er system of one leader

141 A: yeh

142 R: and he has his one woman

143  A:  yeh, oh.

144  R:  its, its, er contrary to anyone's idea of a decent
         way of life...

145  A:  yes, mm ... okay

146  R:  you see its not just a childish er er...

147  A:  do you know what ages they are ... do you know
         what ages these lads are?

148  R:  anything from seventeen up to twenty odd...

149  A:  yeh, I see, what about ... do ... do you have I
         mean do you have any contact with the, the er Boris
         and Jim who er are supposed to be working down
         there?

150  R:  with who?

151  A:  Boris and Jim, you know the two guys who are
         supposed...

152  R:  I've not myself no...

153  A:  yeah, I was just wondering er cos...

154  R:  ... they're certainly not children

155  A:  yeh, yeh ... no I was wondering - you know -
         whether they were sort of er backing these fellas up
         and supporting them and this sort of thing

156  R:  oh I've no idea I've had no contact with Boris or
         anyone at all myself

157  A:  yeh

158  R:  I've just been down there and seen them at night
         and they just get some old wood together, sleep
         down on the ground on the deck and er light the fire
         and er things like that

159  A:  yeh

160  R:  I mean to say if er if an African came and built a hut
         in the middle of town and er lived like that, there'd
         be a real outcry

161  A:  yeah

162 R: but if a white man does it...

163 A: well they are out (o) sight there, aren't they?

164 R: pardon?

165 A: they are out of sight there, heh?

166 R: aye, well out of sight perhaps out of mind

167 A: yeh

168 R: but its th ... erm the young ones that look up to these people

169 A: yeh, do they?

170 R: the example they set is er shocking

171 A: yeh

172 A: is it actually against the law, I mean I just want to know legally where we stand erm as well.

173 R: er - no - not really but er there are a number of moral things which even though they're not er against the law are certainly not desirable, are they?

174 A: no - no quite

175 R: its the effect it has on younger people

176 A: yeh

177 R: the impressionable ones

178 A: yeh, mmm, ah well its very tricky this, very tricky - anyway thanks for your help erm

179 R: okay

180 A: I think I've got a much clearer idea than I had

181 R: anyway, well there is some erm some sort of enquiry going on about it er but er what stage its actually reached I don't know - I've not taken any...

182 A: well there is supposed to be going to ... oh oh yeh I mean from our end yeh, yeh, there is supposed to be going to be a meeting between the police and the town council and er th ... er trust at some stage as which might help matters

183  R :  yes I know we are collecting certain information as
         to what we know about it but er...

184  A :  yeh

185  R :  its er its not my particular job

186  A :  yeh

187  R :  but I don't know what stage its reached really

188  A :  okay, fine, many thanks

189  R :  right thank you

190  A :  yep cheers, bye bye.

# Social enquiry reports data

I

## GENERAL REMARKS

Kenneth's mother is a native of M and lived there until seven years ago when she left her husband and came to A to live with a Mr Y, a divorced man. At the time she had three children (an elder daughter is now married) and Mr Y had two. The two youngest children were born after Mrs P and Mr Y started living together.

From what I have heard, Kenneth's father was a man who drank heavily and set a poor example to his children: I understand that he has made no efforts even to enquire about their well-being, since the family split up. Kenneth's step-father, who was known to me, was at least as unsatisfactory. A lazy man and a gambler, he made little secret of his dislike for Kenneth, and was responsible for a great deal of unhappiness and poverty. He finally left home two years ago, after taking the contents of the electricity and gas meters. Since then, the quality of family life has improved and financially Mrs P has been slightly better off and able to provide better for the children. There has also been less tension in the home, but she has never found it easy to control the older boys. She is a woman who has tried to do her best for her children despite being beset by many problems.

## SUBJECT

Kenneth is a healthy boy of at least average intelligence and ability. The pleasant sides to his character have been becoming more apparent as he grows older, although he has remained moody, restless and inclined to act impulsively. This is perhaps not surprising when one considers his unhappy early life described above. At the time that he was placed on Probation 2½ years ago he was resentful, cheeky and unpopular with other boys: his way of trying to get the admiration of his colleagues was to indulge in stealing and other unlawful activity. During the course of the Probation Order the home situation and his conduct improved, as did his behaviour and attainment at school. After the ending of the order he voluntarily remained in contact with me, and I used to receive good reports on him from the leader of Z Youth Club.   On the more negative side, although he has never, until now, been out of work for long, he quickly left the firm where an apprenticeship had been found for him when he left school at Easter last year, and has worked since at repetitive jobs which have not used his full potential.   He himself now regrets leaving his original apprenticeship, and realizes that he has let an opportunity slip.

During the past few weeks there has been a marked deterioration in his behaviour.   He has had frequent disputes with his mother which have resulted in him leaving home on several occasions;   his behaviour generally has deteriorated and he has been drinking.   All this, and his re-appearance before the Court in March and now for these mean offences are disappointing, and a major setback in what was an improving situation.   His mother is at the end of her tether and has no idea how to handle Kenneth.   Both she and Kenneth need help if this depressing situation is to be improved, and in view of his ability to accept help in the past the Court may feel that the making of a new Supervision Order would be more appropriate than custodial treatment.

1st May, 1972


II

GENERAL REMARKS

Mr and Mrs K married in 1953 and lived all their married life in O (except for nine months at B in 1968) until their move to A in March, 1970.   Mr K's family are well-known to the Social Agencies in O, but he himself is an honest, quiet and sober man who normally holds a good job, and is currently employed by Grasswell and Taylor.   Unfortunately in the past he has taken little part in the upbringing of his sons, leaving the decision making and administration of discipline to his wife.   Mrs K is an intelligent, articulate woman who maintains high standards in the home but who has been inconsistent in her treatment of the two older children.   Andrew, the favourite son, has been spoiled, whereas she never felt able to give John sufficient care and affection in his early years. Mrs K feels guilty about this and has tried to make up for it in recent years.   She is now very worried and anxious and her present poor health appears to be attributable to this situation.   Mr and Mrs K's marriage, although quite settled now, has not been without its difficulties and this has been unsettling for the children.

SUBJECT

John is a boy of below average intelligence, but of good
physical health.   Despite living his early years in an area of
O where delinquency and violence was rife, it was not until
his Father took the family away in 1968 that he and his
brother both came to the attention of the Courts.   A year
after committing his first offence he ran away from home (by
then back in O), returned to the scene of his previous
offence and committed another.   This resulted in his second
Probation Order (both were of a year's duration) but in
September 1970, with the agreement of John and his Mother,
this Order was extended because his behaviour continued to
present serious problems.

The family moved to A in March, 1970 in order to enable
John 'to make a new start.'   Unfortunately, however, the
root of the trouble seems to lie not only in the environment,
but also in John's relationship with his Mother.   She has told
me that he was not 'planned' but that in any case she wanted
a girl and I believe he experienced almost total rejection at
birth.   Matters have not been helped by the fact that he
lies to his Mother and not only wets the bed but soils his
clothing when under stress.   Attempts to get psychiatric
help for this problem and the other nervous complaints from
which this lad suffers have been unsuccessful.

From October, 1969 to March, 1972 he committed no offences
and seemed to benefit from being under Supervision.   He had
a better school record after his move to A and remained working at the same firm from leaving school in the Summer of 1971
to committing the offence of Theft in June this year.   After
that he quickly gained new employment, but as quickly lost it.
Since being bailed by your Court last week, however, his
efforts to find work have been rewarded and he has obtained
employment in a handbag factory where he will earn £9 per
week.

Both John and his Mother make as much use as they can, in
their different ways, of Supervision, and my relationship with
this boy and his family is an intensive one.   However, after
four years of being supervised John still tends to wander the
streets at night and behave in an unbalanced way, and relations between him and his Mother have remained 'overcharged'.
When I first heard of this latest offence my initial reaction was
to consider recommending to Your Worships that he should be
sent to a Detention Centre.   Since his release from Realey,
however (where he spent a week after telling a lie to the
Court about his age), he has shown small signs of a change of
heart.   He has indicated his regret at the way his conduct
has affected his mother's health, has been prepared to spend

time talking about his life, and has gone out and got himself
a job.   In the circumstances the Court may feel that to give
this boy one more chance of remaining under supervision
would be a risk worth taking.

Appendix 5

1 If a = number of relevant elements comprised in the term
used to denote the act

  c = number of elements comprised in term used to denote
  the consequences

  t = number of relevant elements comprised in description
  of whole episode

then

$$a = t - c.$$

2 <u>Action Ascription 1</u>     Action (Consequences)
                                <u>Ascription 2</u>

(A)  He shot John intentionally.   Entertained his friends.

(B)  He fired the gun.             Shot John intentionally.

3     <u>Action</u> A $(T_1)$           <u>Action</u> B $(T_2)$

Description D (A)              Description D (B)

4  A: So you gave him the sleeping pills and you struck him.

   B: Well, it was after/

   A: Yes or no?

   B: I gave him the pills, but he did not fall asleep – he
      was full of energy ... he wouldn't fall asleep ... it
      was getting towards midnight, so I thought if I could
      knock him out some other way; so I waited behind the
      door; I didn't mean to kill him.

5  A: So she gave him the sleeping pills and struck him on
      the head.

   B: No, not straight after ... *that* was three hours later.

   A: Oh?  So what happened?

# Group therapy data

1  A:  Well, for a start I (do) think he should tell us how his weekend went at home what he did and what happened, how he feels about it.

2  B:  I've got that much to say, so I'll have to wait till this chap comes.   ((     ))

(Someone laughs softly.)

3  A:  So it's up to Dr Smith or William as he prefers it.

4  C:  D'you call him William?

(pause)

5  A:  In here?   Ya.

(Someone mutters.)

6  C:  Do you?   Why why do you sor' of er (let's) say, in here, d'you call him, why don't you call him William all the time?

7  D:  *You* don't call him William, do you?

8  E:  Who d'you mean?

9  D:  Dr Smith.

10  C:  *I* don't call him William ... nor anything.

11  E:  ((     ))

12  A:  Well, the thing is you'll find if you (were to) call him in here, if you say Dr Smith, 'e'll say my name is William.

13  C:  Mmm.

14  F:  Ya.

15  A:  You see...eheh.

16 F: Ye ... don't seem right to call him William outside here, though does it?

17 C: Well, if you call him William in here you may as well bloody call him William outside.

18 F: Ehahaha ... yehehe.

# NOTES

## INTRODUCTION

1  This distinctive approach to sociological inquiry, focusing upon the practices and methods whereby social order is constructed, was initiated by Harold Garfinkel. See his seminal 'Studies in Ethnomethodology' (Prentice-Hall, 1967).

2  For a comprehensive introduction to the formal study of communicative interaction, see Jim Schenkein (ed.), 'Studies in the Organization of Conversational Interaction' (Academic Press, 1978).

3  See, inter alia, H. Sacks, An Initial Investigation into the Usability of Conversational Data for Doing Sociology, in David Sudnow (ed.), 'Studies in Social Interaction' (Free Press, 1972); H. Sacks, On the Analyzability of Stories by Children, in Roy Turner (ed.), 'Ethnomethodology' (Penguin, 1974); and H. Sacks, Hotrodder: A Revolutionary Category, in George Psathas (ed.), 'Everyday Language: Studies in Ethnomethodology' (Irvington Press, 1979). For a brief overview of Sacks's contribution, see Jeff Coulter, Harvey Sacks: A Preliminary Appreciation, 'Sociology', vol. 10, no. 3, September 1976.

4  This term was coined by Sacks, An Initial Investigation, op. cit. For a summary of his formal findings in respect of membership categorization, see Appendix 1.

5  D.Z. Phillips and H.O. Mounce, 'Moral Practices' (Routledge & Kegan Paul, 1969), pp. 20-1.

6  This notion is taken from Gilbert Ryle. See his Formal and Informal Logic, in 'Dilemmas' (Cambridge University Press, 1954).

7  Cheyney Ryan, The Normative Concept of Coercion, 'Mind', October 1980.

8  Ibid., p. 492.

9  Hayden White, Historical Text as Literary Artifact, in R.H. Canary and H. Kozicki (eds), 'The Writing of History: Literary Form and Historical Understanding' (University of Wisconsin Press, 1978).

10  Ibid., p. 46. For a related discussion, see also his Fictions of Factual Representation, in A. Fletcher (ed.), 'The Literature of Fact' (Columbia University Press, 1972).

11  R.M. Hare, 'Freedom and Reason' (Oxford University Press, 1972 ed.), passim.

12  Ibid., p. 126.

13  Kai Nielsen, On Being Morally Authoritative, 'Mind', July 1980, p. 427.

14  David Cooper, Moral Relativism, in Peter A. French, Theodore E. Uehling, Jr and Howard K. Wettstein (eds), 'Midwest Studies in Philosophy, Vol. 111: Studies in Ethical Theory' (University of Minnesota Press, 1978).

15  Donald Davidson, Thought and Talk, in S. Guttenplan (ed.), 'Mind and Language' (Oxford University Press, 1975).

16  Cooper, op. cit., p. 101.

17  Ibid.

18  Ibid.

19  See Jeff Coulter, Beliefs and Practical Understanding, in George Psathas (ed.), 'Everyday Language: Studies in Ethnomethodology' (Irvington Press, 1979).

20 Nielsen, op. cit.
21 Ibid., p. 428.
22 F.E. Snare, The Diversity of Morals, 'Mind', July 1980, p. 355.
23 Peter Winch, 'Ethics and Action' (Routledge & Kegan Paul, 1972),
   p. 152.
24 Phillips and Mounce, op. cit., p. 105.

## CHAPTER 1  MEMBERSHIP CATEGORIZATIONS

1 This data, which I shall refer to as 'The Hell's Angels Data' (hence:
   H.A. Data), was provided under the auspices of work undertaken for
   an SSRC-sponsored project, Community Reactions to Deviance (Dr J.M.
   Atkinson, Principal Investigator), Manchester University, 1973-74.
2 Our knowledge that this is a group comes by virtue of our ability to
   hear 'Hell's Angels' as a proper collective name;  our knowledge of
   what the group is is substantive, and like all substantive knowledge
   may be differentially available to members of a culture.
3 This question will be answered in Chapter 3.
4 The use of the notion of 'clusters' here (drawing on Wittgenstein) is
   not intended to be identified with its use in the cluster *theory* or the
   cluster-of-descriptions theory of naming discussed by Saul Kripke and
   John Searle.    (S. Kripke, Naming and Necessity, in G. Harman and
   D. Davidson (eds), 'Semantics of Natural Language' (D. Reidel Co.,
   1972);  John Searle, Proper Names, 'Mind', vol. 67, 1958.)
5 A category such as 'doctor' functions somewhat differently as an explanation.    Although its use in that capacity does not furnish *grounds*
   for action (and thus may contrast with that option where available), it
   nevertheless strongly provides for *reasons for* action (but no specific
   reason).    Where provided us an explanation for some action it may be
   used as a formulation of a domain of practice and a set of obligations
   and rights that provide reasons for acting.    We shall look at such
   categories in more detail in the next section.
6 Albert J. Reiss, Jr, The Social Integration of Queers and Peers, in
   Howard S. Becker (ed.), 'The Other Side' (Free Press, 1964), pp.
   183-4.
7 This issue is taken up in Chapter 8.    For further instances of double
   categorization, see Chapter 4.
8 This data was made available to me by Professor Richard Frankel.    I
   understand that it comes from a corpus collected and transcribed by
   Professor A. Adato.
9 This data is drawn from official transcripts of the Scarman Tribunal
   hearings into Violence and Civil Disorder in Northern Ireland, 1969
   (hence:  S.T. Data) and was very kindly made available to me by Dr
   Paul Drew, York University, England.
10 It is clear that Q in the data orients to one set of category terms as
   being 'stronger' than the categorizations and descriptions provided by
   A:
       Q:  These are irresponsible youths.    You would not put it higher
           than that?   Are they vandals?
   One of the features of such a possible contrast may be that whilst
   'hooligan' and 'vandal' both provide a sense of deliberateness to actions
   that generate the ascription of such categories, 'irresponsible' and
   'hot-headed' maintain or project an *indeterminacy of intention* involved
   in relevant actions.    Specifically, where it is the same kind of action
   or set of observable consequences that could generate either categorization for practical purposes, then the use of one rather than the other
   may be hearable as being a 'stronger' or 'weaker' action (or involvement) attribution.    For some related issues, see Chapter 6.
11 I am grateful to Earl Taylor for this observation.
12 Harvey Sacks, On the Analyzability of Stories by Children, in Roy
   Turner (ed.), 'Ethnomethodology' (Penguin, 1974).

13   D.R. Watson, Categorization, Authorization and Blame-Negotiation in
     Conversation, 'Sociology: Special Issue on Language and Practical
     Reasoning', vol. 12, no. 1, January 1978.
14   W.W. Sharrock, On Owning Knowledge, in Roy Turner (ed.), 'Ethno-
     methodology' (Penguin, 1974).
15   An occasioned accomplishment which is, it would seem, constrained in
     important respects by the syntactic-pragmatic limits to options for
     transformation.   In this way, whilst you may not have a category-
     transformation like 'She's a get-books-back-to-the-library-on-time*r*'
     from a description such as 'She gets her books back to the library on
     time', you *could* have 'She's a get-books-back-to-the-library-on-time
     *type*'!   (Contrast 'She's a Johnnie-can-do-no-wrong-*er*' with 'She's a
     Johnnie-can-do-no-wrong *type*'.   Cf. the Adato data earlier: 'He's a
     Romney-can-do-no-wrong type'.)   The concept of 'type' may be in-
     voked, amongst other ways, when a complex construction is being
     packaged into a single predicate, for which no appropriate suffix is
     available (e.g. '-er', '-ist', etc.).   I owe this point to Jeff Coulter.
16   The notion of 'category-generated activities' belongs to Roy Turner and
     is discussed in his paper Words, Utterances and Activities, in J.D.
     Douglas (ed.), 'Understanding Everyday Life' (Aldine, 1970), reprinted
     in R. Turner (ed.), 'Ethnomethodology' (Penguin, 1974).
17   L. Wittgenstein, 'Philosophical Investigations' (Basil Blackwell, 1968),
     para. 164.
18   For some excellent theoretical discussion of this and related issues, see
     John Heritage, Aspects of the Flexibilities of Language Use, 'Sociology',
     vol. 12, no. 1, January 1978.
19   Gilbert Ryle, 'The Concept of Mind' (Penguin University Books, 1973),
     pp. 28-32.
20   Which is *not* to say that they alone are open-ended but rather that they
     have a specific horizon of open-endedness which might be different from
     other category-concepts.
21   G. Ryle, op. cit., p. 58.   Ryle overlooks here that one *can* be 'part-
     informed' of a *domain* or *set* of facts.
22   John Searle, What Is a Speech Act?, in P.P. Giglioli (ed.), 'Language
     and Social Context' (Penguin, 1973);   D.S. Shwayder, 'The Stratifica-
     tion of Behavior' (Humanities Press, 1963).
23   Although, alternatively, such a formulation can get extended to cover
     all the periods they are supposed to work within.   Then the distinc-
     tion comes to demarcate not the division between their private and work
     time, but between *their* work time and that of lay persons.
24   Sharrock, op. cit.
25   Ibid., p. 49.
26   Ibid., p. 50.
27   E.E. Evans-Pritchard, 'Witchcraft, Oracles and Magic Among the
     Azande' (Oxford University Press, 1937), p. 219.   (Cited in Sharrock,
     op. cit., p. 48.)
28   Ibid., pp. 223-4.
29   Watson, op. cit., p. 107:
        we have the turning of categories from being members of categoriza-
        tion devices into devices in their own right.   Thus, the categoriza-
        tion 'Protestant' may be either treated as a category in the device
        'types of faith' (or 'churches'), or as a device with categories of its
        own, such as 'vicars', 'curates', 'members of the congregation', and
        so on.   Moreover, some devices, like 'Protestant church', can be
        teated as duplicatively-organized, that is, as being organized into
        team-like units (in this case, into individual churches)....

CHAPTER 2   THE SOCIAL ORGANIZATION OF CATEGORIAL INCUMBENCY

1   This term belongs, of course, to Wittgenstein.   See his 'Philosophical
    Investigations' (Basil Blackwell, 1968), passim.

2 Ralph Linton, Status and Role (excerpted from his 'The Study of Man', 1936), in L. Coser and B. Rosenberg (eds), 'Sociological Theory' (Collier Macmillan, 1966), p. 360.
3 See Harold Garfinkel, 'Studies in Ethnomethodology' (Prentice-Hall, 1967), chapter 1.
4 Alan F. Blum, The Sociology of Mental Illness, in Jack D. Douglas (ed.), 'Deviance and Respectability: The Social Construction of Moral Meanings' (Basic Books, 1970).
5 Ibid., p. 45.
6 Ibid., p. 46.
7 Note that in the description 'The vandal walked up to the car and kicked it' the categorization term is given *before* the action which warrants its use. This observation was suggested to me by Max Atkinson, who also gave me the above example (from a newspaper report) at Manchester University in 1974. Such an ordering as the above is, in fact, routine in headlines of newspaper accounts: Killer Goes on the Rampage in Manhattan, Bandits Rob Major London Bank, Thugs Beat up Old Lady in Parking Lot. All these categorizations are (i) action-consequent and (ii) negatively morally implicative. It is interesting that if we compare them with other action-consequent (or activity-consequent) categorizations which are *positively* morally implicative, the same sort of ordering is not routinely employed. We do not generally find headlines such as Hero Saves Little Girl from River - we might, instead, find something more like Teacher Saves Little Girl from River, with the categorization 'hero' coming in (if at all) in the text *after* the description. (Yet we might find a caption such as Hero Returning Home.) Indeed, if we *were* to read a title Hero Saves Little Girl from River, we might take it that the one saving the little girl had already achieved some heroic act in the past for which he was (and is now being) designated as a 'hero', prior to and quite *independently of* the present action or situation being reported upon.
8 Of course, cultures may differ as to *which* categorizations are applicable by any member and which categorizations have an organization that exhibits a distinction (culturally specific) between communities of categorizers.
9 The categories 'bride' and 'bridegroom' are usable of members some short while before the wedding, and not just on the wedding day itself. In some cultures (the Arab Middle East), they are also extendable beyond the wedding in certain contexts of use.
10 For an investigation of Formulations as Conversational Objects, see the paper of this title by J.C. Heritage and D.R. Watson in George Psathas (ed.), 'Everyday Language: Ethnomethodological Approaches' (Irvington Press, 1979).
11 On the notion of 'defeasibility', see H.L.A. Hart, The Ascription of Responsibility and Rights, in A.G.N. Flew (ed.), 'Logic and Language', 1st and 2nd Series (Doubleday, 1965).
12 Paul Drew, Accusations, 'Sociology', vol. 12, no. 1, January 1978.
13 For some instances of this, see Matthew Speier, 'How to Observe Face-to-Face Communication: A Sociological Introduction' (Goodyear, 1973).
14 In *one* display, *three* categorizations are made relevant and available. In the example from the Lebanese civil war, we had *two*. Earlier in Chapter 1, we discussed how other interactional contingencies can generate the relevance of more than one categorization for practical purposes. We shall deal with such issues in detail in Chapter 4.
15 This issue will be taken up in detail in Chapter 4.
16 For members such an issue is politically important. This is not to say that this is the only kind of locus for political interest that members may have with respect to categories such as 'police' and 'army', etc. Another one may be where such a category incumbency as 'policeman' is glance-available, and incumbents are seen to engage, openly and routinely, in certain sorts of repressive activities; members take it that such behaviour is *trading on* the availability of the category

incumbency (to discourage resistance, to secure 'co-operation', enforce certain accounts, etc.) and the category-specific resources available to category incumbents.

17 H. Garfinkel, Passing and the Managed Achievement of Sex Status in an Intersexed Person, in his 'Studies in Ethnomethodology' (Prentice-Hall, 1967).

18 It would be interesting to examine the use of other categories which are treated by members as 'dominant'. Examples would include 'mental patient' which gets reformulated into 'former mental patient', 'schizophrenic' which becomes 'schizophrenic in remission', 'prisoner' which becomes 'ex-convict' and 'President' which becomes 'ex-President'.

## CHAPTER 3  LISTS, CATEGORIZATIONS AND DESCRIPTIONS

1 Many puzzles and riddles turn on a cumulative list structure, e.g. the famous riddle of the Sphinx: 'What goes on four legs in the morning, two in the afternoon and three in the evening?' The answer is, of course, 'man'. This is a complex structure, however, since embedded in the list items is a further feature, that of physical change.

2 Some further instances of category lists constituted by the use of both descriptor categories and organizational categories might be 'agitators and Communists', 'rightists and Phalangists', 'republicans and IRA men', 'fascists and Nazis', etc. Such constructions are very common in certain sorts of discourse. The systematic equivocality that characterizes our analysed data routinely characterizes the use of these category lists also. Once a *third* item of either category type is added (e.g. in 'rightists, fascists and Phalangists' or 'rightists, Nazis and Phalangists'), the list loses some of its equivocal character as to the referents of the different categorizations, and its indeterminacy is resolvable by the added specification. Sometimes, an utterance may be designed with an equivocally hearable two-category list format: (Descriptor Category) + (Organizational Category) in order to accomplish *derogatory* reference.

3 Here we are reminded of Donnellan's point about mistakes in reference. (Keith Donnellan, Reference and Definite Descriptions, in S.P. Schwartz (ed.), 'Naming, Necessity and Natural Kinds' (Cornell University Press, 1977).) We can put the matter this way: if you mean to refer to some person X, in order to say something Y of him, then, for *some* occasions, it is not a problem if you *mis*describe him as Z, as long as you manage to achieve reference to *him* in saying Y. In our case, as in this, it is clear that practical hearership can consist in specifically *disattending* to certain aspects of utterance design.

4 Harvey Sacks, Initial Investigation of the Usability of Conversational Data for Doing Sociology, in David Sudnow (ed.), 'Studies in Social Interaction' (Free Press, 1972). See also Appendix 1.

5 There are contexts in which *hybrid* categorizations are generated or used (e.g. Italian-American); this is an issue which cannot be examined in these pages, however.

6 Paul Drew analyses what would be, in our terms, an indexically generated device ('sectarian groups') as an example of a strictly implied MCD. In other words, instead of treating it as an 'upshot' of the talk, he treats it as an a priori resource for the talk. In the terms of our discussion of the modes of availability of device-categories or device-categorizations, he treats an instance of mode (3) as an instance of mode (1). See his otherwise excellent piece, Accusations, 'Sociology', vol. 12, no. 1, January 1978, p. 12 and p. 21, n. 14.

7 Peter Hoffman, 'The History of the German Resistance 1933-1945', (MIT Press, 1977), p. 15.

8 Routinely, a device-category is offered in talk at the end of some list of co-selected categories, e.g. 'communists, socialists and other radicals', or 'Dukes, Counts, and other aristocrats'.

9   Harvey Sacks, 'Aspects of the Sequential Organization of Conversation' (unpublished manuscript) (September 1970, University of California at Irvine), chapter 3, p. 9.

10  On the notion of 'preferences' and some uses, see, inter alia, A. Pomerantz, 'Second Assessments' (unpublished PhD thesis, University of California at Irvine, 1975); H. Sacks and E.A. Schegloff, Two Preferences for the Organization of Reference to Persons in Conversation, in George Psathas (ed.), 'Everyday Language: Ethnomethodological Approaches' (Irvington Press, 1979).

11  J.F.M. Hunter, Telling, in his 'Essays after Wittgenstein' (University of Toronto Press, 1973), p. 114.

12  Roland Hall, Excluders, in Charles E. Caton (ed.), 'Philosophy and Ordinary Language' (University of Illinois Press, Urbana, 1963).

13  Early in Chapter 1, we posed a series of questions for which our notion of a 'practical translation problem' may serve as an analytical resource in furnishing a solution.   The data ran as follows:

    27  A:  Yeah, were there some skinheads or...
    28  R:  no, no, not skinheads, these are Hell's Angels types.
    29  A:  I see, er, do you get a lot of bother from skinheads as well?
    30  R:  Not particularly.
    31  A:  Yeah.
    32  R:  er the Hell's Angels types are the people who er *don't* stop at home ... they sleep out, they sleep rough, they're a dirty, scruffy, idle shower, they live off social security er plus er thieving er things here and there.

Our issue was: does the category 'skinhead' not take *some* of the list items, or does it not take the list as a *collection*?  We can now argue that, given the mutual elaborativeness of list items, it is the collection as a whole that is ascribed to the Hell's Angels and withheld from the skinheads

14  After all, as members of this culture we know the ways in which concepts and categories are interrelated and the ways that features of the social world are interrelated (although much of this knowledge is non-propositional).  As Cavell notes, in acquiring language we acquire the conventional implications of conceptual usages.  See Stanley Cavell, Must We Mean What We Say?, in Colin Lyas (ed.), 'Philosophy and Linguistics' (St Martin's Press, 1971).

15  For this material, I am grateful to the Probation Service in a large British city.  I am especially indebted to Dr John Lee for facilitating my entry into this service.  The data extracts are taken from two 'Social Enquiry Reports'; hence they are referred to as S.E. Data (see Appendix 4).

16  We can immediately see from the foregoing that for various contexts and tasks a version of the 'practical translation problem' might be or involve the 'practical induction problem', or 'the practical instantiation/exemplification problem', or 'the practical warranting problem' or yet 'the practical documentation problem'.

17  For detailed work on 'formulations', see D.R. Watson and J.C. Heritage, Formulations as Conversational Objects, in George Psathas (ed.), 'Everyday Language: Ethnomethodological Approaches' (Irvington Press, 1979).

18  For a discussion of the ways in which 'formulations' in talk yield further indexical particulars, and thereby cannot be relied upon by analysts to furnish determinate and definite renditions of intersubjective sense, see the classical discussion of Harold Garfinkel and Harvey Sacks in their paper, On Formal Structures of Practical Actions, in John C. McKinney and E.A. Tiryakian (eds), 'Theoretical Sociology' (Appleton-Century-Crofts, 1970).  See also the excellent theoretical discussion in John Heritage's paper, Aspects of the Flexibilities of Natural Language Use: A Reply to Phillips, 'Sociology', vol. 12, no. 1, January 1978.

19  Indeed, these implications are fitted together too, i.e. not only are similar implications attendant upon each of the items, but the implica-

tions themselves are congruent with each other:   this makes sense in that attributes, actions, beliefs, behaviours, etc. are treated by members as organized in *clusters*.

20   An 'illocutionary act' is an act performed in the saying of something, whereas a 'perlocutionary effect' is accomplished by the saying of something.   This distinction belongs to J.L. Austin.   See his 'How to Do Things with Words' (Oxford University Press, 1962).

## CHAPTER 4   CATEGORY-OCCASIONED TRANSFORMATIONS

1   Stephen A. Tyler, Introduction, in his edited collection, 'Cognitive Anthropology' (Holt, Rinehart & Winston, 1969), pp. 8-10.

2   Mick A. Atkinson, Some Practical Uses of 'A Natural Lifetime', 'Human Studies: Special Issue on Ethnomethodological Studies', vol. 3, no. 1, January 1980.

3   W.W. Sharrock and Roy Turner, On a Conversational Environment for Equivocality, in Jim Schenkein (ed.), 'Studies in the Organization of Conversational Interaction' (Academic Press, 1978), p. 183: 'In assembling a complainable over time, *what* is occurring is not necessarily ascertained independently of *who* is seen to be responsible ("who" in this context standing for a category incumbency rather than a name as an identifier).'

4   Ibid.

5   This thought was touched off by a reading of Herbert H. Clark, Word Associations and Linguistic Theory, in John Lyons (ed.), 'New Horizons in Linguistics' (Pelican, 1970).

6   Mrs E. Gaskell, 'North and South' (Everyman's Library, 1975).

7   Ibid., p. 387.

8   My use of 'attributive' and 'referential' here is to be distinguished from K. Donnellan's (see his Reference and Definite Descriptions, in Stephen P. Schwartz (ed.), 'Naming, Necessity and Natural Kinds' (Cornell University Press, 1977)).   By the 'attributive use of categorizations', I mean to specify their in situ inferential consequentiality, implicative strength, and the feature-delivery character of categorizational usage. (I shall henceforth use 'attributive(ly)' in this sense.)   Whilst Donnellan was attempting to correct some classical positions in the theory of reference, his treatment of definite descriptions in terms of *either* referential *or* attributive uses remains artificial and insensitive to practical interactional contexts, in which to use a definite description attributively can involve also making reference to someone, and achieving reference with a definite description can involve attribution(s).

9   D.R. Watson, Some Conceptual Issues in the Social Identification of 'Victims' and 'Offenders', in E. Viano (ed.), 'Victims, Criminals and Society' (Leiden, Sitjhoff, 1980).

10   Harvey Sacks, An Initial Investigation of the Usability of Conversational Data for Doing Sociology, in David Sudnow (ed.), 'Studies in Social Interaction' (Free Press, 1972).

11   Watson, op. cit. (mimeograph copy, University of Manchester).

12   For some explorations of the relevance of 'presuppositions' to practical understanding, and for the distinction between conventional and pragmatic presupposition, see Jeff Coulter, Beliefs and Practical Understanding, in George Psathas (ed.), 'Everyday Language: Ethnomethodological Approaches' (Irvington Press, 1979).

## CHAPTER 5   CATEGORY-GENERATED PROBLEMS AND SOME SOLUTIONS

1   Harvey Sacks, An Initial Investigation of the Usability of Conversational Data for Doing Sociology, in David Sudnow (ed.), 'Studies in Social Interaction' (Free Press, 1972).   For a full account of this notion, see Appendix 1.   In this work, I am extending the use of the

notion 'standardized relational pairs' to cover any category pair that constitutes a locus for a set of rights, obligations or expectations which are not necessarily restricted to the giving of 'help' (as they are in Sacks's formulation).   In the text, I shall sometimes employ the abbreviation 'S-R pair'.

2　Jeff Coulter, Beliefs and Practical Understanding, in George Psathas (ed.), 'Everyday Language: Ethnomethodological Approaches' (Irvington Press, 1979).

3　Sacks, op. cit., pp. 39-40.

4　Sacks's notion of 'Pn-adequacy' is discussed in Appendix 1.   Essentially, it refers to the property of population-exhaustiveness for any categorial device.

5　Roland Hall, Excluders, in Charles C. Caton (ed.), 'Philosophy and Ordinary Language' (University of Illinois, 1963).

6　Indeed, were a member of a collectivity such as 'the police' to be publicly categorized as a 'criminal', he might cease to be officially a member of that collectivity and would become an ex-member; or he might have impeachment proceedings initiated against him.   This can maintain the character of the collectivity as one with certain and variously realizable relationships to persons who are not members of that collectivity and sustains the possibility of the hearing maxim we have indicated.   If such procedures, however, are not observably followed in such circumstances as the above, then that is implicative for the understanding of the entire character of the collectivity and for the usage of the 'police/people' category set.

7　Membership Categorization Device (Sacks).

8　Two senses of the concept 'or' are formulated in the logic literature as either the weak/inclusive sense or the strong/exclusive sense.   See Irving Copi, 'Introduction to Logic' (Macmillan, 1961), p. 240.   My use is cognate but not identical to Copi's.

9　This disjunction may, of course, remain *contained* within one speaker's talk.

10　The report is a category-rich environment.   The *same* activity, 'demonstrating', is used to generate different categorizations: 'demonstrators', 'marchers', 'protesters', which focus upon various features of this activity.   In *some* contexts, of course, the proliferation of categorizations may be treated as simply a matter of *stylistic* preference, where they cannot be seen to be doing further implicative work.

11　Mrs E. Gaskell, 'North and South' (Everyman's Library, 1975), p. 260.

12　This data is cited with permission of the publishers of Richard Arens, 'Make Mad the Guilty' (Charles C. Thomas, 1969).   It appears on pp. 64-5.

13　Some instances of knowledge-claim/belief-claim disjunctions are treated in Jeff Coulter, op. cit.

14　See Sacks's discussion of the constraints upon admitting an activity type into the set of category-bound activities, in his On the Analyzability of Stories by Children, in Roy Turner (ed.), 'Ethnomethodology' (Penguin, 1974).


## CHAPTER 6　WAYS OF DESCRIBING

1　J.L. Austin, 'How to Do Things With Words', ed. J.O. Urmson (Oxford University Press, 1973 ed.), pp. 106-7.

2　Jerry A. Fodor, Methodological Solipsism as a Research Strategy in Psychology, 'Behavioral and Brain Science', vol. 3, no. 1, March 1980.

3　James D. McCawley, Where Do Noun Phrases Come From?, in D.D. Steinberg and L.A. Jakobovits (eds), 'Semantics: An Interdisciplinary Reader' (Cambridge University Press, 1971), p. 224.

4　Ryszard Zuber, Semantic Antinomies and Deep Structure Analysis, 'Semiotica', vol. 13, no. 3, 1975, p. 268.

5　Fodor, op. cit., p. 10.   I should add here that I am not endorsing

Fodor's mentalistic thesis on the 'causation' of human behaviour.   For
fuller discussion of this matter, see Jeff Coulter, The Computational
Theory of Conduct: An Assessment, forthcoming.
6   Eric D'Arcy, 'Human Acts: An Essay in Their Moral Evaluation'
(Clarendon Press, 1963), esp. chapter 1.
7   Ibid., p. 18.
8   Ibid., p. 19.
9   Ibid., p. 16.
10   Ibid., p. 17.
11   Ibid., p. 32.


CHAPTER 7   THE INFERENTIAL ENVIRONMENT OF HIERARCHIES AND
CONTRASTS

1   This extract comes from materials collected under the auspices of the
SSRC project, Community Reactions to Deviance (Dr J.M. Atkinson,
Principal Investigator).   The setting is a therapy session.   (See
Appendix 6.)
2   An example was observed in a magistrate's court by Dr J.M. Atkinson
during field work conducted under the auspices of the SSRC project
he was heading (see above).   During the trial of a group of Hell's
Angels, a number of 'skinheads' in the public gallery, who were talking
and laughing, were told by the chairman of the bench, not to 'Stop
laughing and talking', but that 'This is a court of law'.
3   Clearly, I am here outlining only *one* modality of inferential procedure,
that which is tied to *negatively* assessed actions and action-relevant
features.
4   Jeff Coulter, Basic Structures for Arguments in Interaction, paper
delivered in a public lecture to the Third Annual International Institute
in Ethnomethodology and Conversation Analysis, Boston University,
June 1978 (mimeograph version).


CHAPTER 8   RATIONALITY, PRACTICE AND MORALITY

1   Richard Arens, 'Make Mad the Guilty' (Charles C. Thomas, 1969), p. 64.
2   The grounds for treating the subject's behaviour as a serious attempt
rather than a bluff are provided in the description – the fact that the
subject was 'prevented only by physical intervention'; that this intervention involved at least 'one person, maybe two or three'; and that
this scenario was repeated on another occasion.   Given the seriousness
of the judgment being provided as relevant by the defence (i.e. that
Stewart was not 'normal'), the strongest possible indication of the
*seriousness* of the attempt in question is required.
3   For some discussion, see Jeff Coulter, 'Approaches to Insanity: A Philosophical and Sociological Study' (Martin Robertson, 1973), Section 2.
4   This is done on occasion.   But in such a case, the attributions of
'collective madness' or 'mass psychosis' operate only as devices of moral
denigration or moral exclusion, since *intelligibility* per se is not an
issue in such cases.   The collective framework provides for a *rationale*
for action, but not a *justification* of it.
5   Arens, op. cit., p. 183.
6   The work by Arens already cited is replete with examples of such disagreements.
7   The Reverend Jim Jones of the People's Temple, based in San Francisco,
USA, who led most of his followers at their Jamestown, Guyana, commune
to mass suicide in the winter of 1978.
8   This notion is taken from Wittgenstein.   For an excellent account, see
J.F.M. Hunter, 'Forms of Life' in Wittgenstein's 'Philosophical Investigations', in E.D. Klemke (ed.), 'Essays on Wittgenstein' (University of
Illinois Press, 1971).

9  These specific judgments are conventionally available in *this* culture and, where made, display a specific moral view.    The point holds, however, regardless of how one substantively fills in what a 'morally proscribed action' is.

10  Indeed, 'possession' is still used as an explanatory and excusing device by some agents of such actions, but nowadays this accounting scheme is further usable as criterial evidence of insanity.    An instance in which this occurred was the case of the 'Son of Sam', a killer responsible for the murders of a number of young women in New York City in the summer of 1978.

11  Julius Kovesi, 'Moral Notions' (Routledge & Kegan Paul, 1967).

12  Ibid., p. 112.

13  L. Wittgenstein, 'On Certainty' (Basil Blackwell, 1974 ed.), para. 139.

14  Ibid., para. 140.

15  Kovesi, op. cit., p. 51.

16  Ibid., p. 109.

17  Ibid., p. 135.

18  Eric D'Arcy, 'Human Acts' (Clarendon Press, 1963), pp. 25-6.

19  Wittgenstein, op. cit., para. 124.

20  As in, for instance, the case of the Texas Penal Code, Article 1220, which made the killing by a husband of a wife's paramour taken in the act of adultery 'justifiable homicide' (H.L.A. Hart, 'Punishment and Responsibility' (Oxford University Press, 1966), p. 256).

21  Keith Graham, Moral Notions and Moral Misconceptions, 'Analysis', vol. 35, no. 3, January 1975.    The notion of 'saving-deceit' is introduced by Kovesi as a way of further differentiating the notion of 'lying', so that lying can then be treated as a *complete* moral notion which logically entails the condemnation of the action so described.    'Saving-deceit', on the other hand, would describe only those instances where prevarication may be appraised positively.

22  'For each alternative course of action, there will be not one but a plurality of morally relevant descriptions...' (Graham, op. cit., p. 76).

23  Ibid., p. 73 and passim.

24  Kovesi, op. cit., passim.

25  Graham, op. cit., p. 70.    (Although I would question Graham's 'common properties' account of the logic of classification, his point still stands.)

26  Kovesi, op. cit., p. 161.    Kovesi's final chapter is preoccupied with elucidating this contention.

27  In this connection, D'Arcy speaks of *morally significant* acts:
    It is of them particularly that I want to say, not that moral judgment must always pronounce them wrong:  but that whenever their definition is verified they must be characterized in isolation before moral judgment can be passed on the whole incident of which they are a part.    Perhaps they are not always morally wrong;  but they are always morally significant.    There will be much wider agreement about what kinds of act are morally significant than about the moral significance of each.    (op. cit., p. 39)

28  Rush Rhees, Some Developments in Wittgenstein's View of Ethics, 'Philosophical Review', vol. 74, no. 1, p. 19.

29  L. Wittgenstein, 'Philosophical Investigations', trans G.E.M. Anscombe (Basil Blackwell, 1968 ed.), para. 217.

30  Wittgenstein, 'On Certainty', paras 611-12.

31  The sociological study of 'deviance' may fruitfully be redirected towards the study of topically normative and moral assessments, judgments and inferences.

32  R.M. Hare, 'Freedom and Reason' (Oxford University Press, 1963), pp. 89-90.

33  Ibid., p. 195.

34  G.J. Warnock, 'The Object of Morality' (Methuen, 1971), p. 149.

35  Alternatively, one may try, as a member, to argue for a particular morality in a theoretically and analytically sophisticated way:  this is a

different enterprise and one which, I believe, would be enriched and deepened by a serious investigation into members' moral methods. An interesting avenue of analytic concern would be the further study of how certain moral concepts came into use, their various historically developed contexts of use, the language games in which they were used and the changes which were introduced into these language games over time.

36  Hanna F. Pitkin, 'Wittgenstein and Justice: On the Significance of Ludwig Wittgenstein for Social and Political Thought' (University of California Press, 1972).
37  Ibid., pp. 140-68.
38  Ibid., p. 140.
39  Ibid., quoting Wittgenstein, 'Philosophical Investigations', paras 90 and 18.
40  Ibid., p. 141.
41  Ibid., p. 146.
42  Ibid.
43  Ibid., p. 149.
44  Ibid., p. 153.
45  Ibid., p. 155.
46  Ibid., p. 156.
47  Stanley Cavell, 'The Claim to Rationality:  Knowledge and the Basis of Morality', unpublished doctoral dissertation, Harvard University, 1961-62.
48  Pitkin, op. cit., p. 146.
49  Ibid.
50  Ibid., p. 144.
51  Ibid., p. 142.
52  Ibid., p. 143.
53  Ibid., p. 142.
54  Ibid., p. 140.
55  F. Waismann, Language Strata, in A.G.N. Flew (ed.), 'Logic and Language', 1st and 2nd series (Doubleday, 1965).
56  Wittgenstein, 'Philosophical Investigations', para. 23.
57  Harold Garfinkel, 'Studies in Ethnomethodology' (Prentice-Hall, 1967), pp. 73-4.
58  Wittgenstein, 'On Certainty', para. 124.

## APPENDIX 1   HARVEY SACKS ON CATEGORIZATION: AN OVERVIEW

1   Harvey Sacks, 'The Search for Help: No-one to Turn to', unpublished doctoral dissertation, University of California at Berkeley, Department of Sociology, 1966, pp. 15-16 (Sacks's emphasis).
2   This concept was first introduced by Sacks in his paper, On the Analyzability of Stories by Children, in Roy Turner (ed.), 'Ethnomethodology' (Penguin, 1974).
3   H. Sacks, 'Transcribed Lectures', University of California at Irvine, 1966-67.
4   Harvey Sacks, An Initial Investigation of the Usability of Conversational Data for Doing Sociology, in David Sudnow (ed.), 'Studies in Social Interaction' (Free Press, 1972).
5   Ibid., pp. 33-4.
6   Ibid., p. 34.
7   H. Sacks and E.H. Schegloff, Two Preferences for the Organization of Reference to Persons in Conversation and their Interaction, in George Psathas (ed.) 'Everyday Language: Ethnomethodological Approaches' (Irvington Press, 1979).
8   H. Sacks, An Initial Investigation, p. 36.
9   Ibid., p. 431, note 19.
10  Ibid., p. 37.
11  Ibid.
12  Ibid.

13  Ibid.
14  Ibid., p. 38.
15  Ibid., pp. 39-40.
16  In Roy Turner (ed.), 'Ethnomethodology' (Penguin, 1974).
17  Ibid., pp. 219-20.
18  Ibid., p. 220.
19  Ibid., pp. 220-1.
20  Ibid., p. 221.
21  Ibid., pp. 221-4.

# SUBJECT INDEX

Ability, -ies, 40, 41, 42-3; *see
also* Skills
Account(s), 37-8, 46, 52, 69, 85,
89, 93, 96, 105-7, 115, 122-3,
136, 143-4; asymmetrical constructions of, 28; category
transformability of, 108, 110;
C-type, 196; P-type, 196;
rights of ratification of, 65;
transforming detail, 143
Accountability, 136
Accounting scheme, 84
Accounting work, 95
Achieved status, 57-8
Achievement, 58-60
Act/Action/Activity, -ies, 137, 148,
158, 160, 177, 184-8, 200, 205,
207; ascription/attribution of,
151, 157, 159, 160, 173; categories, 195, 197; consequence(s)
line, 159; contexts, 137; deemed
good, 191; description, 152, 158,
161, 163, 165, 191, 192-3, 195,
203, 211; deviant, 187; grounds
for, 163-4, 182, 259n; intelligibility of, 183; intentional, 159;
legal description of, 194; legally
sanctioned, 194; literal applicability of description to, 195;
morally implicative, 11, 161;
morally proscribed, 187; morally
right, 190; morally significant,
267n; morally wrong, 190; negatively assessed, 266n; negatively
implicative, 191; object of, 153;
projections, 28, 178; reasons for,
183, 187, 259n; relevant
features, 266n; setting-inappropriate, 170, 172-3, 177, 209;
setting-tied, 174
Acting on principle, 189
Agreement(s), 8-12, 14, 17, 19, 79,
87-8, 138, 161, 208, 211; moral,
14, 16, 18
Appraisal, 58
Ascribed status, 57-8
Ascription(s), 57-60, 115, 141, 211;
action, 147, 151, 160, 181; category, 147, 259n; contexts of,
154; insanity, 182-3, 186-7;

intention, 151; irrationality, 182,
184-6; knowledge, 151; moral,
197; responsibility, 151, 160;
*see also* Attribution(s)
Assessment(s), 21, 166; context
of, 58; moral, 181; of relevances and consequences, 189
Asymmetric category sets, 122, 124-
5, 171; complementary use of,
127, 130; oppositional use of,
127, 129, 136, 138
Asymmetry convention, 127
Attribute(s), 33
Attributions: of collective madness,
266n; of ignorance, 143; of
knowledge, 151; of membership
category, 145; over-, 152-4, 156,
165; of prejudice, 51, 145-50;
of responsibility, 72, 151; under/
over-attributive action description,
158

Beliefs, 12-17, 26; category-organized, 146-7, 149; contextually-
attributable, 112; moral, 14, 15,
210

Categorial precedence, 137
Categorization(s): accounting, 62,
116, 118, 120; action-consequent,
63, 66, 125, 261n; *ad hoc*, 36,
171; age, 105; ascriptive use
of, 27; collective attribute, 35;
descriptor, 28, 63, 80-1, 262n;
event-specific, 62, 66, 115, 116,
118, 119, 125; gender, 68, 73,
106, 108; hybrid, 55, 262n;
morally implicative, 261n; moral
performance, 44, 195; stable,
114, 116, 119, 125; stage-of-life,
67-8, 73, 106, 108, 216-17;
transient, 66; umbrella, 20, 28
Category, -ies; *passim*
Category accretion, 114, 116, 135
Category-bound actions/activities,
38, 148, 212, 217, 265n;
features, 26, 33, 35, 37, 43, 51,
52, 56-7, 103, 106, 108, 110, 113,
131, 134, 146-50, 170, 183, 195,
209, 210; display, 71; know-

# NAME INDEX

Arens, R., 265n, 266n
Atkinson, J.M., 261n, 266n
Atkinson, M.A., 264n
Austin, J.L., 100, 101, 151, 264n, 265n

Blum, A., 60-2, 65, 261n

Cavell, S., 203, 205, 263n, 268n
Clark, H.H., 264n
Cooper, D., 12-14, 17, 258n
Copi, I., 265n
Coulter, J., 123, 179, 258n, 260n, 264n, 265n, 266n

D'Arcy, E., 158-60, 191, 266n, 267n
Davidson, D., 12-14, 17, 258n
Donnellan, K., 262n, 264n
Drew, P., 261n, 262n
Dworkin, R., 6

Evans-Pritchard, E.E., 260n

Fodor, J.A., 153-5, 265n, 266n
Foot, P., 11

Garfinkel, H., 73, 208, 258n, 261n, 262n, 263n, 268n
Gaskell, E., 113, 141, 264n, 265n
Graham, K., 194-6, 267n

Hall, R., 263n, 265n
Hare, R.M., 10, 18, 200-1, 209, 258n, 267n
Hart, H.L.A., 77, 261n, 267n
Heritage, J.C., 260n, 261n, 263n
Hoffman, P., 262n
Hunter, J.F.M., 89, 263n, 266n

Kovesi, J., 188, 190-7, 267n
Kripke, S., 259n

Linton, R., 28, 261n

McCawley, J.D., 265n
Mounce, H.O., 2, 18, 258n, 259n

Nielsen, K., 11, 15, 258n, 259n

Oakshott, M., 202, 205-6

Phillips, D.Z., 2, 18, 258n, 259n
Pitkin, H.F., 202, 203, 205-7, 268n
Pomerantz, A., 263n

Reiss, A.J., 259n
Rhees, R., 267n
Ryan, C., 5, 6, 258n
Ryle, G., 40, 41, 202, 258n, 260n

Sacks, H., 2, 20, 35, 60, 61, 67, 81, 82, 83, 86, 110, 116, 122, 124, 125, 148, 212-17, 258n, 259n, 262n, 263n, 264n, 265n, 268n
Schegloff, E.A., 214, 263n, 268n
Schwayder, D.S., 42, 260n
Searle, J.R., 42, 259n, 260n
Sharrock, W.W., 35, 52, 53-5, 112, 260n, 264n
Sidgwick, H., 18
Snare, F.E., 17, 259n
Speier, M., 261n

Taylor, E., 259n
Turner, R., 112, 260n, 264n
Tyler, S.A., 106, 264n

Waismann, F., 202, 205, 207, 268n
Warnock, G.J., 201, 267n
Watson, D.R., 35, 56, 116, 260n, 261n, 263n, 264n
White, H., 6, 7, 258n
White, J., 185
Winch, P., 18, 259n
Wittgenstein, L., 39, 190, 192, 196, 198, 202, 205, 207, 208, 210, 259n, 260n, 266n, 267n, 268n

Zuber, R., 155, 265n

275